PSYCHOANALYSIS ONLINE 3

Library of Technology and Mental Health

Series Editor: Jill Savege Scharff, MD

Distance Psychoanalysis: The Theory and Practice of Using Communication Technology in the Clinic (2011)
by Ricardo Carlino, translated by James Nuss

Psychoanalysis Online: Mental Health, Teletherapy, and Training (2013)
edited by Jill Savege Scharff

Screen Relations (2015)
by Gillian Russell

Psychoanalysis Online 2: Impact of Technology on Development, Training, and Therapy (2015)
edited by Jill Savege Scharff

Psychoanalysis, Identity, and the Internet: Explorations into Cyberspace (2016)
edited by Andrea Marzi

PSYCHOANALYSIS ONLINE 3

The Teleanalytic Setting

Edited by

Jill Savege Scharff

KARNAC

First published in 2017 by
Karnac Books Ltd
118 Finchley Road
London NW3 5HT

British Library Cataloguing in Publication Data

A C.I.P. for this book is available from the British Library

ISBN-13: 978-1-78220-518-0

Typeset by V Publishing Solutions Pvt Ltd., Chennai, India

www.karnacbooks.com

Dedicated to analysands who led me to teleanalysis

CONTENTS

ACKNOWLEDGMENTS xi

ABOUT THE EDITOR AND CONTRIBUTORS xiii

INTRODUCTION xvii

CHAPTER ONE
Teleanalysis beyond Skype 1
Jill Savege Scharff (USA)

CHAPTER TWO
Analytic dialogue: its multiple transformations—clinical implementation through telecommunication 21
Ricardo Carlino (Argentina and Mexico)

CHAPTER THREE
Privacy, telecommunications, and the psychoanalytic setting 35
John Churcher (UK)

CHAPTER FOUR
The analyst's closeness in long-distance psychoanalysis 53
Claudia Mizrahi (Argentina)

CHAPTER FIVE
Light and shadow in online analysis 65
Andrea Marzi and Giuseppe Fiorentini (Italy)

CHAPTER SIX
The space and place of psychoanalytic treatment: a philosophical meditation 85
José A. Saporta (USA)

CHAPTER SEVEN
The effect of the analytic couple's shared physical presence on transference fantasy 97
Lin Tao (China and UK)

CHAPTER EIGHT
The setting, the screen, and the conveying of unconscious dynamics 105
Caroline Sehon and Jill Savege Scharff (USA)

CHAPTER NINE
Technology: convenience and therapeutic leverage 129
Dina Oren (Israel and USA)

CHAPTER TEN
Screen images: transitional and defensive internet use among LGBTQ adolescents and adults 153
Andi Pilecki (USA)

CHAPTER ELEVEN
Couple psychotherapy settings and change in the digital age 169
Amita Sehgal (UK)

CHAPTER TWELVE
Listening and therapeutic alliance online 187
Lea S. de Setton (Panama)
Commentary 198
Caroline Sehon (USA)

CHAPTER THIRTEEN
Thinking ethically about terminating therapy after trying new technologies 207
Ernest Wallwork (USA)

INDEX 221

ACKNOWLEDGMENTS

Jill Scharff's chapter is an expanded version of "The pros and cons of Skype analysis," a presentation in a panel chaired by Maria Teresa Savio Hooke at the International Psychoanalytical Association Congress, Boston 2015.

John Churcher's chapter "Privacy, telecommunications, and the psychoanalytic setting," based on a paper read at the 28th Annual Conference of the EPF (European Psychoanalytical Federation), Stockholm, 26–29 March 2015, was previously published in the *Bulletin of the European Psychoanalytical Federation*, 69: 221–233 (1 Aug. 2015) and is reproduced here with minor revisions, courtesy of the editor. http://www.epf-fep.eu/eng/article/privacy-telecommunications-and-the-psychoanalytic-setting

Lin Tao's chapter "The effect of the analytic couple's shared physical presence on transference fantasy" was modified from a short article "Sense of possibility coming true" first published on the IPA website July 2015, http://www.psychoanalysis.today/en-GB/PT-Articles/Lin154993/Le-sentiment-dune-possibilite-de-realisation.aspx, with permission of the website editor.

José Saporta's chapter is based on an earlier and shorter version: "Digitalizing psychoanalysis and psychotherapy: possibilities and downsides," published in American Psychoanalytic Association's quarterly magazine, *The American Psychoanalyst* 42(2), 1–2 & 9, Spring/Summer 2008, courtesy of the editor, Douglas Chavis.

In Andi Pilecki's chapter, the song Arachne from *Dreams of Hope* was reproduced courtesy of Judith K. Avers.

ABOUT THE EDITOR AND CONTRIBUTORS

Ricardo Carlino, MD (Argentina and Mexico): psychiatrist and psychoanalyst, full member, Asociación Psicoanalítica de Buenos Aires (APdeBA), Argentina; associate member, Sociedad Psicoanalítica de México (SPM), México; full member, Federación Psicoanalítica de América Latina (FEPAL) and International Psychoanalytical Association (IPA); author of *Psicoanálisis a Distancia* (Lumen, 2010), translated as *Distance Psychoanalysis* (Karnac, 2011).

John Churcher (UK): psychoanalyst based in Manchester, retired from clinical practice; member, British Psychoanalytical Society; formerly lecturer in psychology, University of Manchester; researcher in visual perception, infant development, computer-mediated communication, and the psychoanalytic setting; and co-editor with Leopoldo Bleger for the first English edition of J. Bleger's 1967 book *Symbiosis and Ambiguity* (Routledge, 2013).

Giuseppe Fiorentini, MD (Italy): IPA training analyst; psychiatrist, formerly with the National Health Service; formerly professor of psychology, University of Turin and of Milan; European Chair, IPA Committee for Public Information; author of articles on the psychoanalytic setting, psychoanalytic education, and teleanalysis; faculty, Milan Training Institute, Italian Society of Psychoanalysis (SPI); in private practice in Milan.

Andrea Marzi, MD, PhD (Italy): psychiatrist, psychoanalyst, supervisor in institutions and the national health service; full member, International Psychoanalytical Association and Italian Psychoanalytical Society (Società Psicoanalitica Italiana); formerly visiting fellow in forensic psychopathology, University of Cambridge and professor of developmental psychology at the University of Siena; author of *Ciak si gira, Psicoanalisi al cinema*, and editor, *Psicoanalisi, Identità e Internet* (*Psychoanalysis, Identity, and the Internet* (Karnac, 2016)).

Claudia E. Mizrahi (Argentina): Vocal Member of Psychoanalytic History Department at the Argentine Psychoanalytical Association. Full member International Psychoanalytical Association; full member training and supervising analyst, Argentinian Psychoanalytic Association; teaching analyst at the analytic institute of the Argentinian Psychoanalytical Association; in private practice of psychoanalysis, psychotherapy, and tele-analysis with adults, children, adolescents, mothers, and babies. Past Newborn Individualized Developmental Care and Assessment Program (NIDCAP) specialist, the neonatal intensive care unit at the Fernandez Hospital, Buenos Aires.

Dina Oren, PhD (Israel and USA): certified family and couple therapist, teacher, and supervisor in Israel and New York; clinic administrator and training program director in Tel-Aviv.

Andi Pilecki, MS, LPC (USA): psychotherapist in private practice in Pittsburgh, Pennsylvania; member of the International Psychotherapy Institute and candidate at its International Institute for Psychoanalytic Training; member of the American Counseling Association (ACA) and its Association for Lesbian, Gay, Bisexual and Transgender Issues in Counseling (ALGBTIC), and the Association for Women in Psychology (AWP); formerly adjunct faculty, Carlow University.

José A. Saporta, MD (USA): faculty member, Center for Psychodynamic Treatment and Research, Massachusetts General Hospital, Harvard

Medical School; faculty member, Advanced Psychotherapy Training Program, Boston Psychoanalytic Society and Institute.

Jill Savege Scharff, MD, FABP (USA): adult and child psychiatrist, fellow of the American Board of Psychoanalysis, certified adult and child analyst of the American Psychoanalytic Association (APsaA), certified child and adolescent analyst of the International Psychoanalytical Association (IPA), co-founder of the International Psychotherapy Institute (IPI), founder and supervising analyst of the International Institute for Psychoanalytic Training (IIPT), author and editor of books on object relations individual, couple and family therapy including *The Interpersonal Unconscious*, and *Psychoanalysis Online, volumes 1 and 2* (Karnac).

Amita Sehgal, MA, PhD (UK): psychoanalytic couple psychotherapist accredited by the British Psychoanalytic Council (through the Tavistock Institute of Medical Psychology); practising in Central London; specializing in out-of-court divorce as registered collaborative practitioner with Resolution (formerly the Solicitors Family Law Association); visiting lecturer and clinician at Tavistock Relationships; author in the field of couple psychotherapy.

Caroline Sehon, MD (USA): psychoanalyst, adult and child psychiatrist, fellow of the American Academy of Psychoanalysis and Dynamic Psychiatry, member of the American Psychoanalytic Association (APsaA) and the International Psychoanalytical Association (IPA), Chair of the International Institute for Psychoanalytic Training program (IIPT) at the International Psychotherapy Institute (IPI), past chair of the Washington, DC program of IPI (IPI-Metro), and author of publications on object relations, individual, couple and family therapy, including chapters in *Psychoanalysis Online, volumes 1 and 2* (Karnac).

Lea Setton, PhD (Panama, RP): IPA training and supervising analyst, Panama City, Republic of Panama; supervising analyst, the International Institute for Psychoanalytic Training at the International Psychotherapy Institute in Chevy Chase MD, USA; formerly chair, IPI-Panama; co-editor with R. Losso and D. Scharff of *The Linked Self in Psychoanalysis: The Pioneering Work of Enrique Pichon-Rivière* (Karnac, 2017).

Lin Tao, MD (China and UK): psychoanalyst, interim IPA training analyst for China, couple psychoanalytic psychotherapist, vice-chief psychiatrist; direct member, International Psychoanalytical Association (IPA); member, IPA China committee and Couple and Family Psychoanalysis committee; guest member, British Psychoanalytical Society (BPAS); formerly director, ward for neurosis and associate director of the Department of Clinical Psychology, Beijing Anding Hospital, affiliated with Capital Medical University, Beijing, China.

Ernest Wallwork, PhD (USA): psychoanalyst in private practice in Washington DC and Syracuse, New York; professor of religion and ethics at Syracuse University; faculty, Washington Center for Psychoanalysis; author on ethical topics including *Psychoanalysis and Ethics* (Yale University Press), *Durkheim: Morality and* Milieu (Harvard University Press) and *Critical Issues in Modern Religion* (Prentice-Hall).

INTRODUCTION

As the practice of teleanalysis and teletherapy has grown, so has the literature on teleanalysis. Joining in that burgeoning conversation, here comes the third edited volume of *Psychoanalysis Online*, bringing together contributions from analysts who collaborate in the precongress workshops of the international work group on teleanalysis at meetings of the International Psychoanalytical Association.

The contributors explore the strengths and weaknesses of the teleanalytic setting and the essential aspects of the technology-assisted frame. In my opening chapter, I examine the pros and cons of Skype and make a plea for the use of a secure videoplatform instead. I look at the limitations and challenges of teleanalysis and consider whether it is real analysis: for instance, how can the patient imagine lying on the analyst's lap in a state of fantasied fusion with the mother's body across virtual reality?

Ricardo Carlino sets the parameters for a framework and roles within which a valid psychoanalytic project takes place, and shows that teleanalysis evolves from the same foundation. John Churcher, noting evidence that no telecommunication is secure and that privacy in teleanalysis is likely to breached, concludes that at least analysts can focus on this reality and analyze its impact on treatment. Claudia

Mizrahi fought her fear of disapproval to write about teleanalysis, and asks us to allow experience to temper our prejudices against innovation, as it did for her. She thinks of teleanalysis as real analysis in which the patient can feel incredibly close to the analyst despite the distance separating them. Andrea Marzi and Giuseppe Fiorentini warn against dangerously overlooking assumptions, ethics, and particular technical and theoretical features of teleanalysis; for remaining alert to these will help us to grasp the full potential of psychoanalysis online. José Saporta grounds his discussion of teleanalysis in philosophy, reflecting on the analytic pair's experience of technology, space, and physical context. Lin Tao moves into the clinical realm as he illustrates his reflections on the setting with an account of a patient who experienced the full impact of her fantasy about the analyst, made much more frightening when she was in the same room as him.

Caroline Sehon, co-authoring with me, leads off with a clinical narrative to show how unconscious dynamics are conveyed by the patient's presentation on screen. The offer of teleanalysis is usually made for the patient's convenience, but in the next chapter we are shown how it was used for the convenience of the analyst as well as the benefit of her patients while she was on a six-month journey. She learned the value of analyzing the impact of the setting on the analytic process, as Churcher recommends in his earlier chapter.

Defining internet use as defensive against interpersonal interaction or as transitional towards full social acceptance and engagement, Andi Pilecki illustrates these two aspects in examples drawn from the LGBTQ community. Teletherapy is not just for individuals who are marginalized or who live at a distance from a therapy center. It can be for couples too. Amita Sehgal shows how the digital age has required flexibility in thinking about the setting for couple therapy and she illustrates transformational change in couple therapy settings conducted in cyberspace.

Teleanalysis privileges the words and the music of the words. Drawing from literature on auditory reception and vocal production Lea Sofer de Setton shows how the voice in analysis online represents the body in the analytic conversation, as the speaking and listening analytic pair maintain a therapeutic alliance across a temporary distance. As Caroline Sehon points out in her commentary, Lea Setton values the therapeutic alliance as the primary agent of therapeutic action.

Ernest Wallwork brings an ethicist's eye to two analyses, one of which brought harm to the patient by perpetuating a less-than-effective treatment online, while the other was immensely helpful in maintaining a drug addict in treatment until it became unnecessary, Wallwork's point being that the ethical position is to explore the pros and cons of online analysis thoroughly so that patients can give truly informed consent as to whether to accept the offer of teleanalysis or referral to a local analyst. As soon as there is a plethora of clinical experiences with teleanalysis, new ethical challenges appear.

CHAPTER ONE

Teleanalysis beyond Skype

Jill Savege Scharff (USA)

I began teleanalysis some years ago because colleagues in another country with no psychoanalysis at all requested analysis conducted on the telephone. I do not like talking socially on the phone, and I was skeptical. But there was no other way for them to get the analysis they sought. So I agreed to try psychoanalysis on the telephone. Then I found that, even though the analysand's body was not in the same physical location as the analyst, and working on the telephone I could not see the patient, unverbalized feelings were transmitted anyway (Scharff, 2012). Two of the patients introduced me to Skype, the most frequently used Voice over Internet Protocol (VoIP), along with the use of a web camera. They preferred the audiovisual dimension offered by Skype because online connection was much less expensive than telephone, and they wanted to see me and be seen as they spoke. So I switched to Skype (at that time believing it to be totally secure).

Whether on the telephone or on Skype, psychoanalysis proceeded. The analytic frame got attacked, resistance stepped in, interpretations were given and responded to, transference and countertransference developed, and an analytic process got underway, as happens in in-the-office analysis. We adapt our psychoanalytic technique to make the innovation of applying technology to analysis most effective. We discover how to use analysis of the new setting and its impact on the transference as grist for the mill until eventually experience of teleanalysis sheds light on analytic processes of traditional analysis (Scharff, J., 2015).

Whether meeting with an analyst in the same room or online, the analytic process thrives on the paradox of intimacy and distance. "The combination of these two elements, of intimacy and distance, conspires to create moments of immense frankness" (Nafisi, 2014, p. 127). Across time and space, an intimate relationship develops, patient and therapist achieve deep unconscious communication, and psychoanalysis arrives in unexplored territory.

Enthusiasm for technology and the outreach potential of teleanalysis should not blind us to its limitations and challenges. For instance, how can the patient imagine lying on the analyst's lap if the analyst is not breathing in the same room? Is it possible to regress to a state of fantasied fusion with the mother's body across virtual reality? How does the analyst cope with greater uncertainty? We need to take an analytic stance and examine both the constraint and the acceleration that technology puts on psychoanalysis. We need to explore and test the value versus harm of technology as a vehicle for conveying unconscious process. We need to talk and think together about our clinical experiences in teleanalysis and teletherapy, and we need systematic research into their clinical effectiveness.

Many patients who live in a remote area or must relocate ask for treatment online using Skype, but it is not yet known how many analysts conduct analyses using Skype. Many do not admit to doing analysis using Skype because it is still controversial. In contrast to this situation, the China-America Psychoanalytic Alliance proudly reports the occurrence in China of distance analysis (three to five sessions a week) with analysts of the American Psychoanalytic Association using VoIP (mainly Skype: sixty-six analyses are currently ongoing and eighty-four have terminated (Fishkin, personal communication)).

Two separate research studies were funded by the International Psychoanalytical Association (IPA) to learn how many analysts use telephone or Skype with or without the use of a web camera in therapy and analysis. The two questionnaire surveys sent to the IPA membership generated response rates of 7.7 percent (Werbin et al., 2014) and six percent (Wanlass, 2015). These percentages seem low but are in keeping with the usual response rate to such surveys sent by email to the IPA membership. Werbin and her colleagues regard the responses as representative of membership experiences and attitudes, whereas Wanlass regrets the effect of the low response rate and sample size on the validity and generalizability of the findings. Nevertheless, the findings of the two studies were fairly close in that the percentages reporting the use of technological means for remote analysis were 62.2 percent and sixty-five percent respectively. Of these Werbin found that 53.9 percent used Skype, and, whether they used it or not, thirty-four percent regarded teleanalysis as psychoanalytic in nature. Wanlass found that 63.2 percent of responders using technology had conducted analytic sessions by phone. The next most common method of technology used was Skype, with 41.8 percent using Skype with video camera and 25.4 percent using Skype with audio alone. Wanlass reports that of the total sample, including both users and non-users of technology, 42.3 percent found it good or adequate psychoanalytic treatment. In Werbin's study forty-one percent reported that technology-assisted analysis is not a form of psychoanalysis, while in Wanlass's study over fifty percent found it marginally or not at all acceptable.

At first glance, the research findings appear to support Bolognini's statement of 29 January 2016 to the IPA members and candidates: "Full remote analysis is not considered by the majority of analysts and by the Representatives at the IPA Board as an acceptable analysis for a future psychoanalyst. We want to develop an open and intensive debate in the IPA, but for now our duty is to preserve the current training education rules and procedures until the Board decides otherwise. This does not mean that some helpful and creative analytic work cannot be done via Skype or other systems, and we respect the professional activity of those colleagues who undoubtedly help patients living in remote areas through this treatment" (Bolognini, 2016).

But the average age of respondents was 60.5, drawing from a population of IPA members where the average age is 63.27 (Wanlass, 2015). Noting this, Wanlass points out that the field of psychoanalysis is removed in age and experience with internet-based communication from the analytic patients and practitioners of the digital generation. These senior analysts may think quite differently from younger, digital generation analysts who are not yet fully autonomous in their mode of psychoanalytic practice but who will become the guardians of best practice in the future. Additionally, we have no empirical data from the analysands themselves, who may take a different view than treaters in the field about the effectiveness of their analytic experience. Younger patients and their younger analysts opt for teleanalysis because it is in keeping with their networked lifestyle and mindset. Certainly, the findings of both research studies support the need for further research efforts to increase understanding of technology use and to generate recommendations for clinical training in technology-assisted methods of intervention. So, it is good that the IPA welcomes intensive debate and hopefully will support more research into the effectiveness of teleanalysis now and into the future. Otherwise, psychoanalysis will be out of step with developments in telemedicine and telemental health in particular and with the digital culture of the patient population in general. "In the age of 24/7 communication through social media, email, texting and video, healthcare is trapped in a world where in-person interaction is still the primary form of contact between patients and providers" (Avizia, 2016).

Skype in particular: pros and cons

Many patients prefer the convenience and familiarity of Skype. They already use it with their families and non-local friends. So it is easy and free. For the analyst, there is the same benefit of convenience and affordability. That is the major "pro" of Skype. The second advantage of Skype over using the telephone is that when using Skype with a web camera the analyst can see the patient's facial expressions and body movements. This counters the frequent objection that when nonverbal communication is lost there can be no analysis. Access to nonverbal body language is the other major "pro" of Skype used with a web camera.

The use of Skype has a number of "cons." There are technical problems with the image on Skype. The image may pixelate, which gives an impression of fragmentation. There are technical problems with the audio on Skype, because although the sound quality may be startlingly good, especially when using a headset, the connection is subject to dropped calls and junk on the line, which interrupts relaxed listening and creates latent anxiety (Lin, 2015). This makes for a frustrating experience of helplessness and instability. So, communicating on Skype is certainly not the same as communicating with the patient in the same room, but the patient and the analyst can accommodate to these technical interferences and can analyze their impact as they connect to earlier experiences of frustration and abandonment. And as I mentioned, it is easy and free.

This is appealing but ultimately has been found to be unsafe. Using Skype to communicate with friends and loved ones, patients and analysts naturally are not concerned about confidentiality. In the treatment setting, however, the analyst's guarantee of confidentiality is an ethical responsibility and a professional commitment. When I used it years ago, Skype was promoted as totally secure for computer-to-computer use (Snyder, 2011a). Now there are major concerns about the level of security that Skype offers. The security studies literature reports that Skype's encryption has never been made available to verify that claim, and breaches have been reported. In my experience patients in teleanalysis or teletherapy do not worry about the security issues even when they are pointed out to them. It is up to the analyst to make sure that patients understand the risks of information leakage and that they co-operate to secure the treatment against those risks. But that is not possible using Skype. In short, the major con of Skype is that it is a consumer-grade platform that cannot and does not claim to be HIPAA compliant. That is to say in the United States it does not meet the requirements of the Health Insurance Portability and Accountability Act of 1996. So it became no longer tenable for me to use Skype. China America Psychoanalytic Alliance (CAPA) now recommends Zoom and VSee. Skype is a compromised means of connection for psychoanalysis. Skype is simply not a medical grade platform. This is the major "con" of Skype analysis.

Teleanalysis in general

Ethical and legal considerations

Having eschewed Skype in favor of secure videotechnology, my argument now expands to teleanalysis in general. Best practice guidelines call for the teleanalyst to sign a business agreement as a business associate of a videotechnology services provider (VTC) that does claim to be HIPAA compliant, and pay the yearly fee as a business expense. However, that is costly. For the analyst seeing just one patient at a distance it is a considerable expense at $200–300 a month. The patient then is given an individual address to access the therapy session through a portal to a virtual waiting room with a connection that is completely private, and secure. There is no recording or storage of data. In the unlikely event of a breach, say by hackers getting through the company's advanced security system, the company reports the breach and appropriate steps can be taken. Unfortunately, the extra step and cost of signing up means that many therapists continue to use Skype instead. Some patients push their therapists to use Skype because they are familiar with it, in disregard of the risk of intrusion to their privacy. The only safe thing is to purchase a subscription to a medical grade platform that offers a signed business agreement that does meet HIPAA requirements. Having made that decision, I am glad to have the reassurance of greater security, no dropped calls, no junk on the line, and no pixelation of the image, but the image is still not vividly three dimensional, and network conditions can still affect the quality of the connection. Patients and analysts using a teleanalytic setting may feel helplessly at the mercy of the internet. Much depends on the available bandwidth at the user's location.

Let's say that patient and analyst agree to stop using Skype and decide to transfer to a videotechnology company. Technical problems still need to be addressed. The image is necessarily flat, like looking at a rectangular photograph that occasionally moves. With the smaller image of the analyst in the corner of the screen, the impression is of an envelope with a stamp on it, an eerie reminder of earlier means of communicating across a distance. It is disconcerting for the analyst to see an image of herself as well until she learns how to move it off the screen. Patients may actually contribute to the technical problems in various ways. They may fail to purchase adequate equipment or bandwidth. They may create the interference by failing to close down other programs that are running on their computer. They may fail to use a headset or forget to charge the iPad. These forms of technical interference are manifestations of anxiety and active expressions of resistance. And technical interference provides a projection screen for the expression of the negative transference in particular.

Although at first teleanalysis may seem cold and distant, lacking the "security, constancy, stability, and intimacy of the mother's womb and her embrace" experienced in the analytic office setting, analyst and analysand nevertheless get used to it and "in their minds create an internal space where both parties are emotionally there" (Lin, 2015). To put it another way, "the analytic space can become libidinous within any technology" (Aryan, 2015). Despite technical problems with sound and image, many people who live at a distance find that technology offers a reasonably manageable experience. For them, teleanalysis with occasional challenges to connection is preferable to the limited audio-connection of a landline telephone; the disruption when a person must relocate to find an analyst; the interference with family life and clinical continuity with patients when a candidate has to travel for condensed analysis; the incestuous crowding when sharing one analyst with the other candidates, as happens in Beijing and Shanghai; or no analysis at all. Teleanalysis permits optimum frequency, augments continuity, enables outreach to patients in underserved areas, and serves potential trainees who live far from an analytically informed center. Compared to the expense of shuttle analysis, teleanalysis provides a relatively inexpensive way to spread the values of psychoanalysis. Many patients who live remotely conclude that teleanalysis is relatively manageable, and better than the alternatives.

Licensure

Licensure and reimbursement are concerns, both difficult to figure out. In the United States the analyst must be licensed by professional discipline both in the state where the analyst practices and the state in which the patient resides. But the ease of application for a license, and the rules about reimbursement vary from state to state. Complying with the rules for just one patient is an enormous burden on the therapist, and so some productive analyses have been dropped because the analyst cannot obtain a full, temporary, or restricted license. Some states have now joined a compact to allow psychologists to do teletherapy across state lines, but it is not actually operational, and movement toward a federal medical license is underway. At first the states opposed such a license, but now many states have signed on and others have the move under consideration in the fall of 2016 (Figure 1).

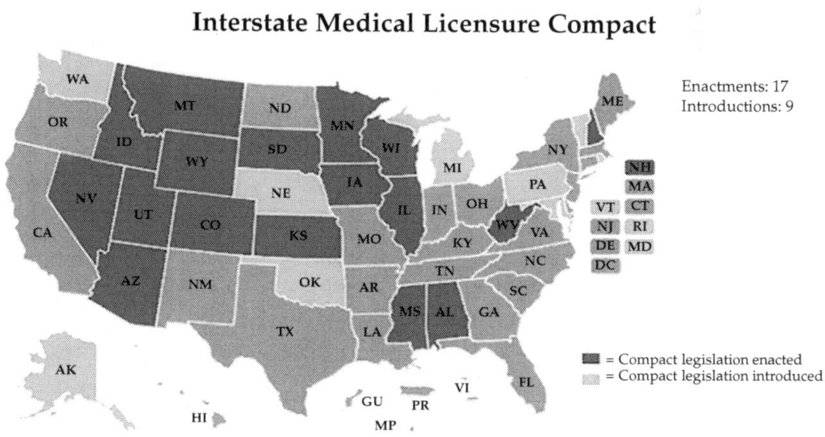

Figure 1. Seventeen states have enacted the Interstate Medical Licensure Compact so far, with nine more states introducing compact legislation. (Map courtesy of the Federation of State Medical Boards, http://license-portability.org/).

Beyond these practical concerns about technology, regulations, and best practice guidelines, there are psychoanalytic concerns about teleanalysis. Are teleanalysts inducing a state of denial of separation and loss? Do they give in to resistance instead of interpreting it? Critics claim that teleanalysis is not really analysis because it has bent the established frame, there is no actual bodily presence, no atmosphere, and no sense of smell. Opponents of teleanalysis claim that it privileges the false self. But any in-the-office psychoanalysis may fail to reach the true self. In teleanalysis the lack of physical proximity may actually fuel disclosure of the true self. For instance, a single teleanalysis session, where the analyst's presence was less immediate than in the analysis routinely held in the analyst's office, offered the patient a degree of anonymity similar to that offered by lying down instead of interacting face-to-face, and allowed the patient freedom to confront the true, grumpy self (Scharff, D., 2015).

Indications and contraindications

If we can settle the licensure and ethical issues, and contemplate recommending teleanalysis, we consider many criteria, not only analyzability (Aryan, 2015). Teleanalysis is usually not for the patient with a really fragile ego that breaks down and leads to hospitalization, with a highly insecure attachment style of the disorganized type, with a psychopathic organization or tendency to act out with frequent suicidal gestures, with a person of interest to the government, or with a parent in a contentious custody dispute where confidential information could possibly be obtained by hacking. Nevertheless, selection is based not only on diagnostic suitability but also on willingness to adopt technology, capacity for commitment, existing therapeutic alliance, local network of support from family and friends, and availability of a local psychiatrist colleague in case of emergency. Indications for teleanalysis include the relocation of patient or analyst, immobilization because of physical or mental illness of the patient or significant others, physical immobility of the analyst, travel that interrupts continuity of care, and, above all, lack of local access to psychoanalysis for patient or prospective analytic candidate.

Modes of resistance

Teleanalysts admit to valuing continuity of care over interpreting resistance to enforced separation and loss, but they certainly do interpret resistance. We find that resistance emerges in various ways as it does in the analyst's office, for instance, through silences, hesitations, coughing at anxious moments, late payment, and non-payment. In teleanalysis, patients may displace anxiety onto technology. They may forget to call or lose the dial-in information. They may speak too softly or too fast. They may fail to use a headset, provide an up-to-date computer with adequate bandwidth, or arrange adequate lighting for the image. They may keep moving away from the microphone, or chat as if on a social call. They may insist on Skype to avoid the formality of connecting to a securely confidential session, or they may avoid using a web camera to avoid the shame of being seen. Each of these manifestations is analyzed as it reflects resistance, defense, affect, and transference tied to early experience and internal object relationships (Sehon, 2015).

One patient persistently failed to enter the private electronic address for the secure technology service I had arranged (and for which I was paying a substantial fee), and contacted me instead on the free consumer-grade version of the platform until I realized what was happening. After this patient eventually complied with my request, she said this: "There is a profound meaning in your wanting to switch to a program with more security. It has had a very strong impact on me. I feel this relationship is much more professional, which is funny because nothing has changed. I now feel like I am really in analysis. I went to another level in the work. I understand now your determination in wanting to do that."

The frame and the setting

Analyst and patient agree on the externals of the frame of treatment regarding establishing the treatment in the analyst's office where the analyst and patient are physically present in the same geographic space for each one to establish their identity, style, role, and expectations in an embodied relatedness before moving to a teleanalysis format. They agree on frequency of sessions, duration of session, and frequency of periods of in-person immersion. The frame is as important as in in-the-office analysis. It is flexible to accommodate those who live at a distance, but the frame is not bent or corrupted by doing so. It is simply adapted to current reality.

The contract includes that the patient (or the analyst if it is the analyst who has had to relocate) returns for a series of visits every few months or so to reconnect to the familiar and trusted holding environment of analysis in the office. This is standard practice at this point in our experience of teleanalysis. But I have questions about it. I worry that it diminishes the value of the teleanalytic work, as if it is just a placeholder for the "real thing." It may not be necessary once we have more confidence in and acceptance of the modality of teleanalysis, but I have not taken that chance. A series of twice a day visits in the office maintains the alliance and provides a venue for exchanges in physical co-presence to elaborate on any transference perceptions (see Lin Tao, Chapter Seven).

With a patient in analysis on the couch using videotechnology, I ask the patient to arrange the computer camera to focus on the couch. The patient initiates the call and I respond to say Hello, the patient lies down and begins the session, she on her couch, and I in my chair looking at the couch displayed on my screen, the same view as I would have in my office. She uses ear buds or headphones connected to the computer so that the sound comes directly to me from the microphone at her mouth, not through the air, which improves the sound quality. This has been described as the patient entering and filling the mind, the line like a long umbilical cord. One patient set up the camera to focus on a couch in front of a long bright window that made her look faded and small. My comment about her choice of setting led her to remember that she had been in an incubator box for the first month of life, and although she had known this, she had not experienced it until it was conveyed so vividly in the analytic virtual space (Scharff, 2013b).

My patients in teleanalysis have all been on the couch. I have trouble imagining myself treating anyone in analysis four or five times per week face-to-face because of my own preferences regarding closeness and distance. I need the degree of physical distance offered by the couch in order to be close. I have treated a college student in once a week teletherapy face-to-face. She sat close to her computer so that she could also check email as it came in (typical of the digital generation). This put her face too close to me, flattened her image, and I couldn't see her whole person as I did when she was seeing me in my office when she lived at home. I found the experience too much in my face. When she was not speaking, I felt under the gun to say something, and when she did speak, I felt pinned listening. But this was not simply my style of intimacy under threat. She was conveying to me, and I was picking up in my countertransference, how she felt alternately controlled by, and demanded to take care of, a frustrating and intrusive father.

In teleanalysis the analyst is not in control of the setting, although some do advise their patients on how to set it up (Estrada, 2015). Even so, the setting is constructed by the patient, and the analyst meets the patient on the patient's terms. From their separate bases in time and space, analyst and analysand meet in cyberspace. Patients' choice of setting reveals aspects of their history, personality, and unconscious. Another patient who connected to analytic sessions from home, from two temporary offices, and from a newly established permanent office, left her analyst feeling unrooted. In response to interpretation based on this countertransference, the patient revealed that she had been raised by an extended family in their various houses, unsure of which was home.

Just as each patient has a unique way of using the couch, each patient has a unique way of arranging the setting. Poor angle of view, a drifting microphone, a dark room, may express resistance to being seen and heard, difficulty in adapting to technology, reluctance to taking care of the analyst's need for the patient to co-create the setting, distress at losing in-person sessions, and negative transference. Complaints about the limitations of technology tend to diminish as both parties get used to the format, but we need to distinguish between a mature adaptation and a fake adjustment that actually covers a psychic retreat. Patient and analyst in separate rooms connect in a third space, the virtual space, and this creates a triangle in which they may pair intensely in gratitude for connection, and exclude some other aspect such as fear and deprivation of actual presence. The analyst is dependent on the patient to provide a secure, private setting. It has been said that the patient's control over the frame leaves the analyst seeming to be a weak and unreliable object, which makes it much harder to offer a secure holding environment.

Is teleanalysis real analysis?

The main objection to teleanalysis from traditional analysis, especially from European analysts, is that in teleanalysis the body of analyst and the body of patient are not in the analyst's office. How can the analyst pick up nonverbal clues to shifts in affect and detect the emergence of unconscious? How can a patient regress to experience preverbal experience and merge with the body of the analyst if the body of analyst and patient are not in physical proximity as protagonists in the cure? Certainly in traditional analytic setting the two bodies are in the same room, but they are not in physical contact. Any physical interaction is a fantasy co-created by the unconscious mind of patient and analyst. That fantasy may be stimulated by the relative proximity of the two bodies, but it is equally likely that the fantasy is stimulated by the deprivation of bodily separation across a distance in cyberspace. Just because the bodies are not co-present does not mean that they are not in relationship. The teleanalyst and the patient do each live in a body and communicate physically through voice, breath, and visible gestures. Like the traditional analyst, the teleanalyst appreciates that the body is a fleshy mass, a volume in space, a source of sensation and movement (Anzieu, 1979). The body is a loved and hated object of the self and of the other. I have found that the teleanalyst can still take the patient into the depths of her psychic body and resonate there with the patient's undreamt traumatic elements and primitive transferences.

Among those who have not engaged in a teleanalytic session, there remain many questions about teleanalysis that are often couched in criticism. Is it analysis at all? How can transference and countertransference occur in virtual space? How can it be analysis if the frame is bent to accommodate the patient's wishes and avoid separation anxiety? Concretely, the body may be absent but symbolically it is as present as in traditional analysis. Even with patient and analyst connected by virtual channels of communication, a relationship of symbolic importance develops as the frame recalls the "most primitive fusion with the mother's body" (Bleger, 1967, p. 518).

I say let's raise the questions, they are all valid concerns, and subject them to the test of experience by asking analysts to present clinical session notes from teleanalysis and studying the material in depth with an open-minded but questioning attitude. Does the analyst work with unconscious process? Does she deal with affect? Does she interpret transference/countertransference? Does the material show analytic process? Is this really analysis?

Using only the telephone an analyst may suffer from the lack of sensory information, facial expression, and tone. When her patient shows a negative transference to the telephone the analyst may doubt the value of her decision to offer teleanalysis. But the emergence of negative transference is not just a resistance to the process, it is a necessary part of the process. But this can be hard to remember because when adapting to using the telephone in the psychoanalytic setting, we feel anxious about doing it well or doing it at all. When we do not have the authorization of our profession—on the contrary, colleagues may be attacking our papers on teleanalysis at meetings or in journals—any ordinary criticism or ill-feeling about the limitations of the telephone from the patient is harder to see as transference. Then the analyst may actually struggle with a negative transference to the telephone. For some analysts, that will be the end of the foray into telephone-assisted psychoanalysis. Others may be persuaded by a patient, as I was, to switch to using a web camera.

Is the web camera really necessary? Yes, when the analyst is not comfortable on the phone without the visual channel of communication. If the patient prefers to use the telephone, I happily agree to that. I find the telephone adequate because with the visual channel missing, other channels assume greater importance and I become more sensitive to changes in tone, hesitations, pauses, and the quality of silence. For some patients it is adequate and for others it is preferable. For some it is less than satisfactory. Persuaded to try using a web camera with VoIP by a tech-savvy patient, the analyst who is uncomfortable on the telephone may warm to the idea of the teleanalysis with a web camera, finding that visual access enables the detection of patients' responses of anger, sadness, shame, and fear.

Once patient and analyst have agreed on the form of technology to be used, there will still be ambivalence. Some patients may need a trial period of technology-assisted psychoanalysis, having been assured that they can stop at any time. Sometimes the analyst may feel more in touch with the visual dimension in place, but the patient may feel more upset—too close, too exposed, or even coerced. This is a reaction to technology, but it is also a repetition of an earlier experience of discomfort over intimacy. What is it that the patient does not want the analyst to see too clearly? What if the patient hates his analyst to see blushing of the skin, sweating, a tic, or other signs of anxiety? In that case the analyst may feel too curious and anxiety-provoking, and this countertransference may lead her to understand the internal object relations that embody the impact on him of a parent experienced as voyeuristic. What if he is embarrassed by pustular acne, facial hair, angioedema of the lip, or other physical attributes that are imbued with feelings of shame? The analyst may feel intrusive, and ashamed in identification with the patient's self-loathing. If coercion is the main feature of the patient's experience, the analyst may feel abusive and traumatizing to the patient. The patient's hatred of the analyst's need for technology that includes a visual image may be a current version of the patient's mental state of victimization by unauthorized looking. When the negative transference is projected into the technology, the analyst may collude with hatred of the technology or she may take a step back and realize that she herself is being viewed as the perpetrator. From there the analyst can appreciate from inside the transference something of the pain the patient has experienced. The analytic couple may then be able to reach the origins of the abuse scenario in early childhood.

Does the analyst work with affect? Yes, with shame, one of the hardest affects to deal with. Does the analyst work with unconscious conflict? Yes, in analyzing the resistance to using the web camera. Does she work with transference? Yes, when she inhabits the role of the perpetrator. Does she experience countertransference? Yes, she experiences herself as an intrusive person who sees too much, and she may disavow this perception at first, by moving her chair back from the screen. Does she work with her countertransference? Yes, if she analyzes her choice to be more distant, draws an interpretation from it, and moves the analysis forward.

The analysis of reactions to the introduction of technology can create a turning point. When you conduct technology-assisted psychoanalysis, the experience of the mode of connection supplies the manifest content that stands in for the latent content. In this way technology is an extension of the holding environment and it receives the contextual transference. Technology provides the metaphors for the elucidation of unconscious material in the analytic relationship. The intrusiveness of the audiovisual dimension of the teleanalytic setting must at some point become the focus of the conversation, and then it will provide the engine of important analytic work. On the other hand, some patients prefer the use of the web camera because the visual dimension lets them feel more secure. They readily accept technology and it does not become the focus of analysis. Yet the ready acceptance must also be examined, since acquiescence may be part of a pattern of avoiding conflict that is agreeable but ultimately self-defeating.

Like traditional analysis, teleanalysis calls forth self-protective defenses and facilitates self-expression. For one patient the visual dimension is a threat, for another it is a reassurance. For one analyst teletherapy is a violation; for another it is a useful way to offer continuity of care.

Unconscious communication through voice

In analysis that occurs in analysts' offices, we are accustomed to noting changes in tone, depth and rate of breathing, and hesitations. We deal with what the patient actually said and how they said it, and with what we said and how it was heard. In teleanalysis, we become highly sensitive to breath, nuances of dialogues, and vocal inflection. We find that, whether we look at an image or not, the voice conjures up a visual image. We see the patient moving and reacting in our mind's eye. In imagination we are co-present. The voice is part of the body, and thus the body enters the analytic space through the voice, and also through bodily sensations that the analyst and patient experience in response to vocal tone and rhythm of the other. The verbal exchanges of teleanalysis recall the auditory environment of infancy, as important as holding and handling of the infant in the development of the self (Anzieu, 1979).

For example, a depressed underfunctioning woman patient fell silent. The lack of auditory input created in the analyst an image of a desolate child alone on a balcony (Scharff, 2013b). The analyst next experienced a sensation of dropping, and shared this countertransference. The patient reported a memory of wanting to jump from a balcony in order to convey to others how she felt. She later said that what mattered most to her in this interchange was that the analyst had been on the balcony with her, and she was not alone. She said that it was a transformative moment after which she returned to full productivity.

The alliance and the transference–countertransference: the real and the virtual

Communication in teleanalysis is virtual. Here we have to pause to consider the meaning of virtual. Virtual communication refers to the engagement of patient and analyst as they speak, listen, emote, and relate while connected by the therapeutic relationship that they establish using technology to bridge the physical distance between them. This setting creates a simulation of the co-presence of patient and analyst, and recreates the environment, experience, and interaction of the in-the-office analytic session. The terms virtual and simulation suggest that teleanalysis is not real psychoanalysis and therefore cannot be as effective as traditional in-the-office analysis. Simulation makes it seem as if what happens between analyst and patient is pretend, fake, less than the real thing. True, at present the technological capacity for simulation is limited, but it is not hard to imagine in the near future affordable access to a virtual reality application for psychoanalysis that conveys sensory experience including tactile sensation and smell.

The term virtual describes communication that is "existing or resulting in essence or effect though not in actual fact, form, or name" or "being such in essence or effect though not formally recognized or admitted" or more simply, "being very like something without actually being it" (Merriam-Webster, 2017). Teleanalysis is of the essence of psychoanalysis. It has all the features of analysis: building therapeutic relationships, working with resistance, transference–countertransference, interpretation, insight, construction and reconstruction, dream analysis, and working through, and, in my view, it has the same effect as traditional in-the-office analysis, though it is not in fact, or in name, traditional psychoanalysis. Virtual implies something that is almost what it simulates, and that it carries the potential to become exactly like it. For instance the "virtual extinction of the dinosaur" refers to extinction that had more or less happened and would become complete. I certainly do not want to see the extinction of in-the-office psychoanalysis, but I think we are moving to a time when teleanalysis can be regarded as equivalent in effectiveness, when combined with in-the-office sessions that set the model for co-presence that can then be simulated.

Virtual seems to me to refer also to the latent content that lies within the manifest content. Even when patient and analyst are meeting solely in the office setting, the transference/countertransference dialectic of the analytic relationship may be described as a virtual reality, an "as if" construction of the infant at the breast and the child in the oedipal triangle, fostering the expression of love, lust, and aggression in the pursuit of the other and the formation of the self. Indeed the analysis is destroyed if that virtual reality becomes real. Corbett (2013) asks: "Do we move too quickly to defend the 'real' of interpersonal exchange as opposed to what is most often called the 'virtual' that occurs in technological exchange? And if we move too quickly to separate the interpersonal and the virtual might we also lose hold of the fantastic potential of psychic equivalence—the potential of psychic reality as it blends and bends material reality?"

Last, a word about the term "in person." Authors frequently describe traditional psychoanalysis as being in person, as if teleanalysis is not in person. In traditional psychoanalysis, the analyst provides the environment, the patient brings his or her body into the analyst's office and onto the couch, the patient gets on with using it, and the two of them develop an intimate relationship full of excitement and frustration all of which are grist for the mill. In teleanalysis, the patient provides the physical setting and puts his body onto his or her own couch, the analyst puts his or her body into the analytic chair with ears tuned in to words and eyes looking at nonverbal language and, with hearts and minds engaged, the analytic pair co-operate to create an environment online and develop an intimate relationship full of excitement, longing, and frustration, all of which gets analyzed. How is that not "in person?" We look beyond the concrete facts of the geographic separation of bodies and the use of cyberspace as the place of meeting, to realize that the unconscious communication takes place in the space between us and in the communicating, mutually affected and affecting minds of patient and analyst. In some situations, of course, cyberspace may be a place of sequestration and hatred, as in psychic retreat or claustrum, but in an effective psychoanalysis, it may be a place of imagination, exploration, and discovery, and, like the dream space, of symbolization.

Conclusions

Most patients over the age of fifty prefer to meet the analyst at the analyst's office, but they accept teleanalysis as an option in exceptional circumstances (Russell, 2015). But some younger patients prefer teleanalysis and even text-based therapy (Carlino, 2011). Adapting analysis to the reality of the changing needs and ways of communicating of patients in a rapidly changing digital culture is essential if psychoanalysis is to survive. And psychoanalysis is needed more than ever to provide a quiet reflective space in the middle of the multitasking, connected, dispersed way of thinking and working. Adapting ourselves to new models is hard, particularly when the analytic establishment reacts against innovation to maintain traditional standards, based not on objective assessment of clinical effectiveness, but on the need to maintain consensus on the quality of power of the institution (Aryan & Carlino, 2013; Scharff, 2013a). Opponents of teleanalysis are usually arguing against it without having tried it, but their voice is compelling. So those using technology for analysis tend to hide what they are doing, stay under the radar, and avoid attack from colleagues, in the name of ethics. As Lemma and Caparotta (2014) noted, "Any pace of change in the psychoanalytic world takes too long or it may even have to occur 'secretly' before unusual or unconventional methods of working become common knowledge and thus influence or are endorsed in our clinical practice" (p. 18). The field of psychoanalysis needs more clinical experience and systematic research on the clinical effectiveness of teleanalysis.

Teleanalysis is not for every patient and not for every analyst. But personal preference and clinical unsuitability should not be arguments for demonizing teleanalysis altogether. Declaring what is and is not psychoanalysis will slow down the evolution of psychoanalysis, and seeing technology as evil will lead to a shutdown that will widen the gap between the generations. The future of psychoanalysis lies in the internet's potential for expanded relatedness. Psychoanalysis needs to open up to a riskier, more unknown, more diverse environment in which to grow and change and meet the needs of the new generation of technology natives.

Certainly, teleanalysis is not my preference, but sometimes it is indicated. Some of those who have avoided teleanalysis moved to accepting it when they needed it, for instance, to maintain continuity for a young patient who had to travel (Ferro, 2016). In some circumstances, for some patients, it is better than traditional in-the-office psychoanalysis. If we accept the reality of what it is, and mourn what it is not without denial, then it can be as vital and effective as any traditional analysis.

References

Anzieu, D. (1979). The sound image of the self. *International Review of Psycho-analysis, 6*: 23–36.

Aryan, A. (2015). Psychoanalytic process within cyber-technology. Panel presentation: Case study and qualitative research in teleanalysis. 49th IPA Congress, Boston, July 2015.

Aryan, A., & Carlino, R. (2013). The power of the establishment in the face of change: Psychoanalysis by telephone. In: J. S. Scharff (Ed.), *Psychoanalysis Online: Mental Health, Teletherapy, and Training* (pp. 161–170). London: Karnac.

Avizia research report (2016). Closing the telehealth gap. *American Telemedicine Association News Brief*, 23 June.

Bleger, J. (1967). Psycho-analysis of the psycho-analytic frame. *International Journal of Psychoanalysis, 48*: 511–519.

Bolognini, S. (2016). Email to IPA members and candidates, 29 January 2016.

Carlino, R. (2011). *Distance Analysis*. London: Karnac.

Corbett, K. (2013). Shifting sexual cultures, the potential space of online relations, and the promise of psychoanalytic listening. *Journal of the American Psychoanalytic Association, 61*: 25–44.

Estrada, T. (2015). Qualitative research on 36 cases in teleanalysis. Panel presentation: Case study and qualitative research in teleanalysis. 49th IPA Congress, Boston, July 2015.

Ferro, A. (2016). Preface. In: *Psychoanalysis, Identity, and the Internet* (ed. A. Marzi). London: Karnac.

Lemma, A., & Caparotta, L. (2014). *Psychoanalysis in the Technoculture Era.* London: Routledge.

Lin, T. (2015). Teleanalysis: problems and limitations. In: J. S. Scharff (Ed.), *Psychoanalysis Online 2: Impact of Technology on Development, Training, and Therapy*. London: Karnac.

Merriam-Webster (2017). https://www.merriam-webster.com/dictionary/virtual

Nafisi, A. (2014). *The Republic of Imagination: America in Three Books.* New York: Viking.

Russell, G. (2015). *Screen Relations*. London: Karnac.

Scharff, D. (2015). Occasional telephone sessions in ongoing in-person psychoanalysis. In: J. S. Scharff (Ed.), *Psychoanalysis Online 2: Impact of Technology on Human Development, Treatment, Training, and Therapy.* London: Karnac.

Scharff, J. S. (2012). Clinical effectiveness of analysis over the telephone or internet. *International Journal of Psychoanalysis, 93*: 81–95.

Scharff, J. S. (Ed.) (2013a). *Psychoanalysis Online: Mental Health, Teletherapy, and Training*. London: Karnac.

Scharff, J. S. (2013b). Technology assisted psychoanalysis. *Journal of the American Psychoanalytic Association, 61:* 491–509.

Scharff, J. S. (Ed.) (2015). *Psychoanalysis Online 2. Impact of Technology on Human Development, Treatment, and Training*. London: Karnac.

Sehon, C. (2015). Can we analyze transference in analysis using Skype? Panel presentation: Case study and qualitative research in teleanalysis. 49th IPA Congress, Boston, July 2015.

Snyder, E. (2011a). How Skype works (PowerPoint slide presentation). Paper presented at the American Psychoanalytic Association winter meeting. New York City, 15 January.

Wanlass, J. (2015). Findings from research questionnaire and interviews of analysts. Panel presentation: Case study and qualitative research in teleanalysis. 49th IPA Congress, Boston, July 2015.

Werbin, A., Burdet, M., Giménez Noble, F., Sahovaler Litvinoff, D., Hirsch Hardy, J., & Ambort, G. (2014). Remote therapy research: A research on distance psychoanalysis sponsored by the International Psychoanalytical Association. http://www.remotetherapy.net/home.html

CHAPTER TWO

Analytic dialogue: its multiple transformations—clinical implementation through telecommunication

Ricardo Carlino (Argentina and Mexico)

The crucial element of clinical psychoanalysis is the dialogue between analyst and patient. For this dialogue to occur, the basic condition must be met: each inhabits a prescribed role in a specific situation agreed upon in the analytic contract, which contains an appropriate framework for the task. If this condition for psychoanalysis can be met while patient and analyst connect using information and communication technology (ICT), then they can conduct an analytic treatment at a distance. This proposition is framed by an already long period of socio-cultural transformation (Carlino, 2000), which is changing our way of conceiving of, and going about, everyday communication, making ICT of utmost importance in contemporary life.

The real and the virtual in the teleanalytic dialogue

We are now far from the dawn of history, when it was essential to recognize reality through sight and touch, the sound of an object, smell, and taste. In those remote early stages of knowledge, sensory experience built up the sense of reality. Beyond what could be touched, seen, smelled, and tasted, there lay the realm of the evocable, and the imaginable, but what could be imagined was not, back then, possible to actualize. What I would like to convey is that several completely new experiences that had always been impossible to imagine began, at some point, to be possible. Suddenly, what had been purely from the realm of science fiction became something real. Couldn't telephone communication, which we've known throughout our lifetime, also be thought of as either virtual or real? It is easy to imagine that the first telephone experiences of the nineteenth century produced affective–intellectual upheavals.

All technological advances of great transformative magnitude are experienced as a type of insurrection against established norms, given that they are contemplated in the preconception of the previous reality. I find it possible to assume that, in order to mitigate the very real intellectual and affective upheavals produced by such transformations, the term "virtual" began to be used as a way of maintaining calm and making the new phenomenon seem less real, and less threatening. My intention is not to criticize but rather to describe a phenomenon that, at the time of impact, creates an understandable reaction of wishing to reduce the threat.

Initial reception of new ideas

When there arrives in a science or a discipline a new concept that implies a departure from the traditionally accepted paradigm, this new concept can be well received or, conversely, be considered misguided, mistaken, or recalcitrant. In some cases, it may even be considered insane. The evolution of knowledge throughout history abounds in stories of this type. Sometimes it is observed that the introduction of an idea that differs from that which is already known and accepted, instead of being discussed in order to add clarity and understanding, is often caught up in what might seem to be a ruthless struggle of interests. The new idea, while trying to find a place in the ideas established within individual minds and social customs, can be perceived as violating the established order, especially by those who hold that which is established to be definitive and unchangeable (Aryan & Carlino, 2012, 2013).

Freud and many of his contemporaries suffered ill-treatment from the Establishment due to their ideas. Nevertheless, they were able to bring recognition for their ideas by making further contributions to already-held beliefs, with no intention of destroying anything. As in Freud's situation, the ideas of a great innovator and the thinkers around him, find support in related ideas and parallel disciplines, and thus their theoretic developments reach their maximum potential. When this occurs, there is a true possibility of contributing new ways of thinking that will either enhance or modify previous concepts. This, however, can cause severe narcissistic disturbance in those who cannot differentiate their own person from the ideas with which they identify, either in order to maintain a narcissistic object relationship (Freud, 1917e) or in order to protect interests linked to hegemonic power.

Historical evolution

Since the sharp increase in the development of mass media in the 1970s, the passing years have lessened the enormity of its impact, given the changes in human behavior and human contemplation of reality that have already occurred in response. The extraordinary reach of the media has changed the established logic of what had been considered remote and inaccessible and has given people the choice to live at a distance from their loved ones or their work. A comparatively high percentage of them are changing their place of residence, either temporarily or permanently. Those who live far from anywhere an analyst may live aspire to undergo analysis because of access to information and communication technology (ICT), following the pattern of how they acquired other services that had not been available to them before the advent of new communication technologies (Carlino, 2011). The number of people who aspire to undergo analysis increases as psychoanalysis, partly thanks to the media, becomes more familiar—and more accessible—to them.

The impact of ICT has led to a new culture of reality, and therefore we are propelled into a new reality in addition to the reality we had known before. The classic interpretation of reality is much like the tangible object that occupies a place in space and can never be in two places at the same time: it can never be ubiquitous. That is the reality that permits the distance between two people to be the determining factor as to whether or not it will be possible for them to connect—a concept as old as the human species. It harkens back to the days in which if two people began to move away from each other, they had to increase the volume of their voices, then shout, and finally, barring the intervention of technological support, discontinue their communication. Some of the first technologies to solve the problem of distance communication were body signals, then smoke signals, and banging in an established sound code. Thereafter, all other forms of technology were born.

As I stated earlier, the conditions and means of communication suitable for analytic dialogue make technology communication a good fit for its purpose. Admittedly, the treatment differs when both members of the duo are in session in the same physical place as opposed to when each one is in a different physical place. The difference between in-the-office sessions and teleanalysis sessions increases when additional communication resources such as text messages, WhatsApp, email, and other means are used between sessions. The adjunctive means of communication are needed to accommodate the facts of the daily lives of patients who are analyzed via technology. Patients live in different countries with different personal and work habits, often occurring in different time zones, and may often need to connect with their analyst between sessions to change the schedule of the session. In Mexico City, for example, unexpected traffic jams, or air pollution alerts can drastically change a patient's routine schedule and therefore should not be conceived of as an aspect of resistance. More and more frequently, patients who have their regular analysis in the analyst's office request that an analytic session be carried out with the help of communication technology because of their circumstantial inability to reach the venue. This flexible movement between in-office and technology-assisted sessions becomes more and more routine as communication technology becomes a regular aspect of modern interpersonal contact.

The spontaneous and coincidental alternation of sessions, as I have just described, leads me to propose a mental exercise. For a moment, let us separate ourselves from the preconception that analysis can only function as such when it is carried out in the analyst's office. Then we can consider various forms of conducting psychoanalysis, which in order to be considered as such, must show that an analytic process emerges and is consolidated. The choice of the term psychoanalysis stems from the fact that originally and for a century, psychoanalysis functioned in close quarters. However, this circumstance should not be used as a defining quality of psychoanalysis, given the fact that for such a long time the only option was to carry it out in that specific way. Now we have telecommunication to make psychoanalysis possible at a distance.

I want to wean teleanalysis away from its subordination to classical psychoanalysis, given that, at this point in time, teleanalysis already possesses an identity based on the coherence between what it has intended and what it has achieved. It is true that more research is needed. However, in order for that research to take place, we must remove the labelling of distance psychoanalysis as that which can only take place when no other possibility exists and in very exceptional situations. At this point it is generally still considered only as a substitute form of psychoanalytic treatment, inferior to psychoanalysis in the analyst's office. Nevertheless, we now have somewhat more than fifteen years of practice with this type of analysis—first by telephone and later by videoconference technology (such as Skype, VSee, Zoom) as its technology has improved in quality and security.

Psychoanalysis via telecommunication should be taken for what it is: a type of psychoanalysis conceived of with psychoanalytic theory, implemented by psychoanalytic technique in a secure setting, the dyad connected physically by means of a technological channel and psychoanalytically by unconscious communication. This type of psychoanalytic approach has its own characteristics, which can be perceived and utilized for the purposes of analysis. What are these specific characteristics? Is it the lack of proximity, which often leads it to be described as "better than nothing" psychoanalysis? Or does it have qualities that are useful for the benefit of psychoanalysis itself, rather than for the benefit of comparison to psychoanalysis.

This telecommunicative approach to psychoanalysis began developing into a recognized treatment after a series of isolated and exceptional distance analyses. These experimental analyses gave encouraging results and showed that technology-assisted psychoanalysis had a good prospect for successful treatment. Accompanying the socially transformative phenomenon of the internet and its effect on human life, psychoanalysis as teleanalysis continues marking a new direction previously unimaginable in civilization.

Jaron Lanier, an American writer and musician, is credited with the creation of so-called virtual reality (Aryan, Carlino, & Manguel, 2014). Virtual reality refers to certain sensory experiences captured through special lenses through which images transmitted by a series of synchronized computers give the sensation of being present. The flight simulator is an example of this. A much less sophisticated medium also produces "reality effects" (Berenstein, 2004), for instance, programs broadcast on television or in cinemas. People look at the screen, knowing that they are seeing broadcast images of what is happening or has already happened elsewhere, and take these images as televisual or cinematographic reality. If I were to assign an adjective to this phenomenon, it would be that of *elusive* reality because their programs are only one of the possible realities that can be captured. Similarly I regard as an elusive reality the comment of a patient, the report of an analyst communicating a session to a supervisor, a statement of a transference interpretation, the description of a dream, the portrayal of fiction by a writer, or a myth, for instance. All of these elusive realities are the result of various phenomena capable of producing, as a result of their descriptive impact in near time, *reality effects*. And yet, each of them is, in itself, a reality of the kind I qualified as elusive. When we listen to music that was recorded in the past, we do not consider it unreal simply because the recording artists are not present with us.

A common assumption is that what is virtual is the opposite of what is real and tangible. I believe that this conceptualization is mistaken when it is intended to be considered as universal but does not take into account non-material realities. At this point in psychoanalytic practice, the analytic dialogue carried out via telecommunication should be considered an instrument for real psychoanalytic communication. Denominating a patient as virtual is misleading and should no longer be used. Similarly, the terms virtual communication, virtual analysis, virtual session, and similar expressions do not do justice the integrity of the analytic process that develops. Patients, analysts, and treatments carried out through telecommunication are real. In these treatments, as well as in those made in the office, we should make the process the subject of our critical observation and discussion, rather than the setting the subject of derision.

Conditions for establishing an analytic dialogue

Just because an analyst and patient can communicate via telecommunication does not mean that an analysis takes place. In order for a dialogue to be considered psychoanalytic, it has to meet the standards for analytic dialogue. That is why before accepting a patient in treatment I usually ask myself several things:

- With the telephone as the means of communication, is it possible to create a dialogue in which the various messages and emotions expressed in oral language can be caught?

- Will the possible amount of verbal and behavioral acting out be perceived, contained, and elaborated for the purposes of analysis?
- Will the degree of emotional comfort that is necessary for sharing experiences and coping with the fantasies that accompany them be properly established with the patient in question?
- Will this method allow us to perceive, and connect with, disassociated feelings and thoughts?
- Through this means of communication, will it be possible to recognize and rectify or fulfil the fantasies of healing that the patient brings?

Although I am fully aware that before beginning an analysis, it is impossible to answer these questions with certainty, it is nevertheless useful to pose them and wait for just a hint of response. If this response is favorable, then once the process is established, it will show the expected results. These same questions are appropriate to ask every time an analyst decides to take on a new patient, notwithstanding the medium through which it will take place. Any attempt at analysis, wherever and however it may occur, is precisely that—an attempt at accomplishing something. The resulting reality will answer the question as to whether this attempt has proved fruitful (Galli, 2005; Paz, 2005). To this exhaustive definition of principles, it is necessary to explicitly state the ultimate requirement, which has been implicit until now: the suitability, experience, and ethics of the analyst to perform the task of analysis.

Following the fundamental rule, the patient communicates to the analyst his feelings and thoughts, while the analyst engages in free-floating attention. While this is an essential aspect of the dialogue, one must also consider what they achieve in that dialogue. Both patient and analyst, each from his or her role, create together a conversational product in which both are involved and engaged in its development. The patient's communication and the analyst's interpretation make their personal contribution at the beginning of the session. However, once this is put into motion, material produced in the dialogue itself becomes the "intersubjective analytic third party," which is the product of an interplay of two separate contributions amalgamated with both the rational conscious and unconscious resonance of both participants (Ogden, 1996). Interventions occur in what I conceive graphically as a "playful space of analytic dialogue." Here each of the "intervening plays" will begin to be constituted, some as warp and others as weft of the web of communicative tissue (Cabanne & Petrucci, 1987).

Clinical material as both a real and virtual phenomenon

One of the greatest criticisms of this method is that it lacks the consistency of reality, that it is somewhat contrived, that there cannot be real and full contact with the patient. That is to say, it is virtual in the classical sense of the term. But many other phenomena of analytic encounter are similarly virtual. When we interpret transference, we refer to something that happened in the past and that manifests itself in the session as psychic reality. This feeling and acting that occurs in the here and now of the session re-presents the feeling and action of the past and brings them to the present here and now. Behavior in the transference is similar to that in the past. It is real now, and a virtual representation of the past, at the same time. A dream is a fictional reality. It is an imaginary construction that produces a psychic representability of images, which, at the moment in which it occurs, creates an effect of something real happening even if it was created by the imagination. Therefore, should a dream be considered as real or unreal? The patient's dream contains elements of the psychic history and traces of its transformational potential, conveyed beyond the dream in language. The dream then undergoes another transformation when it is described to the analyst. Each present moment in the process of having and reporting the dream goes through the transforming process of virtualization in order to move on to the next current state of communication and understanding.

In Freud's (1925i) article "Moral responsibility for the content of dreams" he refers to the virtual and real aspect of dreams. The dreamer has no civil liability for the *occurred* events of the dream. Nevertheless, if under analysis, the *reported* dream is part of the patient's psychic reality to be addressed analytically. The reality imagined or created in the dream comes from feelings that were dormant, much like seeds, which, as censorship lessens, are subjected to the primary process. Within this process the *dreamed* dream is created. This, in turn, will operate as a new latent seed that will contribute to the development that becomes the *remembered* dream, which, in turn, will be another latent seed used to build the *reported* dream, which is the only reality from which the analysis of dreams can take place. In this process, we can see several transformations that start from the original *feeling-idea* of the dreamer—the "O" origin of the dream (Bion, 1965). The *dreamed* dream has two aspects; one real, due to its condition of being the way it is, and the other virtual, because of its potential ability to transform, as has just been described.

Virtual is that which, contained in each present state of something real, has the potential to transform by virtualization into the next new present state of something real. It would be wrong to oppose the virtual to the real. In Lévy's (1995) view, virtuality is a capacity with potential for transformation, contained in something real. Although the caterpillar is identified as a real object, it is known that the caterpillar has the potential of becoming a butterfly. Between the caterpillar and the butterfly a transformative process called virtualization occurs.

The voice that transmits ideas and feelings is not something disembodied. It is a physical expression of feelings and ideas born in the mind and transformed into the words of the language being spoken. However, when listening to someone else, no one argues that the spoken word is something unreal simply because it is a derivative of the virtualization of the speaker's feeling and thinking. The real object that impresses our senses in every present moment is the current chapter of a reality in the process of becoming, promoted by its own virtualization. Lévy illustrates this process by asserting that the seed potentially contains the tree. All one needs to do is to supply water, nutrients, light, and time in order to witness the birth of a tree. Both the seed and the tree are the present in the respective current and future times of the virtualization process.

The virtualization capability of a real object is a latent reserve of differentiation potential. From its multiple virtualization possibilities, the original develops in various, unpredicted dimensions. That which is virtual, contained in that which is real, in addition to referring to a principle of movement to a new state of being, is the source of a generating principle of diversity. In our case, the classical psychoanalytic interpretation of the manifest content brings us to know the real latent content that gives rise to the current content expressed by the patient in the session. That which is transferred (latent content) displays itself as the present (manifest content). If we take the transformative potential of each iteration, the present contains the latent ability of transforming into something new.

Interpretation has the capacity for retrospective transformation but it can also use this capacity in reverse, not as interpretation of the impact of the past on the transference but rather in the service of an elaborative and prospective study of the analytic duo. If we accept that the present comes from a virtualization process of past chapters, in a prospective sense we can consider that the past contains the present given its ability for virtualization into the future. Psychoanalysis has always held that the symptoms and behaviors of the present rooted in those of the past are repeated in the present in life and in the transference. This is still true. Psychoanalysis can take a leap forward if it will also focus its sight on the potential ability of the present from today onwards, as a basis for potential metamorphosis. And that potential includes using telecommunication to bring psychoanalysis to more potential patients, its integrity determined not by the setting, but by the knowledge, skill, and ethical stance of the analyst.

Ubiquity of the voice

The vocal chords of each of the duo form part of their bodies and therefore are located only in the exact places where each of the two people is situated. Nevertheless, the voice that emerges from their vibration, mediated by a telecommunication device, is located simultaneously in both places, operating as an oral communicative element.

a. The *real* aspect of the voice is located:
   - in the vocal chords, which are anatomical material, and in their sound vibration, which is a physical phenomenon;
   - in the voice that creates words that carry meaning and contain and convey the ideas and emotions of the speaker;
   - in the intonation, rhythm, and musicality of its sound and the quality of its silence as a significant reality of the session;
   - in the act of communication itself;
   - in the temporal space (day and time) of the session, with the patient either present or absent. The session always exists as a reality and for this reason it makes sense to take into account the attendance or absence thereto;
   - in what is said and omitted as significant.
b. The *virtual* aspect of communication in a session is found:
   - in the "O" origin of the initial ideo-affective content of the message. This comes through in partial, somewhat distorted form due to repression. It then goes through a second deformation as it reaches the listener by the way in which the dream is described.

The analyst's task is to take this deformation into account. What the analyst hears from the patient is taken as the real aspect, and his interpretive work involves looking for the meaning;

- all verbal material—and also visual material if a web camera is used—is the manifest content. Reaching the latent content, the virtual within it, requires an interpretation, making a journey back in time to arrive at the issues of yesterday that give rise to the issues of today.

A supervisee who was conducting a psychoanalytic treatment by telecommunication and in the English language (the native language of the patient) reported that in one session, the patient described a dream from the night before. The patient did not reproduce the images of the dream but rather transformed them into a storyline in English. In supervision, the analyst presented the clinical material having made a further transformation into Spanish, thus causing the dream to go through several transforming virtualizations by the time it was shared with the supervisor. The dream described by the patient was not the dreamed dream, but rather a product of its secondary processing. His description became the "present state" of the dreamed dream. In turn, the story that the analyst took to his supervisor is another "present state" presented in Spanish based on the previous one in English, along with the deformation that it contains. All the changes that occurred in this chain of communication—and in others similar to those of everyday life—inevitably bring a transformation from the source, yet do not constantly raise the true/false or real/virtual antinomy. These deformations, virtualizations, and transformations occur during in-the-office sessions, as well as in those carried out through telecommunication.

The preceding procedural descriptions were developed in order to substantiate the conceptual error that is committed when we pit the terms virtual sessions or virtual analysis against in-person analysis and real analysis. Let's be clear that analysis carried out in the analyst's office is different from that carried out through telecommunication. The process takes place in a different medium, with different circumstances, and different transformations specific to each method. We need to address in-the-office analysis and teleanalysis singularly and with respect for their unique value.

While the experience of traditional psychoanalysis in the analyst's office is fully documented and its value quite well proven, there is no reason to exclude the possibility that another, equally prescribed, setting, using telecommunication, can offer equivalent value, especially now that teleanalysis is being requested to accommodate the socio-cultural transformations that have changed the distance-time paradigm. Technology has brought to psychoanalysis a new means of communication, and this development is moving psychoanalysis to take on previously unimaginable new forms.

References

Aryan, A., & Carlino, R. (2012). El "establishment" y las ideas nuevas. Unpublished paper. 9th Argentine Congress of Psychoanalysis. Mendoza, Argentina, May 2012.

Aryan, A., & Carlino, R. (2013). The power of the establishment in the face of change: Psychoanalysis by telephone. In: J. S. Scharff (Ed.), *Psychoanalysis Online: Mental Health, Teletherapy, and Training* (pp. 161–170). London: Karnac.

Aryan, A., Carlino, R., & Manguel, L. (2014). Lo real, lo virtual, lo ficcional en la sesión analítica a distancia. Unpublished paper. 30th Congreso Latinoamericano de Psicoanálisis: Realidades y Ficciones. Panel presented at the 30th Congreso Latinoamericano de Psicoanálisis: Realidades y Ficciones. Federación Psicoanalítica de América Latina (FEPAL) Buenos Aires, Argentina. September, 2014.

Berenstein, I. (2004). El sujeto como otro entre [inter] otros. In: G. Fiorini (Ed.), *El Otro en la Trama Intersubjetiva* (pp. 75–97). Buenos Aires: Lugar and APA.

Bion, W. R. (1965). *Transformations*. London: Heinemann.

Cabanne, J., & Petrucci, H. (1988). La urdimbre y la trauma. *Revista de Psicoanálisis, 10*: 185–196.

Carlino, R. (2000). "Transformationes socioculturales: Su incidencia en el encuentro analista-analizando". Proceedings of the Segundo Coloquio Interdisciplinar: Transformaciones, Psicoanálisis y Sociedad. Centre d'Atenció, Docéncia i Investigació en Salut Mental (IPsi), Barcelona, Spain, 11–13 February 2000.

Carlino, R. (2011). *Distance Psychoanalysis*. London. Karnac.

Freud, S. (1917e). Mourning and melancholia. *S. E., 14*: 243–258. London: Hogarth.

Freud, S. (1925i). Moral responsibility for the content of dreams. In: Some additional notes on dream-interpretation as a whole. *S. E., 19*: 131–134. London: Hogarth.

Galli, V. (2005). Psicoanálisis-Psicoterapias psicoanalíticas: sobre diferencias de grado y de cualidad. *Revista de la Sociedad Argentina de Psicoanálisis, 7*: 153–170.

Lévy, P. (1995). *Qu'est-ce que le Virtuel?* Paris: La Découverte. [*¿Qué es lo virtual?* Barcelona: Paidós Ibérica, 1999.] Accessed at www.slideshare.net/marianamarlene/levy-pierre-que-es-lo-virtual

Ogden, T. (1996). Reconsidering three aspects of psychoanalytic technique. *International Journal of Psycho-Analysis, 77*: 883–899. [Reconsiderando tres aspectos de la técnica psicoanalítica. *Revista de Psicoanálisis, 20*, 1998].

Paz, R. (2005). El psicoanálisis también existe. *Revista de la Sociedad Argentina de Psicoanálisis, 7*: 115–138.

CHAPTER THREE

Privacy, telecommunications, and the psychoanalytic setting

John Churcher (UK)

What are the implications for privacy when telecommunications are introduced into the psychoanalytic setting? In the classical setting, shared tacit knowledge about buildings enables privacy to be maintained, but this is insufficient when telecommunications are involved. We find it hard to know where to turn for expert advice, but there are conspicuous examples of bad advice, for example, those concerning Skype. From revelations by Edward Snowden in 2013, we now know that interception of telecommunications, including telephone and video conversations, is occurring on a massive scale and indiscriminately. Our reaction may be to turn a blind eye, disavowing the danger to privacy that this interception entails. As Freud showed, this is a defense against a psychical trauma, the fear of something intolerable happening in the future, and involves a splitting of the ego. José Bleger's view of the setting as a depository for the psychotic part of the personality implies that this splitting will undermine our work in a particular way. It will also tend to happen differently in countries and communities with differing social and political norms. It is unclear whether "good enough" security of telecommunications is in principle available, or what it would cost, but even the best systems are compromised by our poor "endpoint security." Our only option, if we wish to continue using telecommunications as part of the psychoanalytic setting, is to try to analyze these difficulties within the setting itself. This will mean being honest with patients and ourselves about the new situation, undoing the disavowal, and proceeding on the basis of an "acceptance" of the uncertainty.

Introduction

From the beginnings of psychoanalysis there have been experiments with modifications of the classical setting, some more successful than others, most of them controversial. Modern telecommunications, beginning with the telephone and now including videoconferencing such as Skype via the Internet, are increasingly being used to substitute for the physical co-presence of analyst and patient at the same location. This raises many questions for psychoanalytic practice, which are leading to a rapidly growing area of research and debate (see, for example, Björklind, 2014; Churcher, 2015, 2016; Lemma, 2015; Lemma & Caparrotta, 2013; Lin, 2012; Scharff, 2013, 2015; Werbin et al., 2014).

One such question concerns the consequences of telecommunication for confidentiality and the maintenance of privacy, and how this affects the setting. In this chapter I will not rehearse the technical and ethical arguments for maintaining confidentiality between analyst and patient, and therefore the privacy of their conversation in the consulting room, as these have been amply developed elsewhere by others (Bollas & Sundelson, 1996; Cordess, 2001; Forrester, 2003; Gabbard, 2000; Garvey & Layton, 2004; Hayman, 1965; Stimmel, 2013). Instead, I shall assume that as psychoanalysts we are agreed that confidentiality is a necessary condition of our work, and that any modification of the setting must therefore preserve its privacy if it is to be capable of supporting a psychoanalytic process. In a beautiful and compelling book, Cohen (2013) has written: "The conception of privacy implicit in public debates around the competing rights of individual and public interest is a rather impoverished one, mired in the confusion of privacy with secrecy," and that he contrasts this with "another, more essential privacy, namely what I keep private even from myself—and in spite of myself." Unfortunately, we need the first kind of privacy in order to be able to explore the second.

I want to consider the implications for privacy when telecommunications, of any kind, are introduced into the psychoanalytic setting. An adequate assessment of these implications needs to be informed both by an understanding of the technology itself and by a psychoanalytic way of thinking about how the technology and its evolving social organisation come to inhabit the setting, including the internal setting in the minds of both analyst and patient. The concept of the internal setting has been developed by various authors (Alizade, 2002; Bridge, 2013 [1997], 2013; Churcher, 2005; Civitarese, 2013; Labarthe, 2012; Parsons, 2007; Temperley, 1984; and others). Although these authors do not all think of the internal setting in precisely the same way, they all agree that it is precisely when the external setting is disrupted or under threat that the internal setting is most essential for maintaining or restoring the analytic process.

In his discussion of the psychoanalytic setting, José Bleger argued that it functions as a depository for the psychotic part of the personality that is present in all of us as the residuum of early symbiosis with the mother and with the world. According to Bleger, the setting is also a social institution, which forms part of the personality of each individual who participates in it (Bleger, 2013 [1967]). Rosemary Davies has discussed the value of Bleger's ideas for her clinical work within a classical setting (Davies, 2015). Here, I am using the same ideas to help me to think about a specific problem that arises in settings that involve telecommunication.

An implication of Bleger's argument, in my view, is that we tend to establish a symbiotic relation with *any* invariants that we discover and adapt to, whether in our own bodies or in the rest of the world, and that we do so not only in the psychoanalytic setting but also in everyday life (Churcher, 2015, 2016). Wherever we find something stable, secure, constant, we sooner or later "take it for granted," and treat it as something that is not to be questioned. A primitive part of the mind spontaneously establishes a silent and hidden symbiotic relation with the invariant, using it as a depository for undifferentiated parts of ourselves that are always seeking a home. This is both a social and a physical process, as we participate in various institutions.

In a psychoanalysis that is being conducted remotely by means of telecommunications, such as the telephone or Skype, we therefore need to be curious about what may be being deposited silently in the telecommunication system itself.

Shared tacit knowledge and common sense in the classical setting

In the classical psychoanalytic setting, in addition to the elements described by Freud (the fundamental rule, the analytic hour, use of the couch, etc.) there are numerous *implicit* conditions, which are seldom made explicit because they can usually be safely assumed. These include the fact that consultations typically take place in a room within a building, which is reasonably quiet, and where patient and analyst can hear each other but cannot be overheard by others. The acoustic properties of a consulting room are usually stable over time, and its privacy is implicit and assumed. We usually have enough tacit knowledge (Polanyi, 1966) about our immediate physical and social environment to make reliable judgments about whether a conversation is private.

Tacit knowledge of this kind is to a large degree socially shared, and normally the analyst's confidence in the acoustic isolation of the consulting room will be met by a similar confidence in the patient. Indeed, it is only against such a background of shared tacit knowledge (or "common sense"), that occasions when it is called into question, for example, by a patient who repeatedly expresses anxiety about being overheard by a third party, can be taken as indications of pathological functioning. This normative aspect of clinical thinking is unavoidable.

From a psychoanalytic perspective, of course, the idea of tacit knowledge has to be understood in the context of unconscious phantasies that are part of both normal and pathological functioning. Clinical observation repeatedly confirms that buildings, and rooms within buildings, as well as serving in dreams and waking dream-thoughts as symbols for the body, are generally experienced in unconscious phantasy as protective containers, although they may also be experienced as dangerous ones provoking claustrophobia (Meltzer, 1992). Privacy of conversation in the consulting room, although it may be experienced as dangerous, is thus generally experienced in phantasy as an aspect of protective containment, which explains why the emotional reactions of a patient to any deliberate or accidental breach of privacy can be so powerful.

Privacy can be breached in many different ways, but for the purpose of the present discussion the most relevant instance is eavesdropping. The English word "eavesdropping," now frequently applied to interception of telecommunications, derives originally from an architectural term. "The eaves" refers to a projection of a roof beyond the walls of a building, to allow rain to fall away from them, the space beneath being the "eavesdrop," where someone might stand for the purpose of overhearing a conversation within. Eavesdropping has been subject to social disapproval and legal regulation for at least 400 years, although the conflicting interests of governments in wishing simultaneously to allow eavesdropping by the state while disallowing or at least regulating its use by others has led to a complex history of legislation (Spencer, 2009; Stevens & Doyle, 2002).

In the classical psychoanalytic setting, eavesdropping is in principle possible if the walls are thin, or if the arrangements for maintaining acoustic isolation are in some other way compromised, but reports of its occurrence in clinical practice are rare. If there have been times and places in the past where psychoanalysis was practiced under social and political conditions in which eavesdropping was commonplace, we would not necessarily expect it to be openly documented in our professional literature.

Vulnerability of telecommunications and the insufficiency of common sense

As soon as we introduce modern telecommunications into the setting, this background of shared knowledge about the acoustics of buildings is no longer sufficient. We are obliged to consider in addition the knowledge and beliefs of the participants concerning the technology itself.

Interception of telephone conversations by governments and individuals, both legally and illegally, has been occurring since the early 1890s, and, like the telephone itself, is thus even older than psychoanalysis. There is little reason to doubt that interception has been practiced on a significant scale continuously ever since then. In the 1960s, when the global telephone network was still mainly analogue rather than digital, and reliant on electromechanical switching of electrical circuits for the routing of calls, interception typically required the involvement of staff in local telephone exchanges. I can remember my father, who was a telephone engineer, advising me fifty years ago never to say on the telephone anything that I would not be prepared to write on a postcard.

Since the revelations by Edward Snowden in 2013, it has become clear that government agencies in the USA, UK, and various other countries, are routinely intercepting telecommunications traffic of all kinds, including voice and video conversations as well as email and text messages, on an industrial scale and more or less indiscriminately.

Publication of these revelations has led to public discussion and controversy concerning the proper balance of privacy and surveillance in democratic societies faced with dangers from terrorism and organized crime (Greenwald, MacAskill, & Poitras, 2013; *The Guardian*, 2014).

The diversity and sophistication of techniques now available for interception, as detailed in the documents published by Snowden, greatly exceed those employed a generation ago. For the purpose of this discussion, however, the most significant aspect is perhaps the massively increased *scale* of interception, which has been made possible by the development of global digital communications and by advances in techniques such as automatic speech recognition, and the management of large databases. Whereas interception was once necessarily selective, because of the amount of human labour involved, the aim of programmes such as Prism and Tempora is now to be inclusive: to intercept and record *all* telecommunications.

Knowledge of these changes has been widely disseminated since 2013, but the way in which this knowledge informs our awareness is radically different from the way in which we know about the buildings we inhabit. Such is the division of labour in technologically advanced societies that we often rely on the skills of builders, plumbers, and electricians to fix problems in our homes and offices, just as we rely on the skills of computer scientists, electronics technicians, and software engineers to build and maintain our telephones, computers, and the Internet. The difference is that while we retain our common-sense ability to judge if the roof is leaking, or if the walls are permeable to sound, we generally cannot tell whether our phone has been converted into an eavesdropping device, or our emails or Skype conversations are being intercepted. There is too much to know about the digital world, and not enough common sense to guide us through it.

Lacking sufficient knowledge ourselves, we turn to experts: a technician, a colleague who "knows about computers," a younger person. But can we trust whoever fixes the computer or telephone to tell us reliably about the privacy of our communications when we use it? Who really knows, and how do we know that they know? The question is analogous to one that Hanna Segal, quoting the Roman poet Juvenal, once asked about nuclear weapons: *Quis custodiet ipsos custodes*? On the wild frontiers of the Internet, who certifies the certifiers?

There are some conspicuous examples of bad advice being offered recently to the psychoanalytic profession. A recent paper on introducing psychoanalytic psychotherapy into China asserts:

> The special feature that makes Skype uniquely suitable for psychotherapeutic treatment is the security of computer-to-computer video calls. Skype uses a proprietary encryption protocol, which makes it impossible to eavesdrop on any computer-to-computer call (Berson, 2010). With Skype computer to computer connections, there is no central server. Encrypted packets of data are exchanged between many computers so that at any given moment, there is a virtual network that is fluid and continually changing during the same call. … This technology is so solidly secure that it is nearly impossible to detect even whether Skype is in use at any given time. (Fishkin & Fishkin, 2014, p. 206)

These statements are misleading. The fact that Skype uses a proprietary encryption protocol that is not open to scrutiny is one of the principal reasons that many people have argued that it should *not* be regarded as secure. Packet-switching, which the authors describe as if it were a special feature of Skype, is the common basis of *all* communications across the Internet, and offers no special security from interception. Methods for detecting Skype traffic have been described in the literature for at least six years (see Bonfiglio, Mellia, Meo, Rossi, & Tofanelli, 2008), and five years ago the source code of a Trojan was published that taps Skype voice conversations (Symantec, 2009). In December last year, *Der Spiegel* published a document leaked by Snowden that shows that "sustained" interception of Skype traffic by the NSA began in February 2011 (*Spiegel* staff, 2014).

Similarly misleading statements about Skype were published three years ago in the *IJP* (Scharff, 2012a), resulting in editorial correspondence (Churcher, 2012; Scharff, 2012b). Meanwhile, Skype continues to be used on a considerable scale, including for online psychoanalysis and psychotherapy. Alternatives to Skype have been suggested, such as VSee, or WebEx, on grounds of their supposed greater security. As we shall see shortly, such claims are problematic.

Turning a blind eye to the risks

Having come to depend on the Internet in so many aspects of our lives, from maintaining contact with friends to the very operation of the social infrastructure (in transport, health, electrical power distribution, finance, etc.), any knowledge that puts the viability of this dependence into doubt provides an occasion for psychic defence. A widespread reaction to the Snowden revelations is similar to that which Hanna Segal described as a response to the threat of nuclear war (Segal, 1987), and which has more recently been discussed in the context of climate change (Hoggett, 2013; Weintrobe, 2013) and instability of financial markets (Tuckett, 2011). This is the defence of disavowal (*Verleugnung*), which Freud described as the starting point of fetishism, and which Steiner has discussed as the basis of a perverse attitude of "turning of a blind eye" in the direction of reality (Steiner, 1985).

For Freud, disavowal is a defence against a psychical trauma:

> a child's ego is under the sway of a powerful instinctual demand which it is accustomed to satisfy and … it is suddenly frightened by an experience which teaches it that the continuance of this satisfaction will result in an almost intolerable real danger. (Freud, 1940e, p. 275)

The ego responds by disavowing the reality of the situation, "[making] itself believe there is no reason for fear, so that it may be able to retain the satisfaction" (p. 275), while simultaneously recognizing the danger and converting the fear into a symptom. The outcome is a "rift in the ego which never heals but which increases as time goes on" (p. 276).

This describes quite accurately our predicament today faced with new knowledge about the extent of interception of our private communications, and our uncertainty about what it might lead to. In his first public interview for *The Guardian*, later reproduced in Laura Poitras' documentary film *Citizenfour*, Snowden said: "… I can't in good conscience allow the US government to destroy privacy, internet freedom and basic liberties for people around the world with this massive surveillance machine they're secretly building," which he described as "an existential threat to democracy" (Greenwald, MacAskill, & Poitras, 2013; Poitras, 2014).

The fact that disavowal is a defence activated by a *psychical* trauma, an experience that creates a fear of something intolerable happening in the future, is significant for the argument that I am putting forward in this chapter. The concept of trauma, as Freud noted, implies an overwhelming or flooding of the mental apparatus, which normally maintains a protective barrier to prevent this occurring (Freud, 1950a [1895], 1920g). The concept of a psychical trauma implies an incommensurability between the relative peace and calm of the status quo, and the terror of an anticipated future.

As Weintrobe (2013) and Hoggett (2013) have argued in connection with climate change, disavowal can form the basis of a perverse culture of denial. However, it is important to add that our psychoanalytic understanding of such defenses cannot itself tell us anything about the external reality or unreality of what is being defended against. "Denial" can be easily misused as a means of discrediting views with which one disagrees, by suggesting that they are pathologically determined, rather than being based on different experiences and/or different interpretations of the evidence. But the validity of beliefs about the world cannot be determined by examining either the fears that they induce or those that they enable us to evade. Because psychoanalysis cannot decide questions of fact arising outside the consulting room, our beliefs and judgments about the wider world need to be informed by other sources of information and knowledge, and psychoanalysis cannot tell us which of these to believe.

When the organisers of a European Psychoanalytic Federation conference wrote that they wished to dedicate it to "those who live, and who make us live, the too much—not enough, and who make us experience the limits of norms" (Frisch, Ylander, & Bleger, 2015), might they have had Edward Snowden in mind, among others? With any scenario of global disaster (climate change, nuclear war, nuclear power, pandemic, financial crash, or any of a dozen others), we are liable to feel paralysed by the sheer scale of the anticipated consequences, the rapidity with which they could develop, the amount of suffering that would be involved, and the insufficiency of our mental resources for facing them, or for keeping up with developments in the world that might help us to face them. Snowden's comments clearly imply a warning against an "almost intolerable danger" that the surveillance machine might at some point fall into the hands of an undemocratic and oppressive government.

Implications of José Bleger's view of the setting

In Bleger's view, Freud's "splitting of the ego" is "a splitting between a more developed, adult part of the personality that recognizes reality and another infantile part that still adheres to a primitive organization", which is to say "a splitting between the neurotic and the psychotic part of the personality" (Bleger, 2013 [1967], pp. 258–259). The psychotic part of the personality as described by Bion, which Bleger also calls the "agglutinated nucleus," remains ready throughout life to establish new symbiotic relationships characterized by massive projective identifications. In an analysis it is quickly and quietly deposited in the setting, where it remains hidden and unanalyzed, until a disruption of some kind causes it to become manifest.

As long as the setting is not disrupted, it remains unnoticed. The agglutinated nucleus, the undifferentiated and unresolved infantile symbiotic relationship, remains hidden. Like a phantom limb that has not yet been experienced as such because the body is still intact, it silently persists in the setting as a "phantom world," undetected but nonetheless psychically real. The setting thus functions as a tenacious and invisible "bastion" (Baranger & Baranger 1961–1962), a refuge or retreat for the psychotic part of the personality, which demands that nothing shall change. Sooner or later the analyst must therefore try to analyze the setting, and Bleger observes that this meets strong resistance because the symbiosis is something that has never before been recognized by the patient.

In describing the technical requirements for this clinical task, Bleger distinguishes between two different versions of the setting: the one that the analyst provides, and the one that the patient "brings" to the analysis. The analyst, he writes, needs to "accept" the setting brought by the patient because within it will be found, in summary form, all of the primitive unresolved symbiosis. At the same time, the analyst must hold firmly to his own setting in order to be able to analyze both the psychoanalytic process and the patient's setting when this has been transformed into a process. In other words, he "accepts" the patient's setting in order to interpret it (Bleger, 2013 [1967], pp. 240–241).

Psychoanalysis is difficult enough when the reality towards which the blind eye is turned is *not* itself part of the psychoanalytic setting, so that there is at least a possibility of doing analytic work on the patient's use of the setting without compromising the setting itself. Bleger notes that precisely because the setting is respected and preserved in psychoanalysis, much of this area of the mind may never be analyzed.

However, when what is being disavowed is itself an aspect of the setting, the difficulty is potentially much more serious. The use of telecommunications in psychoanalysis presents us with precisely such a difficulty. If, in our work as analysts, we turn a blind eye to something that we know about the setting we are offering to our patients, how can we avoid undermining it as the only resource we have for analyzing the patient's setting?

Different societies, different norms

Norms of expectation concerning the privacy of telecommunications tend to vary between different countries and communities with differing histories of relations between government and citizens. Reactions to Snowden have been markedly stronger in Germany, for example, where memories of surveillance in the DDR are painful and recent, than in Britain, where, with the notable exception of *The Guardian* newspaper, reactions have been more muted. Psychoanalysts and their patients in countries that were once part of the communist bloc may be making different assumptions about surveillance, and have different sensibilities, from those in the West. In China, it seems that government intervention in the Internet is massive and systematic. And if in the West it has hitherto been possible for psychoanalysts to feel safe in the belief that their private communications really were private, the situation should be no longer so clear (see Wright & Kreissl, 2013). Thus the existence of norms, and the variations among them in different locales, raises in a stark way the ancient problem of distinguishing between paranoia and realism.

Are "good-enough" telecommunications for psychoanalysis possible?

Can we find a place somewhere between these extremes, and settle for what might be called "good enough security", by analogy with Winnicott's (1953) notion of the "good enough mother"? After all, it could be said that this is all that the classical setting can offer anyway.

Arguably, a concept of "good enough" has already become the norm in many other uses of the Internet, for example, for personal financial transactions. One form of encryption now widely used for email even has the name PGP, which stands for "Pretty Good Privacy" (Zimmermann, 1995). PGP has been in use for more than twenty years, and there is no clear evidence that when properly used it has yet been broken. On the other hand, another widely trusted form of encryption used in banking, SSL ("Secure Sockets Layer"), was shown in 2012 to have multiple vulnerabilities, and has since been replaced.

Huge resources are expended on IT security: a global estimate for 2014 is $71.1 billion, and rising at about eight percent yearly (PwC, 2014, p. 5). Despite this expenditure, and continual technical innovation, it is not clear that anyone has yet found the security they are seeking. There is, in effect, an arms race between commercial enterprises competing in the market, between hostile nation states, and between all of these and organized crime. As in all arms races, the only certain winners are the manufacturers.

It is possible now to buy a communications system that uses the principles of quantum theory to provide "unconditional secrecy," meaning secrecy whose guarantee is "independent of any assumptions about the resources available to an eavesdropper" (Gobby, Yuan, & Shields, 2004). The physical phenomenon of "quantum entanglement" makes it possible for two parties to communicate by optic fibre in such a way that they can reliably detect any eavesdropping by a third party. This method is used to transmit securely a random key, discarding any intercepted signals, and the key is then used to encode data before sending it over an open channel. A state-of-the-art technology based on this, known as Quantum Key Distribution (QKD), is in use by some banks, military, and governmental organizations, but its high price places it beyond the reach of most users, and take-up is further restricted by current limitations on bandwidth and on the distance over which it can operate. Nevertheless, we can use QKD as a kind of object lesson for psychoanalysis, in two ways.

First, the fact that QKD is already being used for videoconferencing makes the point that for some purposes none of the more widely available and cheaper forms of videoconferencing such as Skype, WebEx, and VSee are seen as sufficiently secure. We might then consider whether a system that isn't secure enough for bankers or government departments can be secure enough for psychoanalysts and their patients.

Endpoint security: our weakest link

Second, and this is the more important point: a secure communications channel is of limited value unless the endpoints of the communication, the computers or telephones or other devices at each end, where the information is decrypted, are also themselves secure. A chain is only as strong as its weakest link, and if your personal computer, tablet, or phone is infected by a Trojan that is quietly copying decrypted information to a third party, then no matter how sophisticated and secure the communications channel, it may be worthless.

In a corporate environment, or in military or governmental organizations, it may be possible to regulate who has access to what equipment, and to establish a strict regime for its use in order to prevent breaches of endpoint security. Large organizations typically define their own "intranets" and require employees to use them. Psychoanalysts, on the other hand, tend to avoid this kind of corporate discipline. We use a diverse range of devices and operating systems, in highly idiosyncratic ways, and often with minimal attention to security. It is important to note that even systems that are advertised as offering "end-to-end security" (such as VSee and MegaChat, which compete in the same market as Skype) do not address this problem. To address it seriously would require a cultural change that I am not at all sure is feasible or desirable.

In my own practice over the past twenty-five years I have not been completely consistent. On the one hand, I have avoided all use of Skype or other VOIP, as well as mobile telephones, for all discussion of clinical material; and I created and stored process notes of my patients' sessions in encrypted files, not on the computer I routinely use for the Internet, but on a separate, "air-gapped" computer that has never been connected to the Internet. On the other hand, I regularly discuss clinical material by land-line telephone, with supervisees and colleagues, and I am party to others doing so when participating by telephone in scientific meetings. I used to justify this to myself by persuading myself that using a land-line was intrinsically less risky than either VoIP or a GSM cellphone, but I didn't really know that, and now Snowden's revelations about GCHQ and Tempora have undermined that belief. My own behavior is thus consistent with a splitting of the ego as described by Freud.

Conclusion: implications for psychoanalyses conducted or attempted by means of telecommunications

In conclusion, I feel that I may be bringing some unwelcome news: that as psychoanalysts we cannot simply continue to drift towards ever greater incorporation of telecommunications and computer technology into our clinical work, without facing radical new uncertainties about whether the work can remain private. We may tell ourselves comforting stories: about why we imagine that no one would be interested in eavesdropping on our work; or why if they did they would learn nothing, because psychoanalysis isn't that sort of talk anyway; or why the patient would not be seriously harmed by it; or that to be concerned about any of this is paranoid thinking; or even that "privacy is dead," and we need to get over it. In discussions with colleagues and friends I have heard each of these presented as an objection; but each could also be a way of turning a blind eye to something unwelcome and potentially frightening.

In this chapter I have deliberately limited myself to just one aspect of the problems created for psychoanalysis by attempting to substitute telecommunications for physical co-presence. We are at a difficult moment in the development of the profession, because a momentum in favour of "psychoanalysis online" has built up in recent years, but there is as yet no real consensus among us about what is possible or desirable. By focusing on privacy and confidentiality, I am deliberately drawing attention to an issue that has clear ethical implications, but I think these need also to be considered together with other consequences of the use of telecommunications. I have discussed elsewhere the problem of how to define "presence" as a condition of the possibility of psychoanalysis (Churcher, 2000, 2015, 2016). Sabbadini (2013) addresses a similar question, as does Lemma (2015) in her wide-ranging keynote paper for the forthcoming IPA Congress in Boston.

If we suppose, for the purpose of the present discussion, that psychoanalysis is *not* rendered impossible by other aspects of a setting that depends on telecommunications, how should we address the issues of privacy and confidentiality? The only clinically viable option, in my view, would be to follow José Bleger's example and to continue trying to analyze them within the setting. This would mean being honest with our patients and ourselves about the uncertainty, and turning a seeing eye instead of the blind one towards it, undoing the disavowal, and proceeding on the basis of an "acceptance" of uncertainty.

I have put "acceptance" in quotation marks because I am not sure quite what this would mean. The patient, from the first moment of an analysis, brings his or her most infantile, primitive, and unformed parts to the setting. The encounter creates an immediate dependency, and the patient's "acceptance" of anything, including the classical aspects of the setting and the contract, has to be understood in this context. As Faimberg (2014) has emphasized, it is Bleger's distinction between *two* settings, the psychoanalyst's and the patient's, that makes possible a solution to an apparent paradox: that in order to have a chance of overcoming the inherent tendency towards a sterile ritualization of the psychoanalytic setting, we need to keep the setting constant.

Should we then hope that the damage to psychoanalysis that results from living under surveillance can also be overcome or mitigated, provided that the analyst's setting can contain the anxiety without splitting, an analytic process can get under way, and the patient's and our own acceptance of these unwelcome realities can be explored and developed over time? The only alternative, it seems to me, would be to avoid the use of telecommunications in clinical work, despite the economic pressures and temptations, and to proceed on the assumption that for psychoanalysis, as for some other forms of conviviality, actual physical presence is indispensable.

References

Alizade, A. M. (2002). *Lo Positivo en Psicoanálisis: Implicancias Teórico-Técnicas.* Buenos Aires—Mexico: Lumen.

Baranger, M., & Baranger, W. (1961–1962). La situación analítica como campo dinámico. *Revista Uruguaya de Psicoanálisis, 4*: 3–54. (2008). [The analytic situation as a dynamic field, S. Rogers & J. Churcher (Trans.). *International Journal of Psychoanalysis, 89*: 795–826.]

Björklind, C. (2014). Psychoanalysis and the new technologies. The future of the talking cure and the bodily ego in the digital era. "Psychoanalysis in 2025" Pre-published Papers. http://www.epf-fep.eu/eng/article/psychoanalysis-and-the-new-technologies-the-future-of-the-talking-cure-and-the-bodily-ego-in-the-digital-era

Bleger, J. (2013 [1967]). *Symbiosis and Ambiguity: A Psychoanalytic Study* (edited by J. Churcher & L. Bleger). London: Routledge. [(1967). *Simbiosis y ambigüedad: estudio psicoanalítico.* Buenos Aires: Paidós.]

Bollas, C., & Sundelson, D. (1996). *The New Informants: Betrayal of Confidentiality in Psychoanalysis and Psychotherapy.* London: Karnac.

Bonfiglio, D., Mellia, M., Meo, M., Rossi, D., & Tofanelli, P. (2008). Revealing Skype traffic: When randomness plays with you. *ACM SIGCOMM Computer Communication Review "4", 37*: 37–48 (October 2007).

Bridge, M. (2013 [1997]). Why five times a week? A candidate's perspective. *Bulletin of the British Psychoanalytical Society, 49*: 3–9.

Bridge, M. (2013). Moving out—disruption and repair to the internal setting. *British Journal of Psychotherapy, 29*: 481–493.

Churcher, J. (2000). Clinical meetings, communication technology and presence. *Bulletin of the British Psychoanalytical Society, 36*: 26–31.

Churcher, J. (2005). Keeping the psychoanalytic setting in mind. Paper given to the Annual Conference of Lancaster Psychotherapy Clinic in collaboration with the Tavistock Clinic, at St. Martin's College, Lancaster, 9 September 2005. https://www.academia.edu/4527520 https://www.researchgate.net/publication/277712165

Churcher, J. (2012). On: Skype and privacy. *International Journal of Psychoanalysis, 93*: 1035–1037.

Churcher, J. (2015). "The psychoanalytic setting, the body-schema, telecommunications, and telepresence: some implications of José Bleger's concept of *encuadre*." Expanded version of a paper presented at the

5th British German Colloquium, 11–13 October 2013, Møller Centre, Cambridge, UK. https://www.academia.edu/12802860 https://www.researchgate.net/publication/277712046

Churcher, J. (2016). Der psychoanalytische Rahmen, das Körperschema, Telekommunikation und Telepräsenz: Implikationen von José Blegers Konzept des *encuadre*. *Psyche: Zeitschrift für Psychoanalyse und ihre Anwendungen, 70*: 60–81.

Civitarese, G. (2013). *The Violence of Emotions: Bion and post-Bionian Psychoanalysis*. London: Routledge. [(2011). *La violenze delle emozioni: Bion e la psicoanalisi postbioniana*. Milan: Raffaello Cortina Editore].

Cohen, J. (2013). *The Private Life: Why We Remain in the Dark*. London: Vintage.

Cordess, C. (Ed.) (2001). *Confidentiality and Mental Health*. London: Jessica Kingsley.

Davies, R. (2015). Closeness and distance within the analytic setting: whose frame is it anyway? Paper presented to a Clinical Panel at the EPF annual conference. March 2015, Stockholm. http://www.epf-fep.eu/eng/article/closeness-and-distance-within-the-analytic-setting-whose-frame-is-it-anyway

Faimberg, H. (2014). The paternal function in Winnicott: The psychoanalytical frame. *International Journal of Psychoanalysis, 95*: 629–640.

Fishkin, R. E., & Fishkin, L. P. (2014). Introducing psychoanalytic psychotherapy into China: the CAPA experience. In: D. E. Scharff & S. Varvin (Eds.), *Psychoanalysis in China* (pp. 205–215). London: Karnac.

Forrester, J. (2003). Trust, confidentiality, and the possibility of psychoanalysis. In: C. Levin, A. Furlong, & M. K. O'Neill (Eds.). *Confidentiality: Ethical Perspectives and Clinical Dilemmas* (pp. 19–28). Hillsdale, NJ: Analytic Press.

Freud, S. (1920g). *Beyond the Pleasure Principle. S. E., 18*: 1–64. London: Hogarth.

Freud, S. (1940e). Splitting of the ego in the process of defence. *S. E., 23*: 271–278. London: Hogarth.

Freud, S. (1950a [1895]). Project for a scientific psychology. *S. E., 1*: 281–391. London: Hogarth.

Frisch, S., Ylander, F., & Bleger, L. (2015). Too much—Not enough: Argument of the EPF conference in Stockholm, March 2015. *EPF Bulletin* 69: 20–22.

Gabbard, G. O. (2000). Disguise or consent. *International Journal of Psychoanalysis, 81*: 1071–1086.

Garvey, P., & Layton, A., (Eds.) (2004). *Comparative Confidentiality in Psychoanalysis*. London: British Institute of International & Comparative Law (in association with the IPA).

Gobby, C., Yuan, Z. L., & Shields, A. J. (2004). Unconditionally secure quantum key distribution over 50 km of standard telecom fibre. *Electronics Letters, 40*: 1603–1604.

Greenwald, G., MacAskill, E., & Poitras, L. (2013). Edward Snowden: the whistleblower behind the NSA surveillance revelations. *The Guardian*, 10 June. *The Guardian* (2014). The NSA files. http://www.theguardian.com/us-news/the-nsa-files

Hayman, A. (1965). Psychoanalyst subpoenaed. *The Lancet*, 16 October: 785–786.

Hoggett, P. (2013). Climate change in a perverse culture. In: S. Weintrobe, (Ed.), *Engaging with Climate Change: Psychoanalytic and Interdisciplinary Perspectives* (pp. 56–71). London: Routledge.

Labarthe, C. (2012). El encuadre interno del analista. http://www.revistapsicoanalisis.com/el-encuadre-interno-del-analista/

Lemma, A. (2015). Psychoanalysis in times of technoculture: Some reflections on the fate of the body in virtual space. Keynote paper presented at the IPA Congress, Boston.

Lemma, A., & Caparrotta, L. (Eds.) (2013). *Psychoanalysis in the Technoculture Era*. London: Routledge.

Lin, T. (2012). Skype analysis: problems and limitations *Bulletin of the British Psychoanalytical Society, 48*: 1–10.

Meltzer, D. (1992). *The Claustrum: An Investigation of Claustrophobic Phenomena*. Perth, Scotland: Clunie.

Parsons, M. (2007). Raiding the inarticulate: the internal analytic setting and listening beyond countertransference. *International Journal of Psychoanalysis, 88*: 1441–1456.

Poitras, L. (2014). *Citizenfour*. https://citizenfourfilm.com/

Polanyi, M. (1966). *The Tacit Dimension*. Chicago: University of Chicago Press.

PwC (2014). Managing cyber risks in an interconnected world: Key findings from The Global State of Information Security® Survey 2015. http://www.pwc.com/gx/en/consulting-services/information-security-survey/download.jhtml

Sabbadini, A. (2013). New technologies and the psychoanalytic setting. In: A. Lemma & L. Caparrotta (Eds.) *Psychoanalysis in the Technoculture Era* (pp. 23–32). London: Routledge.

Scharff, J. S. (2012a). Clinical issues in analyses over the telephone and the internet. *International Journal of Psychoanalysis, 93*: 81–95.

Scharff, J. S. (2012b). Reply to "On: Skype and privacy". *International Journal of Psychoanalysis, 93*: 1037–1039.

Scharff, J. S. (Ed.) (2013). *Psychoanalysis Online: Mental Health, Teletherapy, and Training*. London: Karnac.

Scharff, J. S. (Ed.) (2015). *Psychoanalysis Online 2: Impact of Technology on Development, Training, and Therapy*. London: Karnac.

Segal, H. (1987). Silence is the real crime. *International Review of Psychoanalysis, 14*: 3–12.

Spencer, J. R. (2009). Telephone tap evidence and administrative detention in the United Kingdom. In: M. Wade & A. Maljevic (Eds.), *War on Terror? The European Stance on a New Threat, Changing Laws and Human Rights Implications* (pp. 373–400). New York: Springer.

Spiegel Staff (2014). Prying eyes: Inside the NSA's war on Internet security. *Spiegel Online International,* 28 December 2014. http://www.spiegel.de/international/germany/inside-the-nsa-s-war-on-internet-security-a-1010361.html

Steiner, J. (1985). Turning a blind eye: The cover-up for Oedipus. *International Review of Psychoanalysis, 12*: 161–172.

Stevens, G. M., & Doyle, C. (2002). *Privacy: Wiretapping and Electronic Eavesdropping*. New York: Novinka Books.

Stimmel, B. (2013). The conundrum of confidentiality. *Canadian Journal of Psychoanalysis, 21*: 84–106.

Symantec (2009). Trojan. Peskyspy—Listening in on your conversations. http://www.symantec.com/connect/blogs/trojanpeskyspy-listening-your-conversations

Temperley, J. (1984). Settings for psychotherapy. *British Journal of Psychotherapy, 1*: 101–111.

Tuckett, D. (2011). *Minding the Markets: An Emotional Finance View of Financial Instability*. Basingstoke, UK: Palgrave Macmillan.

Weintrobe, S. (2013). Introduction. In: S. Weintrobe (Ed.), *Engaging with Climate Change: Psychoanalytic and Interdisciplinary Perspectives*. London: Routledge.

Werbin, A., Burdet, M., Giménez Noble, F., Sahovaler Litvinoff, D., Hirsch Hardy, J., & Ambort, G. (2014). Remote therapy research: A research on distance psychoanalysis sponsored by the International Psychoanalytical Association. http://www.remotetherapy.net/home.html

Winnicott, D. W. (1953). Transitional objects and transitional phenomena—a study of the first not-me possession. *International Journal of Psychoanalysis, 34*: 89–97.

Wright, D., & Kreissl, R. (2013). European responses to the Snowden revelations: A discussion paper. *IRISS (Increasing Resilience in Surveillance Societies) Consortium*. http://irissproject.eu/wp- content/uploads/2013/12/IRISS_European-responses-to-the-Snowden-revelations_18-Dec-2013_Final.pdf

Zimmermann, P. R. (1995). *The Official PGP User's Guide*. Cambridge, MA: MIT Press.

CHAPTER FOUR

The analyst's closeness in long-distance psychoanalysis

Claudia Mizrahi (Argentina)

Introduction

Technology has greatly affected the practice of psychoanalysis. A new setting has been introduced to us. While working in technology-assisted distance analysis, I have often seen my prejudices and principles questioned. Why do we talk about long-distance psychoanalysis if the patient feels very close despite communicating through technology? Is it psychoanalysis at all? What are the differences between teleanalysis and co-present psychoanalysis with the body of patient and of analyst in the same room? How do new technologies affect us? We frequently think that technology stimulates the development of a narcissistic psychic apparatus—much like the one Freud described in his early paper (Freud, 1911)—which is apparently eager to get rid of its drives without regard to its need for objects. However, we live in complex times. On the one hand, while we observe increasing disconnection in very small children who are overexposed to technology, we also observe, on the other hand, an important gain in many other areas. I think it is important that we adopt an open attitude toward this, avoiding prejudices in order to try to deepen our understanding of the phenomena that we observe and experience. I do not support the demonization of technology. I agree that it may have risks, but I think the value of technology depends on the use we make of it, and I believe that it may well be an important resource.

To present a dissertation on this subject, as I did at an International Psychoanalytical Association Congress, seemed like science fiction (Mizrahi, 2015). There were moments when the voice of authority urged me not to write about this subject, and choose instead to write about "more psychoanalytic" matters. Indeed, I do not know if the impact of technology on psychoanalysis is a strictly psychoanalytic subject, but I do know that it is relevant to today's clinical practice and that it is part of my own experience as an analyst. I have wanted to write about these experiences for some time.

When writing about teleanalysis, as about any topic, we leave a long-lasting impression. We make a commitment to show with honesty what we do. Writing is the analyst's elaboration on the work of psychoanalysis. Writing allows us to define our practice, recreate the experience, and, as Joseph Sandler says, encourage ourselves to find our own private theories, those that we use in the intimacy of our offices (Sandler, 1983). From these proto-theories that we use in private comes the possibility of deepening the investigation of psychoanalysis. Thus, when we make the decision to continue analysis with a patient who has to leave his country by using technology, we think about the possibility of applying the psychoanalytic method to a new model, one that was not available at the time of the origin of psychoanalysis. Inevitably, the mind of the analyst is crowded with new ideas, conscious and unconscious, new ways of thinking about the theory, the clinical practice, and the setting.

My aim in this work is to discover my intimate, private theories and to compare and confront them with the fundamental concepts of psychoanalysis in the light of this modern, new, and complex practice that is long-distance psychoanalysis.

Development

Present-body and long-distance analysis

While reflecting upon this subject, a question came to me: What would Freud have done in our times? Would he have accepted a long-distance treatment? While we do not have access to an exact answer, we have the example of his experience with Mahler, the composer, in 1910. Theodor Reik narrates in his book *The Haunting Melody* (1953) (translated into Spanish, 1975) the encounter that Freud had with the musician. It was a single psychoanalytic session that took place one afternoon in Leyden, in Holland. Reik says:

> A long list of members of our psychoanalytic profession will pull their hair out when hearing about the utterly unorthodox practice holding one single, psychoanalytic session that lasted the whole afternoon, but extraordinary situations and circumstances demand extraordinary measures. (1975, p. 153, translated from Spanish)

According to Freud, this session lasted for hours and had a deep, lasting effect. Freud speaks about this encounter with a completely natural tone in a letter to Reik in 1935. Here, he comments about the points of Mahler's life that could be analyzed, and those that could not even be touched. Freud considered Mahler a person with an admirable psychological understanding, which promoted interesting incursions into his history. Despite the unorthodox nature of this intervention, it was clearly fruitful.

So, Freud gave us an example of psychoanalysis being conducted in an exceptional circumstance. In my own practice I had an experience of closeness and distance in the traditional setting of a child analysis in which the body of the analyst and the body of the patient are in the analyst's office. I refer to these as "present-body sessions." Pedro, a six-year-old-boy used to enter our present-body sessions with an electronic tablet, and kept on playing a football game while he narrated me his winning feats. I understood that Pedro needed time and distance from me. One day, when I saw that he was physically coming closer, I told him: "That's a good game, but it is single-player." He looked at me and said: "If you have a ball we can play together." We started playing and, after a few minutes, I was getting warm and interrupted the game for a second to take my jacket off. I laid my jacket on the same chair where Pedro's coat was. He looked at me distrustfully and lifted his jacket and put it on another chair to keep it apart from mine, to keep himself apart from me. His body was close to mine as we played, and Pedro had to take distance in this way. When he came closer to me, he could not tolerate the contact between our coats, as if we were touching each other by the work of magic.

Now I want to think about Carlos. Carlos is an Argentine living in the Cantabria region of Spain. He had tried to begin an analysis previously, but had to move to a distant city, which meant missing a day off work for every session. He preferred to be analyzed by an Argentine analyst, but there was no Argentine analyst working in his region of Spain. He contacted me, and decided to come to Argentina to meet me. For fifteen days we held daily sessions. When that period ended, he went back to Spain and decided to continue his analysis long-distance for fifty minutes twice a week. What was interesting was that, initially, Carlos refused to use a computer. He called me by phone. Despite it being a long-distance analysis, Carlos imposed even more distance, just like Pedro.

I asked Carlos why he did not want to use the computer and the web camera that would provide us with the image of each other. A question that had occurred to me was whether Carlos could masturbate while we were speaking on the phone. This did not seem at all likely, both by what I knew about him and by the tone of the conversation in the phone sessions. However, the thought crossed my mind.

Carlos began to comment about his persecutory phantasies regarding the possibility that his girlfriend Marta, with whom he lived, could be listening to our conversations. Marta was Spanish and had been living with Carlos for about five years. Carlos had doubts about staying in Spain, marrying and having children, or going back to Argentina. Then at age thirty-three he developed asthma, which was what motivated his consultation. Among other things, we saw that Carlos lived in a state of suspense that was linked to his asthma and his fears. Interestingly, this health-related symptom gave in much more quickly than the refusal to use the web camera. Carlos was haunted by the idea of Martha messing with his sessions. Phantasies around the three of us joining together in a scene often emerged. We started reconstructing these childish phantasies, and eventually we were able to use the web camera. Today, Carlos is a patient with whom I can alternate analysis with web camera and present-body sessions. He comes once a year to Argentina, and we can then establish a period of frequent sessions. When I had to travel to different cities in Spain, Carlos traveled to the place I was visiting, and we held sessions in a room in the hotel where I was staying. This experience with Carlos, of alternating long-distance with "present-body" sessions, was positive for the conduct of the analysis.

In different places in Freud's work, he dealt with the basic pillars of psychoanalytic theory, between which lies "the assumption that there are unconscious mental processes, the recognition of the theory of resistance and repression, the appreciation of the importance of sexuality and of the Oedipus complex" (1923, p. 247). In my brief story about Carlos these concepts—and transference too—were shown. However, we know that the relationship with the analyst cannot be the same through a screen as it is with a physical, present body. So how is it different?

I now want to think of the impact of the *present* body in a heightened emotional situation such as mourning. I have observed that the presence of the body at a mass makes the experience more vivid for the mourners: the dramatic impact of death and the intensity of the relatives' feelings are increased. There are certain things transmitted by the body that are not transmitted through the screen. The present body in the office has the ability to affect analyst and patient as it speaks beyond words and awakens emotions that are dead or sleeping. We can compare the difference between teleanalysis and traditional psychoanalysis with that between theater and cinema. In the cinema, when the lights go out and we disconnect our psyche from the outer world, what we experience is similar to a dream. In the theater, where the body of each actor is present, the whole atmosphere is different, and what happens affects the spectator—who is, in some ways, part of the scene—with greater intensity. At the theatre and in the cinema the capacity for penetrating and living the scene depends on many factors that do not discriminate between the two audience experiences, but cinema and theater are different in the ways they provide for experiencing a story.

More often than not, when I think about teleanalysis I think about transference love. Therefore, I must pose the following question: Is a love in which experiences are lived through a computer screen the same as a love that is experienced through live action? Evidently not. Sexuality cannot be lived virtually. The contact with the analyst when coming in, saying hello, lying on the couch or talking face to face, makes the relationship with the analyst more tangible, more vivid, just like in theater. In fact, not all people can maintain a long-distance analysis, something it is important to evaluate when starting an analysis. However, if we manage to isolate our minds from external stimuli, as we do in the cinema, if we can clear our minds and concentrate on the patient, perhaps we can reach dream-like states like those in the movies. If analyst and patient can enter wholeheartedly with great concentration into the fiction, there is a lot we can do. I call it a fiction because we don't touch while saying hello, because we are inside a screen, and because the analyst is a mere image for that patient, especially true for those whose sessions have only been virtual and never in the analyst's office. A question that emerges then is whether the analyst is a representation or not. I do not have the answer. But if we say that there is transference, then the analyst on the screen may be that same representation that incarnates the objects of childhood in a traditional analysis. Is not analysis with the body present not the same then as analysis in cyberspace? Is not the analyst, while a person in flesh and blood, with whom the patient relates, whether in the office or online, always a representation that incarnates the objects of childhood?

The first time I held long-distance sessions for psychoanalysis was about ten years ago. The patient, Mariano, was a young twenty-eight-year old, a fraternal twin who had been born in Mexico during his parents' exile, and had come back to Argentina at age six after the return of democracy in our country. For Mariano, the return from exile for his parents felt like an exile for him. The loss of his dear Mexico was a permanent topic of analysis—the smells, the neighborhoods, the traditions, his friends. He felt like an *Argenmex*. About a year into analysis, Mariano had to leave for six months to go to an area close to Mexico in the US, which in fact is called New Mexico. Mariano surprised me, then, with the proposition of continuing the analysis through phone sessions. Mariano used to prepare for our sessions by reading about the weather in Buenos Aires. One time, a severe storm was thundering over Buenos Aires. When Mariano called me for his session, he surprised me with the following opening comment: "What a storm! It is raining so hard today! I will have to come by boat to our session." He dealt with the experience of the session with him in New Mexico and me in Argentina in a way that made him feel less like an exile from either country. Using the phone to maintain the analysis allowed the experience of preserving the object, the places, and even the little details of daily life. It was possible to evoke and analyze transference and reconstruct infant sexuality through dreams, memories of the Mexico of his childhood, and the encounter with his twin sister, who was also living in New Mexico.

From all these experiences I learnt that psychoanalysis is embedded in me, and that every situation allows a new articulation and calls for greater flexibility from me, and a capacity to play with the seriousness of children, in different stages of the work. All of these experiences enriched my development as an analyst in terms of my way of thinking about practice and theory of the neuroses and the most severe pathologies, and enabled the creative implementation of all I have learnt and lived in my years of psychoanalytic practice. Each of these cases was a challenge that allowed me, each time, to have a new integration of theory, practice, and technique of psychoanalysis.

The closeness of the analyst at a distance

Marcela is an Argentine who moved to Mexico when her husband was transferred for work. The whole family had to move with him to a region far from Mexico City, where there were no Argentine psychoanalysts. Marcela was disgusted with the new environment, the Argentines who lived there, and the Mexicans as well. She could not adapt. She decided to begin an analysis, as her anguish and depression made the adaptation much more difficult. She was a doctor and had had to leave her profession to follow her husband. We held sessions for two years, twice a week, via Skype. On many occasions she came to her home town near Buenos Aires to visit her family, but only once did she come to meet me. It was nearly Christmas. This time Marcela came to Buenos Aires and had a session in my office. She said she found it different to have me physically close, and she was moved by the experience. When she left the session, she said she would miss me. Never again did she come to visit, despite having traveled a number of times to Argentina, because when she was in her native province, she disconnected from me. I did not have news from her, even though she was nearby, and we did not continue over Skype either. When she returned to Mexico, I was resurrected in her mind.

After two years, the company where her husband worked decided to repatriate them to Argentina, and to her home town. Then, I thought it was time to refer Marcela to another analyst. While we had built a very good bond, and we could work quite satisfactorily, I thought that she, from the beginning, felt the need of physical presence, and yet she would not physically cross the distance to see me when it was geographically possible. In any case, I support the idea that if there is a local analyst who can offer the patient analysis with the body present, that possibility should be offered.

Marcela came to Buenos Aires so we could together close that period of work. She was sad because of our parting, and also grateful. She brought me a gift of one of those aromatized oils with a very sweet fragrance. I told her that I was now going to be impregnated with her perfume. That moved her. She talked about the possibility of contacting me through email if she needed to, to which I said yes, but I referred her to an analyst I trusted who lived in her city.

Two months later, I received a long email from her telling me that she could not get into her new analysis, that her analyst was very competent, but that she missed me. She also said that she was about to retake her old job and that she was making a great effort helping her children adapt to the new environment. She asked whether she could contact me via Skype, at least once. The new analyst, who had seen her only a few times, communicated to me that she thought Marcela was still engaged in transference with me and that she did not understand why we could not continue the analysis through Skype.

I understood that I had been a bit rigid in my conceptions. That my ideas had worked as maxims. The referral had been rushed. We re-established the analysis via Skype, and since then we have not seen each other again, other than on screen. Not long ago, the patient fantasized about going away from the country to get rid of her mother, with whom she had a conflicted relationship. When I asked about me as a part of that fantasy, she answered, "I take you with me everywhere I go." We may venture the hypothesis that distance protected her from her bad mother, while it was also a way of avoiding that same relationship being evoked between us. We will see whether the transference neurosis develops fully when the analysis is conducted using Skype.

It is interesting to think of the transference in these long-distance treatments: The person feels alien in the environment to which he has migrated and the analyst is experienced as the sole spokesman from his own culture. When having difficulties identifying oneself with the new environment and with its people, that new place is often regarded as dangerous due to its differences with the previous one. To understand a bit more of what is going on in the minds of patients living abroad and preferring an analyst from their own country, I have found it helpful to think in terms of a reactivation of the infant's processes of identification with the mother and the resulting "complex of the fellow human-being" (Freud, 1895, p. 331). Freud shows that the infant's experience with the other who is seen as being like oneself gives rise to a process of identification intimately linked to thinking. When encountering the other, the baby looks for and finds coincidences between his movements and those of the other, between his visual impressions of his body and those of the other. Following Freud's ideas on identification, Winocur shows that the perception of the other stimulates the evocation of the common elements that are part of our own experience, which includes physical experiences and the emotional experiences with the first objects (Winocur, Weber, De Carrica, & De Carrica, 1989). Thereby, we can identify with the other and find something of ourselves in the other, which is the basis for the understanding of the other. These authors assert that the experience with the other evokes a *theoretical* interest. However, some people who for different reasons have had to migrate to foreign countries do not have a theoretical interest in the other. They have difficulty identifying with the people of the new country where they live—even if those people are of their own nationality, migrants like themselves. Even if they do identify with them, once they need an analyst, they need a familiar voice that, even though mediated by technology, is the one that can evoke that primitive experience of recognizing the other and recognizing themselves. In the process of analysis, they see themselves reflected in an analyst with whom they share the same origin. This can even happen in cases when the person (such as an Argentine in Mexico) lives in a country where his mother-tongue is spoken. This is even more interesting if we remember that the possibility of identifying with the other is intimately bonded with the process of thinking. It seems that patients feel that they can think more effectively when they are with another they recognize as similar. Looking at it from this point of view, what analyst and patient are doing is not a long-distance analysis, but an analysis that allows the closeness of the similar across a distance, through technology, almost magically. The crucial element of distance is put into the analytic environment, not by geographical separation, but by patients who cannot find themselves in the analyst and cannot succeed in identifying themselves.

Conclusion

Technology and psychoanalysis

Thinking about the relationship between technology and psychoanalysis reminds me of an article on science fiction as an expression of the fetal regression of the psyche (Lustig de Ferrer & Tomás, 1960). Lustig de Ferrer and Tomás observed that there was a time when the development of science caused fears and anguish about the future of mankind. The genre of science fiction was based on the actual progress of science and technology and imaginative construction of the fabulous development that they could have in the future. The actual progress can be observed in our own time, but the catastrophes predicted by the novels have not happened: human beings have not developed physical aberrations and monsters are not living among us. Even more, we can say that, in different clothing, concerns remain the same. Love, work, and the vicissitudes of the external world are still, in the big picture, the main motives for seeking psychoanalytic consultation. I know that the world has changed, but I am saying that, in essence, we are still today, as human beings of 2016, quite similar as those of the past.

There is a resemblance between the frightening prospects of science and its progress as seen in the past, and the fears that they evoke today. In those times, dangers referred to the uncertainty of how science was going to be used by man. The fear was that we might see the return of the repressed forces through the same technological instruments with which it was hoped to control them. It may seem that what we value as culture, which has brought progress, is the same entity that could destroy us. However, and I think that it is important to emphasize it, the danger is, actually, what we ourselves are capable of doing with our own destructive impulses driven by the death instinct. Accepting that responsibility lies within ourselves allows the analyst to disengage from any prejudice against technology, and instead to address the patient's material psychoanalytically—including analyzing the actual and unconscious use the patient makes of technology.

From the magic board to the PC

In his time, Freud wrote about the cultural acquisitions of civilization, which, just like a fairy tale, make us feel as if all our desires can be fulfilled through access to devices that can improve our sensorial functions (the telephone, movies) or our muscle power (tools) and our perceptions (radar). He described the surprising emergence of a new device, the "mystic writing-pad," which emulates the functioning of our psychic apparatus. "Our mood apparatus [...] doesn't have a limit in its reception for perceptions, which are always new and also [...] provides lasting mnemonic prints" (Freud, 1925, p. 244). Our "mystic writing-pad," namely the personal computer, is even more capable of doing that. In fact, we know that even when we delete information it tends to linger in some part of the rigid disc and that, in order to erase it completely, we would have to destroy the entire disc.

I admire Freud's eagerness for understanding his time, the nature of human beings, and the culture that we live in, in an unprejudiced way. I think that his is a good example to follow in order to understand this intersection between technology and the demand for long-distance analysis. Communication online with voice and image on Skype or similar software is another cultural achievement like those mentioned by Freud in *Das Unbehagen in der Kultur* (*Civilization and its Discontents*) (1930). We can see the other person, talk to distant places, shorten distances, and see the environment the patient chooses. We can write and store our documents. We can make and store images. We have memory for text, photo, video, and music. Nothing escapes us because it is stored in our technological memory. In his time, Freud observed that man, with the cultural acquisitions of the moment, has turned into a god. What should we say in ours?

Science and technology continue to advance, introducing hitherto unimagined devices that will change our behavior, our view of ourselves, and our culture. Culture keeps building itself on the base of instinctual resignation, "it is based not on the satisfaction (by means of suffocation, repression …) of powerful drives" (Freud, 1930, p. 96). Despite the strengthening of culture, the power of self-destruction due to the death instinct has grown stronger. This must be the field of work in analysis, whether through long-distance communication using a computer, or in present-body sessions in the office.

References

Freud, S. (1911). Formulaciones sobre los dos principios del suceder psíquico. *Obras Completas, 12*: 217–231. Buenos Aires: Amorrortu.

Freud, S. (1923 [1922]. Two encyclopedia articles. *S. E., 18*: 233–259. London: Hogarth.

Freud, S. (1925). Notas sobre la pizarra mágica. *Obras Completas, 19*: 241–247. Buenos Aires: Amorrortu.

Freud, S. (1930). El malestar en la cultura. *Obras Completas, 21*: 9–96. Buenos Aires: Amorrortu.

Freud, S. (1950a [1895]). A project for a scientific psychology. *S. E., 1*: 284–346. London: Hogarth.

Lustig de Ferrer, S., & Tomás, J. (1960). La literatura de ciencia ficción como expresión dela regresión fetal. In: A. Rascovsky (Ed.), *El Psiquismo Fetal* (pp. 191–199). Buenos Aires: Paidós.

Mizrahi, C. (2015). The analyst's closeness in long distance psychoanalysis. Unpublished paper. International Psychoanalytical Congress, Boston, 24 July 2015.

Reik, T. (1953). *The Haunting Melody: Psychoanalytic Experiences in Life and Music*. New York: Farrar, Strauss & Young.

Reik, T. (1975). *Variaciones Psicoanalíticas sobre un Tema de Mahler*. Buenos Aires: Taurus Ediciones.

Sandler, J. (1983). Reflexiones sobre algunas relaciones entre los conceptos psicoanalíticos y la práctica psicoanalítica [On some relations between psychoanalytic concepts and psychoanalytic practice]. *Revista de Psicoanálisis, 39*: 579–596.

Winocur, J. O., Weber, C. B., De Carrica, A. I., & De Carrica, S. M. O. (1989). La identificación y su discriminación de la incorporación y la introyección [Identification differentiated from incorporation and introjection]. *Revista de Psicoanálisis, 46*: 863–874.

CHAPTER FIVE

Light and shadow in online analysis

Andrea Marzi and Giuseppe Fiorentini (Italy)

Introduction

New technologies and the current methods of online communication upset the spatial and temporal parameters to which psychoanalysts are accustomed (Shanyang, 2006). They require us to confront and give meaning to the new ways in which our minds increasingly have to interact and our relationships have to take shape. A variety of elements contribute to widening our perspective, including—we would emphasize—the changes induced by contemporary society such as increased mobility, and changed working circumstances. Difficulty in finding patients in large urban areas may also drive us to offer online analysis. It has been pointed out that this practice is very promising in terms of expanding the services provided to a larger number of patients, especially those who may have great difficulty participating in a classic treatment and those who would not be able to do it at all (Martin, 2013).

A raging debate, even fiercer than the one on the interface between psychoanalysis and the Internet and between psychoanalysis and the use of information technology (IT) in the early twenty-first century, has started in analytical circles regarding online analysis—and it is still unresolved. We must critically review the spread of services and publications on the web which seem to "take up the cause" of the Internet at all costs, dangerously overlooking the assumptions, the theoretical and technical features, the ethical caveat, in the name of always being to the fore—and let us admit it—in the name of cheap and simple utilitarianism. These topics have a great theoretical and technical value for psychoanalysis and cannot be ignored. We have to understand this new frontier better and more thoroughly, to grasp the potential of its use.

It is important from now on for training programs to include some classes on this subject and for the different societies to include these courses in their continuing education accreditation policies, so as to train students and professionals in IT as well as in its legal and ethical aspects. However, it is a field that, from an ethical and regulatory point of view, is still very difficult to frame. Something has been said, particularly in terms of analytic training, but the rest of the extra-training world, in analytic circles and mostly outside them, remains a terrain to be explored or, perhaps, a no-man's-land liable to be fraught with risk. As Bob Dylan said, "The times they are a-changing," and we need to pay great attention to the impact of that. There is no doubt a need for research, which can only be carried out by practising these therapies and studying them, in a pure psychoanalytic style.

Virtual reality

At this point, one important aspect emerges that we believe cannot be overlooked when reflecting on online analysis, as this kind of encounter with the patient has certainly to do with the virtual dimension of experience. The concrete and imaginary reality in which our society is plunged is changing. Now we have to take into account that there are not only two types of reality that exist, the concrete and the psychic: concrete reality is external reality; psychic reality is the conscious and unconscious subjective experience of the individual, like the virtual reality of the transference itself.

Beyond those two types of reality, the Internet creates a new form of dematerialised reality or para-reality, a simulated reality better known as *cyberspace*, which can be compared, on the psychological level, to a mysterious abstract area with the potential to expand in many directions and ways. The Internet corresponds to a non-place where events occur not in the countries where the users are located but in an unspecified elsewhere. Yet this non-place, without a space in the commonly understood meaning, lets those who access it meet, get to know one another, and establish relations.

The internet is a universe populated by bits and pixels, by acoustic signals and luminous dots. On Skype, a consumer-friendly Voice over Internet Protocol platform, these show up as lines of light, shadows, colors, beams of particles that animate the images of the participants on their respective screens and reproduce their voices in real time, putting the two people together, even though they are in the remotest corners of the planet (Coleman, 2011). As we know, Skype permits reproduction of the physical reality of the communicating subjects, a reality that seems destined, with the progress of information and communications technology (ICT) systems, to become increasingly indistinguishable from its simulation, to some extent confirming the ancient Hindu belief that the world is nothing but an illusion. It is an illusion made up of the same stuff dreams are made of and experienced consensually in a world suspended on the border between reality and imagination, comparable, according to some authors (Gabbard, 2001; Goldberg, 1999), to transitional space (Winnicott, 1967)—a space situated between external reality and the internal world, which begs the question whether this space belongs to the machine or to the mind. It is a space that is not only an experiment of thought but also, however evanescent it may be, a physical and measurable phenomenon consisting of waves, particles, and energies. Bollas (2007), in a brief and cryptic poem, wonders who there really is on the other side in the "e-world," alluding to the enigmatic status underlying this neo-dimension. According to some cosmological theories, this dimension would represent one of the multiple universes present in a potential state all of which are alleged to radiate out from ours as far as the eye can see, until they form a picturesque hypothetical "multiverse," a universe of all the universes (Barrow, 2011), a phantom world "out there," the existence of which is expressed in terms of waves of probability, like the subatomic kingdom investigated by quantum physics.

We have illustrated this scenario in broad terms to introduce what we consider an important component in online treatments, that is, *place*, the dimension in which we meet our patients via Skype, even though we are sitting in our consulting room near the monitor. Through the monitor, our consulting room, our words and our self, is transported into that other space where the patient is. The latter in turn, thanks to the monitor, feels as though he is where we are, as if through a whirling set of mirrors, as though the actual consulting room (if it still makes sense to talk about it at all) were transferred into cyberspace, a non-place where patient and analyst are in a synchronic and one-to-one contact and feel both distant and deceptively close to one another. As in a polyhedral set of Chinese boxes, we can conceive of our virtual inner room of listening (Di Chiara, 1983) smoothly overlapping with that other room, the room of the encounter—which is just as virtual—located beyond the monitor, like Alice's world behind the mirror, a kaleidoscopic intertwining of nature and culture in which the respective boundaries fade away and overlap.

A recent book by one of us (Marzi, 2013) also emphasizes how virtuality reflects the "mind" (the object of our analytic work) in that both share the same charter of place/non-place that, while having a base that is physical and material (the hardware and the software, the brain and the nervous system), is in fact dematerialized. The subject's mental space, whether the patient's or the analyst's, comes to life and unravels within the analytic relationship, understood as the analytic field, where aspects such as states of mind, fantasies, and dematerialized objects can gradually present themselves, be exchanged, or get connected, as varied relationships are interwoven over time with the events of the analysis. From here the analytic course can set off on its evolving project, endowed with a future. So virtual space succeeds in being mental space (and vice versa, we may conjecture) both of them sharing the character of experiential zones (of exchange, of superimposition) if the subject succeeds in inhabiting this space as a place where "drafts of analytic thought" (Hautmann, 1999, p. 76) are possible, using cyberspace ("dreaming it") as a constant and flourishing source of thoughts. The subject can connect up dispersed or unorganized elements, proto-informatic elements, we might call them (Marzi, 2013), giving to them a form of life, experience, original elaboration (including artistic expressions), and adventures of the mind that are not imbued with omnipotence or destructive narcissism. The person who exchanges emotional–affective communications with the cyber world can draw on the symbolization and constant production of a "relational flow," the fruit of projective and introjective exchanges, aimed at the construction of new elements of thought, endowed with meaning.

This is what happens in the analytic relationship conducted in remote analysis. This technical-clinical mode, this new and at the same time classic setting, shows how essential it is for its proper and genuine realization that a dynamic and creative three-dimensionality is set in the analytic dyad, where the relationship and the field, although infinitely expanded in cyberspace, can contain these processes or transform them, if they present themselves as concrete, asymbolic elements (beta elements, according to Bion, 1962). The apparent dematerialization that is present in cyberspace can be concretized as the personification of a hyper-materiality that cannot be metabolized by the subject. When there is no relatedness capable of giving emotional and symbolic life to the elements scattered through cyberspace, these elements, although deprived of all actual materiality, become absolutely concrete for the subject and indigestible by the mind. The lack of creativity in this case constitutes a psychic risk for the subject himself.

In the field of online analysis, we are concerned not only with the elements that typically belong to the analyst/patient relationship, but also with all the elements of what we can call the online, analytic-digital field. This expansion of our focus offers complex yet enticing new and broader perspectives in clinical practice and theoretical exploration.

Positive and negative opinions

Too strong an emphasis, perhaps driven by the enthusiasm for this technical mode, could lead to a pernicious increase in the resistance to so-called "in person" treatments, that is, resistance to the physical-psychic presence of the analytic dyad. We can identify this danger fairly clearly in those online psychological consultancies that are practised with too poor a filter, in some fairly indiscriminate ways, without any interpretation of the defenses/resistances that are generated there; for instance, when a patient lies down half naked with a macho poster behind him, and the therapist fails to mention or enquire about this situation, or if the therapist were to accept communication from any device such as a smartphone, anytime, anywhere from a patient on her mobile phone in a coffee shop. Furthermore: online psychological services may be provided through a variety of messaging systems using WhatsApp or various apps specifically designed for the teletherapy purpose. Do therapists who use these apps ask how they would affect the therapeutic relationship? The field of telemental health is in pressing danger of indiscriminate flooding by practices that are insufficiently explored in terms of their symbolic meaning to the patient.

In the specifically psychoanalytic field, over the years, a condemning, highly critical approach to this topic has tended to endure alongside its opposite, an excessively enthusiastic acceptance of the IT world and everything surrounding it. Vigorously claiming that either critical viewpoint has the advantage of being serenely objective in fact reveals a heavy ideological bias. On the one hand, for example, Argentieri and Amati Mehler (2003) claim that the analytic process is not compatible with online sessions. Habib (2003) says that there is no authenticity in that kind of distance analytic setting, so much so that one author (Brainsky, 2003) thinks it is a "ghost relationship" that makes the analyst's voice a concentrated persecutory part-object. Chodorow (2004) describes having been afraid of potential regression in teleanalysis, which she had expected could be better controlled in person. On the other hand, an anything-goes attitude runs the ever-present risk in the post-modern climate and post-modern analysis of ramping up the "turbo"-relational or "turbo"-intersubjective dimension. Indeed, we should be very cautious, starting with the formulation of technical and ethical guidelines. In this respect the International Psychoanalytical Association (IPA) stands out for issuing a document (2014) illustrating some procedures for the definition of remote analysis: "Remote analysis takes place when analyst and patient are not present in the same room. It can be conducted by phone or Skype (with or without a webcam). Shuttle and Concentrated analysis, although often used in conjunction with remote analysis, are carried out 'in the room' and are not therefore remote analysis." The IPA also considers some special aspects of concern, for example, the use of online analysis for training analysis and teaching, which is still under discussion. We appreciate the suggestions made by Stefano Bolognini (2015) in his opening talk at the recent IPA Congress in Boston on the significant differences between the "not in the room sessions" and sessions in the consulting room. He also recalled the likelihood that the use of new technologies could allow the development of some audio-visual functions in a compensatory Lamarckian sense so as to replace bodily expression that is lost in the psychoanalytic encounter in the Internet.

Remote therapy and variations of the setting

Another extremely important issue, both theoretically and technically, is whether online analysis is functionally equivalent to in-person analysis—as many authors state—in facilitating dreams, free associations, resistance, and the experience of transference–countertransference oscillation as well as the work of the unconscious in all its dimensions with sufficient intensity to evoke in the subjects the conviction of the existence and the work of the unconscious, the existence of defenses, and the autonomous capacity to work with analysis. It is a complex topic where we need to bear in mind a variety of points of view, including conflicting ones. This problematic issue is inevitably interlocked with the setting and the formal and environmental variations that we make in online analysis.

When we make a connection with a patient who lives at a distance we remain in our consulting room and the patient occupies a specific place he has chosen. We effectively share with him a virtual room, a sort of "cyber-room" surrounded by invisible electronic walls. The temporal frame of the setting (times, length of the sessions, frequency) remains and is more essential than ever, whereas the spatial one takes on completely different connotations. There is something like a fork, a strabismus between time and space, between these two cardinal elements of the framework of the treatment. This "other" room is obviously nowhere, yet it is occupied by the patient and by ourselves, or to put it better, by our respective simulated doubles. It is a reticular space without a centre where everything is near and far away at the same time, the other is there but is not there, in a place that exists but at the same time does not exist. It is a place that transcends those places portrayed on the screens of both the subjects engaged in the therapy.

The setting is made up not only of formal rules and of a concrete spatial frame, but also by a mental attitude of commitment to psychoanalysis, even across a distance. This frame does include a room, namely the analyst's inner room of listening. Our analytical attitude (Di Chiara, 1983; Fiorentini, Frangini, Molone, Mori Ubaldini, & Robutti, 1995) aims at offering a mental space, like a room prepared for a guest, for the purpose of bringing out contents which otherwise would be inaccessible, and fostering the activation of particular functions of the mind brought out by the relationship. However, the technology we have to use breaks into and modifies the closed and confidential space of the session, just as it conditions the internal structure of the analyst and the relationship between the subjects in an articulation of levels that are often difficult to distinguish, as we will see in the clinical material we will present. What we are talking about examines one of the fundamental cornerstones of the original Freudian analytic receiving apparatus on several levels, triggering a conflict between the setting and the requirements of the analytic method. The conflict over the setting is, so to speak, "ironed out" by the patient's needs for access to treatment (and at times by the needs of the analyst to provide continuity of care and to keep up his income). But then the argument over the purity of the psychoanalytic method intensifies.

Although we agree with those who view psychoanalysis as a way "to enter a relationship with the other and with oneself" (Hautmann, 1981) as an exploration of psychic reality, we do not believe that we can dispense with the level of communication that goes through the body in the presence of the body itself. In our view, online analysis runs the risk of emphasizing the body/mind dichotomy to the detriment of the body. In these circumstances, as a shared physical space is lacking, we are not able to seize that particular "atmosphere" that every human being seems to release around himself (Matte Blanco, 1968), and a direct relationship with the reciprocal sensory channels conveying responses of anger, fear, excitement, and so on, through projective identification, gets lost. Bearing these limitations in mind, we believe that teleanalysis is in many respects adequate, as long as the patient has already attended for psychoanalytic sessions in the analyst's consulting room.

We keep all these ideas and arguments at the centre of our attention as we determine the conditions that are necessary for the patient to benefit from psychoanalysis using Skype. The cornerstone that sustains the building of our practice of telanalysis is an approach that alternates flexibility (the search for compromise, with the intention of offering what for patients is the best treatment possible at that particular time in the therapeutic journey) and purism (observation of the psychoanalytic ethic and the search for psychic truth).

We need to exercise caution about online analyses that start immediately using electronic means, without the analyst having met the patient in person. It seems to us that it is appropriate to require the physical presence of the analytic dyad, at least occasionally, so as to avoid blind spots that can occur in the dyad, if remote analysis never returns to in-person treatment. This position is what emerges fairly constantly in all the reports and papers that have appeared over the years. The IPA Panel in 2009 (Panel Report, 2010), collecting several international contributions, pointed out the positive analytic dimension of this form of analysis, where other communication channels may take over when the visual aspect is missing (in that case referring to analysis conducted over the phone) (Scharff, 2010).

Mirkin (2011), talking about analysis by phone, was not able to identify any difference between analysis in person and analysis conducted over the telephone. Although unconscious communication occurs with any means, not all means are the same in terms of analysis. Traditional analysis, phone analysis, and Skype analysis are different, even though all of them foster unconscious communication. Referring to their experience with remote analysis via videoconferencing (such as Skype) with a web camera, many authors emphasize that no difference can be detected in terms of transference/countertransference dynamics, compared to phone and classic analyses. This is definitely in line with the fact that analysis is essentially the encounter with an understanding mind, no matter what the setting. We do understand, however, that some statements increase enthusiasm for this form of analytic experience, but when they tend to remove the boundaries between different parameters and forms of setting, they create the conditions for a risky lack of distinction.

Technological crashes

Another problematic aspect related to the setting has to do with the interactions around the technological crashes that can occur. There can be no doubt that crashes of the online connection are, to various degrees, inevitable at this stage of the state of technology. Technical disruptions to the connection create a condition that needs to be worked through analytically. They may be equated with sudden, intentional or unintentional ruptures of the setting or disturbances of the empathic level, which may have an impact on the continuation of the treatment. Ruptures of the setting can reveal things that might have remained hidden for ever, and this is the very reason why they need extra attention in analysis. This dimension is often overlooked because we cannot tolerate technical crashes. Even minor crashes wreck the illusion of IT's supposed omnipotence, omniscience, and magic. This triggers a defensive denial of the impact of technical difficulties by analysts, who should be closer to their own emotions, including those of this kind.

To illustrate the importance of the issue of technological problems that can occur in online analysis, we will use some clinical material from patients. Patient and analyst each have a webcam and a personal computer so that they are able to see and talk to each other. The patient is asked to lie down, preferably always in the same place. The camera is placed behind the patient, so that the analyst is faced with the same view of the patient on the couch as in a traditional analytic setting. If the patient turns around, she will see her therapist on the monitor just as she can when she lies on the couch.

Giovanna

Giovanna is a thirty-year-old woman in treatment four sessions a week to work on a clear difficulty—ensuing from remote events in her history—in perceiving her right to "exist." After about two years of analysis in my consulting room, Giovanna had to leave Italy for family reasons. She moved on to treatment via Skype. Giovanna immediately expressed a particular concern about the possibility of "crashes" of the connection during the sessions. Once analysis began, technical crashes indeed happened with a predictably unpredictable frequency and the patient, nostalgic for her sessions with her analyst "in flesh and blood" in the consulting room, wondered where the virtual room "went" when the monitor went dead. She added, "It seems that a virtual session is like making an appointment on the dark side of the moon!"

Very briefly, the level of the relationship with the analyst could be described as showing the following central dynamics: the patient is afraid of disappearing from the analyst's mind during the technical interruptions, just as she felt, as a child, that she was vanishing from the mind of her mother who suffered from a severe form of neurodegenerative brain disease. For the purposes of this paper, we want to emphasize in particular the uncanny aspect Giovanna describes in relation to the encounter in what she perceives as an undefined and indefinable context. We are referring here to the random nature of the interruptions, to the lack of a defined shared physical space with corporeality, even though the patient herself had suggested with apparent conviction that we should move the analysis online and had experienced pleasure and relief from this new situation that allowed us to carry on the treatment despite the distance between us.

In addition to revealing this uniquely personal trait, this patient's vignette points to the dark shadow of ambiguity that is hidden under the dazzling omnipotence (Lemma, 2015) of technology that ensures instantaneous travel. When the monitor, which showed analyst and patient together at work fictitiously eclipsing separation, became dark and silent due to malfunctioning of the network, a silent and deadly "uninvited guest" appeared in the analytic scenario equating to when the patient's mother was lost in a mental void. This condition evoked in Giovanna the past cut-off from the mother, keenly felt as vanishing from her mother's mind and becoming once more inexistent. Returning to Giovanna's question about her experience in the virtual room, patient and analyst were catapulted into one of the almost infinite configurations of the enigmatic multiverse (Barrow, 2011), or into a non-relational mental area where culture in the form of technology and nature echo each other in mutual oscillation.

Skype vs. *telephone*

It is particularly interesting, both in terms of technique and of theory, to examine differences between remote analysis via telephone and via videoconferencing. By precluding direct visual observation, the telephone not only does not suit the setting and work habit of the traditional analytic dyad, but also it risks being experienced by some people as a general kind of communication, good for all occasions. The use of the telephone is an everyday activity that does not offer any relational specificity and does not open or maintain any "special" setting for analytic or psychotherapeutic purpose. Videoconferencing via Skype is a newer, less general but at the same time more viable setting for our specific purposes, being more like the traditional analytic setting in that the body is visible. It can also be felt as a new experience in direct continuation with the previous patient-analyst relationship, most likely because it has not been exploited and exhausted by any other previous usage. Moreover, as we have said, the patient can be seen (and so can the analyst be seen, if desired), as in the traditional analytic relationship. By that we do not mean that the traditional setting has to be taken as the gold standard, but it is an established setting effective for analysis, conceived as it was for the patient to be present. Therefore, videoconferencing offers an already experienced analytic dyad the possibility of feeling comfortable in a familiar spatial couch-chair relationship, without going through upheavals in the setting that could have damaging outcomes.

To reiterate, with online analysis we can achieve an analytic relationship that broadly recreates the classic analytic relationship as long as some characteristics are respected, such as the importance of analysis having been established in the traditional setting prior to switching to teleanalysis (for example, when continuing treatment after a move), specific agreements about the setting, in-depth consideration and acceptance of the technical difficulties and interruptions that can occur at any time, a lot of common sense, and consensus on the value of analyzing every manifestation of the remote setting's impact on the analytic process of the couple at work. This dedication to analyzing the inevitable manifestations of the technological support of the encounter becomes a crucial element in the metabolizing work of the analytic dyad, every time they occur—and they always do (IPA, 2016).

More clinical material

We will now report some brief vignettes from analyses conducted through the Internet. We will see together how the changes in the formal arrangement of the setting in teleanalysis, such as the anomalous presence of the technological device, the physical distance between patient and analyst, and the absence of the classical scenario of the analytic encounter, have affected in different ways the development of the treatment, even triggering levels of the relationship that had remained unexpressed before the teleanalysis began.

Francesca

After one year of analysis in the analyst's consulting room, Francesca's analysis was continued via Skype for about four years. A more extensive case report may be read elsewhere (Fiorentini, 2012). Francesca is a cultivated and intelligent foreign woman in her thirties. She asked for help because of isolation and narcissistic fragility attested to by a feeling of inadequacy and lack of self-esteem. Francesca was born prematurely, and since her early childhood had been exposed to sudden and long separations from her parents for several months because she was often sent to stay with some cousins who lived on another continent. Her parents made this choice so that Francesca would learn a foreign language, but Francesca experienced it as an expression both of their narcissistic need for a bright, polyglot prodigy and of their rejection—and she was left feeling as though she had been sent for adoption. The mother was described as a person with little empathy, self-absorbed in her own academic career, and often quite critical of her daughter. With her father she had an essentially good, but somewhat ambivalent relationship. Conversely, with her mother she had a highly conflicted relationship. After about one year of analysis in the analyst's consulting room, Francesca had to return to her home country because of visa problems. She asked me not to stop the sessions and to continue via Skype. The threat of stopping the treatment aroused in Francesca feelings of anger and loss related to when, as a child many years ago, she had to leave her home against her will. The analysis of her request for teleanalysis highlighted not only her clear investment in our work, but also her wish to obtain the narcissistic compensation of a tailor-made context for the particular psychic pain that follows a trauma she had been helpless to avoid. Bearing in mind her history, characterized by countless separations, the analyst thought it appropriate to privilege some continuity instead of sticking to the purism of traditional analytic communication. Teleanalysis would embody the attitude of a father and a mother willing to give her time to bring her analytic gestation to term and help her master the "language" of affects, both of which she had been deprived of. An agreement about doing analysis was set up. The same frequency of sessions would be maintained remotely, and we would resume in-person treatment whenever it became possible again.

In his first experience in this field, the analyst was strongly impressed by the originality of this new way of meeting in the condition of digital abstraction. Everything was as before and yet everything was different. The images and voices of the two participants, even though they were identical to the original ones, were also different because they were processed by the electronic medium. And in the meantime the display of their images on the screen revealed the separation between them, just as, at the same time, it saturated their togetherness fictitiously, becoming the non-limit that broke down the time barrier and tamed the actual physical distance. The analyst required a special effort to oscillate between such different levels, bearing in mind their different valences and yet being able to integrate them, as if seeing the props that make a play possible or watching a movie and seeing the machines that produce the "special effects." In teleanalysis we see a film within a film, a dream within a dream. The repetitive and regular fabric of the sessions constituted an element of containment and gave meaning to a threatening "dark wake from the past" (in Francesca's words), the result of old wounds and aphasia about the anger and pain in them. The presence of cyberspace—like a hologram—gave new meaning to things, session by session, multiplying epistemological possibilities and interlocking and broadening the realm of fantasy. This was similar to what happened when the patient, as a child, enjoyed inventing tales with her father or day-dreaming in the company of an aunt with whom she lived. The idea was to foster the transformation of the digital illusion into a potential space between analyst and patient: a *Zwischenreich*, a middle kingdom of imagination. A particular aspect of countertransference emerged in the middle of the relationship. Similar to what the patient had experienced when she was away from home, the analyst also seemed to find himself listening to a foreign language unknown to him, experiencing feelings of disorientation and uncertainty. These perceptions had been induced in him not only in response to the patient's disorientation but also because of the "foreignness" of the electronic medium, compared to his comfort with the usual mode of intervention that he had experienced in the first year of analysis in his consulting room.

We shall now illustrate another peculiar feature of the treatment with this patient. After long separations, misunderstanding, or lack of empathy, a defensive response appeared in which the figure appearing on the screen assumed some sort of concreteness, becoming for the patient the real object to possess totally, while the monitor itself came to be fetishized and used as a kind of mental prosthesis that could resolve "all the sources of anxiety once for all" (Gaburri, 2006, p. 23). The technological object was mistaken for the person of the analyst. Strength-giving illusion was replaced by denial of the impossible. These dynamics are close to what Riolo (2010) says about transformation in hallucinosis, the goal of which "is not a quest for gratification but the avoidance of frustration" (ibid., p. 646) in the maintenance of independence through absolute power.

In treatment, the analyst's interventions addressed the inevitable recognition of psychic reality and the acceptance of the patient's request for a "mother tongue" with which to tell and unravel painful experiential entanglements linked not only to everything that had happened, but also to what had not happened, in her childhood in relations with the primary objects. Progressively, the patient started to show greater attachment to life and to open up to some hope for the future, as she felt less under siege from the fears of not being accepted and loved. It was also important for her to recognize her parents' narcissistic fragility and start to make a partial integration of her feelings of retaliation and self-blame. The analysis finished about a year ago, unfortunately with a somewhat hasty termination, contrary to what had been agreed, because of inevitable obstacles in her external circumstances.

We will now report the clinical material from another patient.

Cecilia

Cecilia chose to continue her analysis via Skype when she had to move away after she had been in analysis for several years. In one of the first sessions via Skype, Cecilia brought this dream:

> I was at my grandparents'. It is as if all the objects, the sofa, the curtains, the pictures, were alive and I interacted with them. I don't know if they are good or bad. They are "strange." They don't make me feel comfortable. As if they were magical, they go out of the house. Somebody felt unwell and needed help. And these strange objects go to help them.

At first the dream was not clear at all. Then the analyst had an intuition. The analyst said that there were old things that conveyed a feeling of bewilderment that made the patient feel uncomfortable. These things went outside, as if she is now outside the known dimension of her analysis and yet still inside herself. But, the objects in the dream also referred to the Internet and Skype.

The thinking minds of the analytic dyad continue to be at work under the new condition of teleanalysis and do not cease to be fertile, producing in the analyst something that can be called intuition (or even a selected fact). Everything is scary, right now, with these puzzling objects, but if everything is oriented toward help, then it all becomes better known and less threatening and one feels more comfortable. The analyst also comes into this environment. Then if the patient feels helped—or perhaps if she helps others (because of what she is doing and because of her specific profession)—then she is calmer, and the dream becomes more of a fantasy. In addition, what kind of object is in our exchange in this new situation? Where is it? Where does it go?

In other words, the patient starts to think about the therapeutic functioning of this completely new experience, to wonder about it and make sense of it and how it relates to the analytic dyad, to her, and to her previous in-person analysis. She thinks and fantasizes by day, as she does in her night-time dream, as if entering the scene of a Walt Disney movie, where the inanimate, the concrete, the unthought, the asymbolic comes to life in a partially new condition. And all this current experience in teleanalysis intersects with the inner world. We need to address the experience at various levels—at the level of the technical aspects of the digital world, the particular aspects of the analyst-patient relationship in this modality, and the greater difficulty for patient and analyst in tolerating silent moments during the telesession. These intersections of technology and object relations are set in motion by analysis in ways that are still to be understood and discovered.

Sometime later, Cecilia has moved forward, worked through thoughts and fantasies, worries and doubts. She reported a dream:

> It's about the treatment of a woman, many attempts, experimental things, some kind of epidural catheterization. I discuss it with somebody, I do not know who. It's an approach that is outside the box. Something that has never been done for such a suffering person. Then, it seems as if we are in a kitchen, with many people, at a party. The woman is lying in the room next door. She feels unwell, and we decide to carry out this experimental treatment.

The analyst tries to tell the patient that she is still talking about analysis using the internet. Analyst and patient are carrying out "heroic" attempts unlike anything they have done together previously. Who knows what will happen? Teleanalysis is experimental stuff. Perhaps the party appears because there is still nourishment in the analytic setting, but there is also an attempt to "commit to" having fun, a defensive and elusive feature of this patient. Then there is the sick woman, the needy patient lying in a "separate" room (just as the patient actually is now, far from the original and familiar place of analysis), and she needs to be rescued through these "experimental procedures." After all, the catheter goes to the central nervous system, like the microphone cable that connects us with the disembodied voice.

Analyzing external and internal connectivity

With Skype, and perhaps with the telephone, there is a difficulty beyond that we experience in traditional analysis. All the complexity and intricacy inherent in the analytic relationship is augmented by the e-medium, making us reconsider in this specific context all the theoretical parameters and those of the theory of the analytic technique. This variable of the analytic setting forces us to think not only about the meaning of a specific communication of the patient at a given time in the course of analysis, but also about the potential impact on that communication and in the listening of the analyst, of the actual unavoidable presence of the internet dimension, its facilitation of continuity, and its interference with it when the connection crashes. The internet is a "third party" that is neither a third ear nor an analytic third: it is a given, an element that is there permitting the dyad to work but also entering the work of the dyad. It is at the same time an external and an internal element that can be managed, dreamed, and processed like an element of analysis itself, and it is, in fact, inevitably intrinsic to it. This is not an unknown situation for traditional analysis either—just think about the accidental interruptions of the setting in the consulting room, a topic that has been discussed many times in the course of the last decades in the analytic field. This similarity with other familiar settings for treatment helps us to see analogies and overlapping areas of concern, as well as clear differences. Such reflective thinking is an absolute requirement for the teleanalysts. Psychoanalytic theory deals not with the concrete matter of the subject, the facts of his life, and the history of everyone in his life, but is concerned with the internal world. This focus on internal reality is what allows psychoanalysis to extend beyond its original, contingent conditions for work and apply equally well in new situations in the current context (Ceserani, 1998). The mind's psychoanalytic function operates as usual, and at the same time finds multiple new paths for its implementation (Ogden, 2003, 2010).

Teleanalysis is a way of thinking that is the same as in traditional analysis and at the same time different. Patients (like our patients with amazing oneiric intuition) and analysts who engage in teleanalysis agree, sometimes to their surprise, that also in an online analytic relationship they enter an analytic space where emotional experience becomes thought and dangerous inanimate and asymbolic material is transformed into the animated, symbolic flow.

References

Argentieri, S., & Amati Mehler, J. (2003). Cited in: J. S. Scharff, Clinical issues in analysis over the telephone and the Internet. In: J. S. Scharff (Ed.), *Psychoanalysis Online: Mental Health, Teletherapy, and Training* (p. 65). London: Karnac, 2013.

Barrow, J. D. (2011). *The Book of Universes*. London: The Bodley Head.

Bion, W. R. (1962). *Learning from Experience*. London: Heinemann.

Bollas, C. (2007). Cyberspace. *Psychoanalytic Review, 94*: 6–9.

Bolognini, S. (2015). *Rivista di Psicoanalisi, 2014, LX*: 3.

Brainsky, S. (2003). Cited in: J. S. Scharff, Clinical issues in analysis over the telephone and the Internet. In: J. S. Scharff (Ed.), *Psychoanalysis Online* (p. 65). London, Karnac, 2013.

Ceserani, R. (1998). Forme del postmoderno. *Psiche, VI*: 19–25.

Chodorow, N. (2004). Creating a physical surround in the absence of physical presence: Clinical observations on phone treatment. Unpublished paper, cited in: J. S. Scharff, Clinical issues in analysis over the telephone and the Internet. In: J. S. Scharff (Ed.), *Psychoanalysis Online: Mental Health, Teletherapy, and Training* (p. 66). London: Karnac, 2013.

Coleman, B. (2011). *Hello Avatar: The Rise of the Networked Generation*. Cambridge MA: MIT Press.

Di Chiara, G. (1983). L'assetto mentale dell'analista quale invariante tra terapia e conoscenza. Unpublished.

Fiorentini, G. (2012). L'analisi via Internet: variazioni di setting e dinamiche transferali-controtransferali. *Rivista di Psicoanalisi, 58*: 29–45.

Fiorentini, G., Frangini, G., Molone, P., Mori Ubaldini, M., & Robutti, A. (1995). Dalle regole del setting all'assetto mentale dell'analista. *Rivista di Psicoanalisi, 41*: 67–79.

Gabbard, G. O. (2001). E-rotic transference on the Internet. *Psychoanalytic Quarterly, 70*: 719–737.

Gaburri, E. (2006). La promessa delirante e i pifferai magici. *Psiche, 14*: 13–27.

Goldberg, B. (1999). Spatial transitions: contesting the limits of social and psychic space. *Psychoanalysis and Contemporary Thought, 22*: 315–341.

Habib, Y. (2003). Cited in: J. S. Scharff, Clinical issues in analysis over the telephone and the Internet. In: J. S. Scharff (Ed.), *Psychoanalysis Online: Mental Health, Teletherapy, and Training* (p. 65). London: Karnac, 2013.

Hautmann, G. (1981). Il mio debito con Bion: dalla psicoanalisi come teoria alla psicoanalisi come funzione della mente. *Rivista di psicoanalisi, 27*: 558–572.

Hautmann, G. (1999). Immaginazione e interpretazione. In: *La psicoanalisi tra arte e biologia*. Roma: Borla.

IPA policy on remote analysis in training (2014). Approved by the Board of Representatives, electronic vote, December 2014). IPA website. http://www.ipa.org.uk/en/IPA/Procedural_Code/IPA_POLICY_ON_REMOTE_ANALYSIS_IN_TRAINING.aspx

IPA practice note (2016). On the use of skype, telephone, or other VoIP technologies in analysis. IPA website.

Lemma, A. (2015). Psychoanalysis in times of technoculture: Some reflections on the fate of the body in virtual space. *International Journal of Psycho-Analysis, 96*: 535–551.

Martin, A. (2013). Legal, clinical, and ethical issues in teletherapy. In; J. S. Scharff (Ed.), *Psychoanalysis Online: Mental Health, Teletherapy, and Training* (pp. 75–84). London: Karnac, 2013.

Marzi, A. (Ed.) (2013). *Psicoanalisi, Identità e Internet*. Milano: Franco Angeli. [*Psychoanalysis, Identity and the Internet*. London: Karnac, 2016.]

Matte Blanco, I. (1968). Comunicazione non verbale e suoi rapporti con la comunicazione verbale. *Rivista di Psicoanalisi, 14*: 3–34.

Mirkin, M. (2011). Telephone analysis: compromised treatment or an interesting opportunity? *Psychoanalytic Quarterly, 80*: 643–670.

Ogden, T. H. (2003). What's true and whose idea was it? *International Journal of Psycho-Analysis, 84*: 593–606.

Ogden, T. H. (2010). On three forms of thinking: magical thinking, dream thinking, and transformative thinking. *Psychoanalytic Quarterly, 79*: 317–347.

Panel Report (2010). Psychoanalysis and virtual reality. *International Journal of Psycho-Analysis, 91*: 985–988.

Riolo, F. (2010). Trasformazioni in allucinosi. *Rivista di Psicoanalisi, 56*: 635–649.

Scharff, J. S. (2010). Report on panel on telephone analysis. IPA Congress, Chicago, August 2009. *International Journal of Psycho-Analysis, 91*: 989–992.

Shanyang, Z. (2006). The internet and the transformation of the reality of everyday life: Toward a new analytic stance in sociology. *Social Inquiry, 76*: 458–474.

Winnicott, D. W. (1967). *Playing and Reality*. London: Tavistock.

CHAPTER SIX

The space and place of psychoanalytic treatment: a philosophical meditation

José A. Saporta (USA)

Video conferencing allows us to offer psychoanalysis and psychotherapy to previously inaccessible patients. The enthusiasm of psychiatrists and psychologists in countries such as China to learn psychoanalytic concepts and to experience psychoanalytic treatment is matched by the enthusiasm of many American clinicians, such as members of the China America Psychoanalytic Alliance (CAPA), to make supervision and treatment available to patients in China through video conferencing software programs such as Skype, VSee, and Zoom. The International Psychoanalytical Association has voiced reservations for using analysis over video conferencing for training analysis (IPA document, n.d.), and there is a COPE study group at the American Psychoanalytic Association for considering the effects of this sort of technology on psychoanalytic treatment (Jacobs, 2016). I have been pondering the exciting possibilities—and possible downsides—of expanding the reach of psychoanalysis and psychotherapy through the medium of these video software programs. As I have mentioned this to others, I have noticed that some respond with enthusiasm while others instinctively recoil. These two poles in people's reactions may reflect opposing views on the effect of technology and of physical context and space on subjective experience.

What is the effect on patient and therapist of conducting a psychoanalytic treatment through the medium of Skype, VSsee, or Zoom? One possible problem with attempting such an intimate human encounter through this medium was suggested to me while listening to an NPR radio program about reading books on electronic devices such as Kindle. Literary and cultural critic, Svere Birkerts of Boston University, argues that this electronic medium, as opposed to reading the printed page, so alters the subjectivity of reading that it can have more far-reaching consequences for the very structure of subjectivity. In *The Gutenberg Elegies: The Fate of Reading in an Electronic Age*, Birkerts (1994) writes about the subjective and cultural impact of changing the source of our information from the printed word to a digital electronic medium.

There are innumerable physical gestures and rituals around buying, opening, and reading a book. An encounter with a book can be full-bodied experience—tactile, olfactory, visual—in feeling the weight and texture, smelling the newly printed page, seeing the page and the style of the print, cradling the book to read it in our favorite chair. The rituals and gestures around the act of reading place one, according to Birkerts (1994), in a state of reading; "I value the state a book puts me in more than I value the specific contents" (p. 85).

Consulting room or computer screen

There is a dimension of psychotherapy and psychoanalysis, little theorized or even mentioned, that is a ritualized bodily encounter with the physical space of treatment. One can imagine that psychotherapy and psychoanalysis affect the structure of subjectivity in part through repeated sharing of physical gestures and rituals and physical space. We see, smell, and feel as we approach the office. We are greeted and cross the threshold and enter the space provided by the analyst, using our legs, and sit or lie down in the way we have done innumerable times before in that space and in other spaces in our lives and our past. The physical space is bounded. It is the therapist's space we come into, and we experience that space through all of our senses. This physicality and bodily encounter with the space is the background for what transpires affectively and linguistically between therapist and patient.

Now consider patient and therapist going to separate computers and turning them on. Rather than walking to the door and crossing the threshold we type instructions on a keyboard or click a mouse. The space is bounded by a screen. The patient does not enter the physical space of the therapist but stays in his or her own usual surroundings. Beyond conscious perception is the fact that sound and sight are digitalized as opposed to analogical. Voices come over the speakers with a slight, subtle lag between movement of the lips and the matching sound. I have noticed that on Skype one is unable to maintain eye contact. To appear to the other person as if you are looking him or her in the eyes you have to look into the camera, which is just above the screen. Persons cannot look into each other's eyes simultaneously. What does one lose over the computer that is available when we share the same space in an office? Is attachment the same without physical presence? Is affective information equally available? Are we present to each other and to the experience in the same way? Physical contact is possible but proscribed in the office, but not physically possible in virtual space. Does this not alter the experience of the wish and its modulation? The physical presence of both parties presents the possibility of enacting one's fantasies. Would the sense of containment be the same with virtual boundaries as with the physical boundaries of the office? The words may be the same, as well as much of the music, the nonverbal dimensions of speech, and body language. But how do the differences in physical and sensual experience, ritual and boundary affect the subjective impact of the conversation?

The encounter with the space in which psychotherapy takes place is not just physically immediate. In *Culture and Human Development*, cultural-developmental psychologist Valsiner (2000) describes a culturally mediated space where cultural meanings direct our attention and physical encounter with the space. Valsiner (2000) writes:

> We can talk about demands that the meaningful nature of a particular structured environment sets up for persons' feeling, thinking, and acting. Let us call these settings *semiotic demand settings* (SDSs): human-made structures of everyday life settings where the properties of the objects are co-determined by perceptual-actional and cultural-meanings based possibilities and expectations. (p. 124, italics original)

Understanding the role of the physical space in which treatment takes place must include the cultural meanings of the space and how it connects with other culturally arranged spaces and to the culture as a whole. The therapist's office and the Internet are very different cultural spaces, or different "semiotic demand settings," with different relationships to the overall culture, which guide attention and action in our encounter with the space in different ways and with different subjective consequences.

Theorizing space and place

The lack of theorizing about the physical space in which psychoanalysis and psychotherapy take place is due to our inheritance of a Cartesian disembodied and decontextualized model of the mind. Meaning is considered as pre-existing "in the head" and transmitted to another head to be decoded. What transpires between heads is not shaped by body or physical context. The means of communication is incidental to the meaning that is conveyed. The meaning that emerges between two talking heads on a computer screen is essentially the same as that which emerges from two talking heads that share a physical office.

An exception to the inattention to the space in which psychoanalysis and psychotherapy takes place is Madeleine and Willy Baranger's (2008) discussion of the psychoanalytic field and the impact of the arrangement of physical space on the field. They write:

> What we notice most immediately about the psychoanalytic field is its spatial structure. ... Any modification of this spatial structure, empirically adopted as being the most favorable, leads to substantial modifications of the analytic relationship itself.
>
> An analysis does not develop in the same way if the armchair is placed a meter away from the couch or if the couch is placed in the middle of the room instead of being next to a wall. Moreover, the choice of a certain position by the analyst already reveals a particular internal attitude toward the patients.
>
> These placements form a common space for the analytic relationship; but in the transference–countertransference relation, it undergoes important experiential modifications. Although both are in the same place as in all the previous sessions, the patient may ask the analyst why he or she has changed the position of the arm chair, and moved it further away. At other times, patients may experience the distance between themselves and the analyst as being

> annihilated. The space of the analytic relationship may contract until it includes only the analyst and the patient, with denial of the existence of the natural boundaries of the room and the furniture it contains, or may extend itself to include whatever objects (pictures, books, etc.) are in the room, or may even extend itself beyond the boundaries of the room: the other patient in the waiting room who is listening, the noises from the house or the street, may take on important meaning and form a momentary space that is quite different from the common analytic space. (pp. 796–797)

The sensitivity of the Barangers to the space of psychoanalysis must reflect the acknowledged influence on their thinking of the French philosopher, Merleau-Ponti, whose phenomenology was a challenge to the prevailing Cartesian view. One wonders if they were also influenced by another French phenomenological philosopher, Gaston Bachelard, and his classic book, *The Poetics of Space* (1994), first published in France in 1958. Bachelard writes of the importance of intimate, domestic space, such as the house, as containing and cultivating a reflective, imaginative capacity. The house is a "protected intimacy" (p. 3): it houses and protects the capacity to daydream; its nooks and corners are a resting place for daydreaming. It is the "not-I" that protects the "I" (p. 5). We form a deep, primitive attachment to our early space, and our most basic capacity to inhabit space is nurtured there, extending to a capacity to inhabit the self, or to inhabit experience, or to inhabit life. Bachelard (1994) writes, "We should therefore have to say how we inhabit our vital space, in accord with all the dialectics of life, how we take root, day after day, in a 'corner of the world'. For our house is our corner of the world" (p. 4). Psychoanalysis has invested much ink on the holding and protective function of the mother, but little on the role of house, room, and other intimate spaces for holding, protecting, establishing a sense of boundaries, and for the texture of solitude. Inhabiting house, room, nook, and cranny must be related to, though not reducible to, the mother–infant bond. Bachelard (1994) writes:

> Space that has been seized upon by the imagination cannot remain indifferent space subject to the measures and estimates of the surveyor. It has been lived in, not in its positivity, but with all the partiality of the imagination. Particularly, it nearly always exercises an attraction. For it concentrates being within the limits that protect it. (p. xxxvi)

Physical space—the house and the spaces and walls within—give texture to memory and forgetting. Bachelard (1994), who was psychoanalytically informed, writes, "… how can secret rooms, rooms that have disappeared, become abodes for an unforgettable past? … On whatever theoretical horizon we inhabit it, the house image would appear to have become the topography of our intimate being" (p. xxxvi). Memory is fixed to space:

> The finest specimens of fossilized duration concretized as a result of long sojourn, are to be found in and through space. The unconscious abides. Memories are motionless, and the more securely they are fixed in space, the sounder they are … For a knowledge of intimacy, localization in the spaces of our intimacy is more urgent than determination of date. (Bachelard, 1994, p. 9)

Smaller spaces within the house—drawers, chests, wardrobes, closets—are related to the forgotten or the un-thought known:

> What psychology lies behind their locks and keys! They bear within themselves a kind of esthetics of hidden things. To pave the way now for a phenomenology of what is hidden, one preliminary remark will suffice: an empty drawer is *unimaginable*. It can only be *thought of*. (Bachelard, 1994, p. xxxvi, italics original)

Bachelard (1994) also writes of how our early and primitive attachment to the spaces in our lives colors our experience of and ability to inhabit current spaces. The meaning of the analyst's physical space and the objects therein, and our ability to inhabit that space, is colored by our early attachments to the spaces in our lives and our experience of inhabiting them. Such transference to physical space is consistent with my reading of the Barangers (2008). These transferences might be fruitfully analyzed, but only if we acknowledge that space matters. If we deny difference and insist that there is no difference in what unfolds in our physical office and what transpires on our computer monitors, then interesting and useful differences will be missed. Some psychoanalysts, perhaps those from a Kleinian perspective, might see transference to the analyst's physical space as a projection of the patient's internal world, such as fantasies regarding the mother's body. But perhaps psychoanalysts have undervalued the role of the quotidian, such as the daily engagement with the physical spaces in our lives, outside of the passions of the parent–child relationship, in shaping who we are. And we may undervalue the role of the seemingly mundane and repeated encounter with the physical space of the analysis—climbing the same stairs, crossing the same threshold, experiencing the same sights and smells—in shaping the analysis.

Cognitive science and communication studies

Several academic trends, including those in cognitive science and communication studies, are also challenging the disembodied and decontextualized model of the mind and communication. These trends are consistent with observations by phenomenologists such as those Bachelard discussed above. Cognitive scientists and linguists are coming to a new appreciation of Freud's concept of the body ego in their recent emphasis on embodied cognition. This is an appreciation that the experience of the body in motion, and the body's encounter with the world, structure the way we think and the metaphors and language through which we conceive of ourselves and the world (Lakoff & Johnson, 1980). Cognitive functions are no longer seen as occurring essentially "in the head," as in Cartesian psychology. The notions of "embodied cognition" and the "extended mind" recognized that cognitive functions rely on and cannot be separated from the physical encounter with the world and the many material tools we use for thinking (Clark, 2011). Mental functioning is embedded in and shaped by physical context. Clark (2011) tells the story of an interview with Nobel Prize-winning physicist Richard Feynman. The interviewer spoke of how Feynman's notebooks, with their scribbles and diagrams, were a record of his thinking. Feynman insisted that these were not a record of his thinking, they were the thinking itself. Clark (2011) writes, "The loop through pen and paper is part of the physical machinery responsible for the shape and flow of thoughts" (p. xxv). Clark (2011) further states, "Human sensing, learning, thought and feeling are all structured and informed by our body-based interactions with the world around us" (p. xxvi). The prevailing cognitivist model, inherited from Descartes, sees thinking as manipulating and computing symbols in the head. It is this shadow of Descartes that leads psychoanalysts to view meaning as preexisting in the client's mind and transmitted to the analyst. The means of communication and the context in which it occurs, including the material context, does not play an essential role in shaping meaning. The meanings in our heads are the same, as they are pre-existing, whether those heads are on a computer monitor or they share the same physical space. In contrast, the extended mind model is described by Clark (2011) thus:

> … the actual local operations that realize certain forms of human cognizing include inextricable tangles of feedback, feed-forward, and feed-around loops: loops that promiscuously criss-cross the boundaries of brain, body, and world. The local mechanisms of mind, if this is correct, are not all in the head. Cognition leaks out into body and world. (p. xxviii)

Memory does not occur inside the head either but is extended into the environment and includes the various material and cultural tools for remembering (Brockmeier, 2010). Memory storage and retrieval is tied to context, including material context (Brockmeier, 2010; Wertsch, 2002). Finally, academic communication studies emphasize how meaning emerges in the process of conversation and is shaped partly by bodily interaction (Shotter, 2008), context (Linell, 2008), and the material means of communication (Lannemann, 1998). According to these perspectives, meaning does not exist preformed in a person's mind, seeking some form of expression. Meaning emerges through the process of conversation, shaped in part by the person's intention but shaped also by the process of conversation, the person we are addressing, the context (including the material context), and the tools used to mediate the conversation (Saporta, 2016).

If thinking, feeling, remembering, and communicating are shaped by the material context in which they occur and by the material tools used for expression, then the meaning that emerges from the analytic conversation must be shaped, in part, by bodily interaction, by the space in which the analytic conversation takes place, and by the medium of communication. To deny difference between inhabiting together the physical office versus the computer screen is a throwback to a Cartesian view of the mind and communication as I have described, and flies in the face of current academic trends and evidence. Again, these differences might evoke useful meaning that can be analyzed, but difference must be recognized to be useful—that is, space must matter.

However, as I will now consider, it is possible that humans are so adaptable that we can extend our sense of inhabiting to cyberspace and create even there a sense of co-inhabiting space with others. If the mind is extended, as I have just argued, then we can extend ourselves to occupy new and varied spaces.

Human adaptability and expanding contexts

Perhaps then, in my arguments above, I underestimate the power of human identity and subjectivity to adapt and cross into new and expanded media and contexts. Such is the view of philosopher and physician Ray Tallis (2007) who reminds us that in 1850 Wordsworth believed that including illustrations into written text in newspapers would infantilize us and "drive us back to 'caverned life's first rude career'" (p. 6). According to Tallis (2007), Worsdworth "… felt that the endless influx of news from daily papers would incite us to a level of unbearable restlessness" (p. 6). For Tallis, it is the rate of change that is important, and when it is gradual enough our experience of self can appropriate ever-expanding mediums, contexts, and spaces. In his article "Enhancing humanity" published in *Philosophy Now*, Tallis (2007) writes:

> The dramatic electronification of everyday life that has taken place over the last few decades has not fundamentally altered the way we relate to each other. Love, jealousy, kindness, anxiety, hatred, ambition, bitterness, joy etc, still seem to have a remarkable family resemblance to the emotions people had in the 1930s. The low-grade bitchiness of office politics may be conducted more efficiently by e-mail, but its essential character hasn't changed. Teenagers communicating by mobile phones and texts and chat rooms and webcams still seem more like teenagers than nodes in an electronic network. I have to admit a little concern at what we might call the e-ttenuation of life, whereby people find it increasingly difficult to be here now rather than dissipating themselves into an endless electronic elsewhere; but inner absence and wool-gathering is not entirely new, even if it is now electronically orchestrated. It just becomes more publicly visible. What's more, there is something reassuring about electronic technology: because it is widely

> and cheaply available and because it is so smart, it allows us to be dumb, and so compresses the differences between people. (p. 7)

Human identity begins by appropriating its own body and, given time, can appropriate expanding mediums and spaces. Tallis argues that we can expand into cyberspace and appropriate that space into our sense of self. I would add that we intersubjectively create spaces using the Internet and co-create a real sense of inhabiting that space together. I had a recent experience that brought this home to me. I was walking with a five-year-old boy who was looking at his mother's smartphone as we walked, playing Pokémon Go. He said in a hushed tone, "Uncle, do you see that bush in that yard across the street? There is a Pokémon in that bush." I responded, "Oh! Really!" and I was taken with a sense of presence and wonder. We were inhabiting together an intersubjectively created enchanted world, filled with real and invisible presences. Our world felt as real as the enchanted world must have felt for persons in the distant past, filled with mysterious presences. Perhaps in psychoanalysis and psychotherapy over video conferencing therapist and patient co-create and co-inhabit a similar space or field that feels as real and that can be analyzed. The question is how this field in cyberspace, as real as it feels, as real as it is, is affected by the different physical context in which it occurs and what that co-created space contains or omits, or is able to engage, as a result of the different physical, spatial context. And the question remains as to how this different space textures subjectivity differently.

Rather than worry about interactions, including psychotherapy interactions that move from physical space to cyberspace, Tallis (2007) lauds our increasing separation from organic nature:

> If, as I believe, the distinctive genius of humanity is to establish an identity which lies at an ever-increasing distance from our organic nature, we should rejoice in the expression of human possibility in ever-advancing technology. (p. 7)

Tallis (2007) concludes:

> Yes, we shall change; but the essence of human identity lies in this continuing self-redefinition. And if we remember that our identity and our freedom lie in the intersection between our impersonal but

> unique bodies and our personal individual memories and shared cultural awareness, it is difficult to worry about the erosion of either our identity or our freedom by technological advance. (p. 7)

I view psychoanalysis and psychoanalytic psychotherapy as one way to preserve human subjectivity and relatedness against dehumanizing cultural forces. This may be especially the case in cultures that are undergoing massive and accelerated change. But, does the Internet and digital information dehumanize, or does it extend the range of human relatedness? By using the Internet and video conferencing to offer psychotherapy and psychoanalysis to more patients, does psychoanalytic psychotherapy succumb to and even become an agent of these dehumanizing, digitalizing forces? Or will our essential humanity and the essence of the analytic encounter assert itself in expanded and more varied spaces? I would like to say that we will see, but when we as psychotherapists enter and adapt to this new space offered by the Internet our own subjectivity may change as well, so that we may be unable to see its effect. We can see the effect of this new space only from outside of it, from our traditional space. I suppose we will have to see as best we can.

References

Bachelard, G. (1994). *The Poetics of Space*. Boston, MA: Beacon Press.

Baranger, M., & Baranger, W. (2008). The analytic situation as a dynamic field. *International Journal of Psycho-Analysis, 89*: 795–826.

Birkerts, S. (1994). *The Gutenberg Elegies: The Fate of Reading in an Electronic Age*. Winchester, MA: Faber & Faber.

Brockmeier, J. (2010). After the Archive: Remapping Memory. *Culture & Psychology, 16*: 5–35.

Clark, A. (2011). *Supersizing the Mind: Embodiment, Action, and Cognitive Extension*. Oxford: OUP.

IPA Policy on Remote Analysis in Training. (n.d.). Retrieved 7 August 2016, from http://www.ipa.world/en/en/IPA1/Procedural_Code/IPA_Policy_on_Remote_Analysis_in_Training.aspx

Jacobs, D. (2016). Study group on new technologies. *The American Psychoanalyst, 50*: 9–11.

Lakoff, G., & Johnson, M. (1980). *Metaphors We Live By*. Chicago: University of Chicago.

Lannemann, J. (1998). Social construction and materiality: The limits of indeterminacy in therapeutic settings. *Family Processes, 37*: 393–413.

Linell, P. (2009). *Rethinking Language, Mind, and World Dialogically: Interactional and Contextual Theories of Human Sense-making*. Charlotte, NC: Information Age.

Saporta, J. A. (2016). Changing the subject by addressing the other: Mikhail Bakhtin and psychoanalytic therapy. In: D. M. Goodman & E. R. Severson (Eds.), *The Ethical Turn: Otherness and Subjectivity in Contemporary Psychoanalysis*. New York: Routledge.

Shotter, J. (2008). *Conversational Realities Revisited: Life, Language, Body and World*. Chagrin Falls, OH: Taos Institute Publications.

Tallis, R. (2007). Enhancing humanity. *Philosophy Now, 61*: 6–7.

Valsiner, J. (2000). *Culture and Human Development*. London: Sage.

Wertsch, J. V. (2002). *Voices of Collective Remembering*. Cambridge, UK: CUP.

CHAPTER SEVEN

The effect of the analytic couple's shared physical presence on transference fantasy

Lin Tao (China and UK)

Teleanalytic work has been spreading around the world. The technology-assisted setting challenges the traditional analytic format of meeting in the analyst's room in many ways, encouraging us to explore many aspects of the analytic setting and process that we may take for granted. In this chapter, I will describe the first meeting in shared physical space of an analytic couple after long-term teleanalytic work so as to illustrate the clinical meaning of the patient's transference fantasy in the situation where sexual transference emerges because there is then a sense of possibility of its gratification being realized. I will briefly discuss the combination of psychoanalysis in the analyst's room and teleanalysis in cyberspace.

Clinical background

Mrs. A is in her early thirties, married with a five-year-old daughter. She is a teacher in a city in a European country, to which she emigrated years ago. She has been in analysis with a male analyst for over two years, two sessions a week, conducted through the Internet with a web camera, never having actually met her analyst in the consulting room. They had their first meeting online and continued their analytic work through the Internet from then on. In teleanalytic work, Mrs. A mainly talked about what happened in her life. She expressed her feelings about experiences in her childhood. She trusted her analyst, felt close to him despite their geographical separation, was eager to hear how he understood her, and felt supported and contained. In short, she developed a positive transference towards him. At first, she didn't want the opportunity to meet him in person, but as she settled more and more into analytic work through the Internet, she gradually felt, and expressed her wish, that she wanted to meet the analyst one day in the shared physical analytic room. She had some sexual dreams in which she was physically very close to her analyst. Despite that, she couldn't go deeper into exploration of her sexual transference.

Recently, Mrs. A went to the city where her analyst lives. Mrs. A intended to stay there for a few days, and she clearly showed how eager she was to meet him during that time. They discussed her anxiety and excitement about meeting him in the new context of analytic sessions in his physical space. It would be the first time for both of them to be in a shared analytic physical space.

The meeting in the shared physical space for the first time

The analyst had told Mrs. A the time and the address for the session. When the time for the session was coming near, he waited for her. He was not sure what she would look like in reality, whether she would seem familiar or a little strange, and so on. He felt that he wanted to keep the continuity of their perception of each other from the past teleanalytic work, but now he felt a little uncertain about whether it could be done.

Right on time, there was a knock on the door. The analyst came over and opened the door to find Mrs. A standing there. She wore leisure clothes, as if dressed for sport. She looked curiously at the analyst, as if wanting to identify that he was that same analyst she had seen on the Internet. At this first sight of her, the analyst felt something familiar but also something unfamiliar about her and between them, which aroused complex feelings in him at that moment. The analyst invited her to come into the room. Mrs. A walked around in the room a little to examine it. When the analyst invited her to sit down, she took the seat. Very quickly, she moved her body to and fro, and commented that the armchair was not as soft as she had expected. Then she said, "You didn't prepare well for me," a tiny disappointment flashing across her face. Then she said she couldn't enjoy the session because the analyst hadn't prepared a soft enough armchair for her. After a while, she said she had, before the session, wanted to test whether the analyst would provide her with a comfortable armchair. The analyst interpreted that she seemed to be trying to test his care for her physical comfort. She nodded, and said she always cared for herself by preparing a very comfortable armchair in teleanalytic sessions at home, but in the first session when they met in the shared physical space, she wanted to feel cared for by the analyst.

From the start of the session, the analyst felt he paid much more attention to his posture and visual impressions than he did in teleanalytic sessions. He clearly had a much stronger sense of the physical presence of them both and felt the impact of the communication of a rich body language. For instance, he could perceive many details of Mrs. A's physical presentation, such as her vivid complexion, posture, and bodily movement, all of which vividly conveyed material to his senses and his thoughts. Meanwhile, the analyst felt acutely aware of being fully exposed to Mrs. A in terms of his physical presence. All this was quite different from the experience in the virtual analytic space of the Internet. As Mrs. A would prove, this difference led her to a much deeper sexual transference.

In the session, Mrs. A had a free association about being pregnant. She said she had had sex with her husband in the days before she came to see the analyst, and planned to have a pregnancy test after she came back home. However, she said if the test should prove she was pregnant, she would not know for sure whether she had become pregnant before the session or after. The analyst was curious as to why she made the session the time coordinate of her pregnancy. Then smiling, she continued, saying that her friend who traveled on business with her male boss found that she was pregnant after coming back. The friend had a struggle to prove that the pregnancy was related to sex with her husband. The analyst tried to interpret the transference. He said that although it seemed that she was saying that she possibly got pregnant by intercourse with her husband before the session, there seemed to be a hidden fantasy that she could possibly be pregnant from having sex with the analyst in the session. Hearing that, she seemed not be able to understand what the analyst was saying and explained it would take some time after sex with her husband for pregnancy to develop and so it might happen before, in, or after the session. The analyst said to her that what he interpreted seemed to arouse her anxiety related to the fantasy of possible sex with the analyst in the session where they were both physically there, and said she might feel seduced by the physical presence of the analyst in the shared physical space, or worry that her physical presence would seduce the analyst, either of which could possibly lead to sex and thereby to pregnancy. She nodded and then told the analyst that she in fact had had a daydream in which they did have sex in the room where they would meet for the first time. She said her sexual fantasy made her anxious, and she worried that if she told the analyst, he would think badly of her. For instance, she worried that the analyst couldn't manage the analytic work as he had been able to previously, would lose his analytic function, and would think of her as a patient with severe problems.

Discussion

Compared to in-the-room analytic work, teleanalytic work using the Internet has some limitations (Lin, 2015). We need to get to know the meaning of those limitations to analytic work rather than just criticizing them. In this chapter, I have described how the physical co-presence of analyst and patient aroused an emotional storm (Bion, 1979) in, and even before, the first session in the shared physical space after long-term pure teleanalytic work. The shift in the setting shows how a clear and vivid sense of connection emerged in both parties in terms of an emotional link based on physical presence in the shared physical space. Mrs. A seemed to take advantage of the analyst's physical presence beside her to test the analyst's care for her in the shared physical space by checking whether the armchair in the analyst's room was comfortable enough. That seems to indicate that she felt something missing in terms of ways of sensing the analyst's holding function in the previous virtual teleanalytic space, that third space between the analyst's room and her own physical space in which she had to prepare everything—room, armchair, computer, and Internet connection for herself. It stresses the fact that in analytic work in a shared physical space, the patient and the analyst have a significant unity, which means not only the unity of mind and body of each party, but also the unity of both parties' mind and body as a whole. So, compared to teleanalytic work, analytic work in a shared physical space offers a whole situation, specifically in terms of relational connection in which each party's physical presence in front of the other holds clear and vivid psychological meaning. This leads to a whole sense of the situation including the shared unity of mind and body, the shared physical space, and a more vivid sense of being in the here and now (King, 1973) with the other. For Mrs. A and her analyst, the experience of their physical presence in shared physical space gave an objective basis for the emergence of a pre-conscious idea and a related unconscious fantasy.

Mrs. A had the fantasy that she could be pregnant with the analyst in the first meeting in their shared physical space. Even though Mrs. A had had some sexual fantasies related to the analyst in previous phase of teleanalytic work, this fantasy was quite different. In teleanalytic work, her sexual fantasy was just a fantasy, as she knew that the analyst would, in reality, never be able to penetrate her body from far away through her computer screen. However, when they shared the same physical space, she had a sense of the possibility that the wish could become true. The content of the fantasy in this meeting was mainly about pregnancy with the analyst, which, when it was opened up, aroused her anxiety that the analyst would be damaged or she would be thought of as a very severely disturbed patient.

The first meeting with this patient in shared physical space after long-term teleanalytic work indicates a key point about the meaning of in-the-same-room analytic work, that is, when the patient in physical co-presence with the analyst develops a fantasy and transference toward him, there is a sense of hidden possibility that the fantasy can be realized, for instance, the sexual fantasy is now physically possible. Those fantasies in the shared physical space, together with the sense of a hidden possibility of them becoming real in action, can make the fantasy and transference much more real, seductive, and threatening. For the fantasy to feel real is, I think, a necessary part of the natural development of the transference as well as of the effective working on it.

Although teleanalytic work can do much for the patient, this case illustration reminds us of the fact that the teleanalytic setting, which takes away the shared physical space, undoes the link between mind and body, and changes the intensity or even the quality of the transference, which may attenuate the productive analytic work. To compensate for this risk, teleanalytic work should be combined with regular in-the-same-room analytic work, so as to let the patient develop the necessary sense of the possibility of fantasy and wishes in the transference relationship becoming true, even though this possibility may be put into the future meeting in shared physical space when they are still in teleanalytic work. However, things are not as simple as just offering regular analytic work along with teleanalytic work. For instance, the regular analytic meeting may cause the patient to prefer it, and even hope for it in teleanalytic sessions. The problem in such a case may be that what the patient desires is the analyst in another time and space, rather than the analyst in the here and now in virtual space. In some cases, this may reach a level of longing and failed mourning for an ideal of co-presence such that the patient detaches herself from the relationship in the here and now in teleanalytic sessions, which may hinder the work in teleanalytic sessions. In other cases, it can be the opposite, for instance, patients may feel so pressured in shared physical space that they prefer to meet the analyst in virtual space through the Internet, and in such cases, the teleanalytic setting becomes a harbor for hiding those unbearable aspects that might appear in relation to the analyst. In that case, the Internet connection functions like an externalized space for psychic retreat (Steiner, 1993).

Conclusion

Since analyst and patient cannot be co-present in shared physical space, the hidden sense of possibility of unconscious fantasy and wishes becoming true is lost, and that inhibits the natural (and necessary) development of the transference as well as the effective working on it. The solution might be that teleanalysis is combined with co-present sessions in the analyst's consulting room in order for the analytic pair to experience whole mind–body unity as an essential condition in which to analyze the anxiety of the potential for unconscious wishes coming true. It is essential to explore and understand the meaning of each setting for each patient and each treatment when combining co-present analytic work with teleanalytic work. Those analysts who study the impact of the setting on the work in teleanalytic and co-present sessions may contribute much to the new field of teleanalysis.

References

Bion, W. R. (1979). Making the best of a bad job. In: F. Bion (Ed.), *Clinical Seminars and Other Works* (pp. 321–331). London: Karnac, 1994.

King, P. (1973). The therapist–patient relationship. *Journal of Analytical Psychology, 18*: 1–8.

Lin, T. (2015). Teleanalysis: problems and limitations. In: J. S. Scharff (Ed.), *Psychoanalysis Online 2: Impact of Technology on Development, Training, and Therapy* (pp. 105–120). London: Karnac.

Steiner, J. (1993). *Psychic Retreats: Pathological Organizations in Psychotic, Neurotic and Borderline Patients*. London: Routledge.

CHAPTER EIGHT

The setting, the screen, and the conveying of unconscious dynamics

Caroline Sehon and Jill Savege Scharff (USA)

The analyst, Caroline Sehon, presents two teleanalytic sessions six months apart in the context of analysis usually taking place in her office. Jill Scharff provides a commentary, drawing on the analyst's observations and descriptions of her countertransference and on the reactions to this clinical material presented at a teleanalysis clinical research working group in which the co-authors participate to study analytic process material of sessions conducted by telephone and/or encrypted video teleconference (VTC). The material is disguised without disclosure of any identifying information about the patient, and the research group focuses on the relationship between technology and analytic practice. The co-authors discuss the impact of the teleanalysis setting on the analytic relationship and review the patient's choice of setting and its visual impact on the screen to convey the unconscious dynamics.

The analyst's impression of Brent

Brent is a fifty-eight-year-old man who is isolated, obsessive, resentful of a long history of mistreatment, and was an insomniac until successfully managed with a continuous positive airway pressure (CPAP) machine. He is now in analysis with Dr. Sehon on the couch in her office three consecutive days per week. He complains of feelings of emptiness, regret, and guilt. As a younger man he lost job after job because of interpersonal conflict and a sense of identity diffusion, and so he retired early to become a househusband. His wife of thirty-five years died of a severe, chronic disabling condition and he devoted himself to caring for her in their remaining several years together. After she died, he felt that his life was shattered. He relocated to be closer to his family, and soon was caring for his ninety-year-old parents, making reparation after years of limited or no contact. He anticipated that there might be times that his parents' condition would preclude his forty-five-minute commute to analysis, and so, in his careful obsessional way, he asked me in advance for a trial teleanalytic session to get used to it in case it became necessary in emergency. I agreed to this modification in principle for emergency convenience and for rehearsal in case it would be needed, and had given instructions for connecting to me on VSee, the secure videoconferencing software that I use. Brent had downloaded VSee to his iPad without difficulty.

The first session on VTC

The first session using video teleconference (VTC) was about to start. The camera looked on to an empty room with a bed with a very thin-looking bedspread pulled over the left half of the bed. There was one pillow and one cushion placed over the pillow. In the right-hand corner of the screen, there was a small bedside table with a few empty-looking glasses. There was no decorative artwork, clothes, books or any other items within the view of the camera. Most significantly, he was missing but his "Hi" thundered from the background.

ANALYST: Good morning. I can hear you well.

PATIENT: I'm showing you where I'm going to end up. I'm sitting right now where the iPad is located. Can you see what you need to see?

ANALYST: Yes, except for you.

PATIENT: [He laughed a little.] Yes, I was just checking that I set it up okay. [He got up slowly from his bent position near the iPad and moved purposefully onto his bed.]

ANALYST: Okay, can you hear me all right?
PATIENT: Yes, I can.

Commentary

Being unable to leave the home on occasion may be viewed as an action that avoids the analytic relationship and dilutes the transference. In Brent's case, it seems more likely that he wants to be sure that his analyst will be there for him at all times, as he has been there for others. Admittedly his request for a trial session carried an insistent quality, but his analyst welcomed it as an action to conserve the relationship in the future. We cannot know, ahead of time, exactly what his desire signifies, but hope to learn from the experience.

The analyst-patient interaction about securing the connection is a fairly common necessity, part of the learning curve when doing teleanalysis for the first time. This type of exchange recurs at times when there are bandwidth problems and equipment failures. The beginning of the session is businesslike, as Brent gives lists of what he will discuss, but he warms up as the analyst speaks to him about whether she can hear him and see what he needs her to see. What is unusual in this case is the presentation of the image prior to the sound and the absence of the patient on the screen in the opening moments.

We are aware of a sense of emptiness and the expectation that someone will fill it. Brent relocated to take care of his parents, and that may be his way of avoiding the loneliness of the empty bed. He seems hopeless about life and seems to be living through others to keep himself alive. While helping others he may feel less worried about his own death.

Of the image he had constructed, Brent said off camera, "I'm showing you where I'm going to end up." We think of the image on the screen as a portrayal of his life setting since his wife's death before he arrived in analysis, and as a symbolic preview of that setting after his own death.

We notice his attention to detail, and his compulsive doing, and we think of these as defenses first employed during latency. Perhaps he suffered a trauma or a loss in the latency years, and so holds on to those defenses because now death is his life. We have the impression that Brent has already arrived there, and is dealing with a great deal of death anxiety, triggered by recent loss of his intimate partner, fear of future loss of his parents, and presumably the presence of dead internal objects based on his past about which we have no information. Is Brent preoccupied with death since being so close to the process of death, or has he been feeling dead before then?

We think of Brent's construction of this image as a message about the impact of the missing wife and Brent's loneliness since losing her. At the next level we experience his own emotional absence, which may have preceded the loss of his wife. Does the thin bedspread allude to a thin skin of the sort that would explain his resentments and cut-offs from work and family? Does the bedspread over the left half of the bed suggest the development of the left half of Brent's brain (the verbal, planning part of the brain) and the bareness of his right brain, (the part responsible for emotional color)? The image has a ghostly feel to it, like "being on the other side" and leads us to imagine how dead Brent may feel beneath his compulsive caretaking and preparing for all eventualities. As he says, "I don't know the particulars of what I feel" and, later, "my emotions are gone."

The first session continued

PATIENT: (continuing) After I've described to you my father's condition, I want to go on to what we're needing to work on. On Friday, we went to the oncologist. It's metastatic esophageal cancer. The doctor used the word "systemic" which means it's everywhere. The nuclear medicine doctor used the word "numerous" to describe the many spots all over his back. The pain doctor last week didn't want to touch it. He referred us to the palliative care unit. The oncologist is talking about the quality of life. They know when you're going to die. At ninety-five, your life expectancy is just less than three years. Metastatic cancer is a matter of months. The palliative care unit is a code for him not having more than six months of life. It's incurable. The side-effects are worse than the treatments. The treatments are surgery, chemotherapy, and radiation treatment. The side-effects are depression, memory loss, and emotional instability, which is the opposite of what defines my father [an intimidating parental figure who served as a vice-admiral in the US coastguard]. The oncologist said we should just hold off from using the treatments where the side-effects are terrible.

ANALYST: So there have been many significant, ominous developments since you and I last met.

PATIENT: Yes, and what you and I need to work on is how this situation is replaying the things that I experienced with Elizabeth [his late wife]. In a way, this is a laboratory for what I experienced, and if I'm clever enough to tell you, it may allow us to see the antecedents of my symptoms before even meeting Elizabeth. For example, my emotions are gone. That's what happened with Elizabeth. I wasn't distressed. I wasn't distraught. I was then, and I am now, all business. I'm the steady, focused caregiver, and I'm saying things to my father in ways I wouldn't have said to Elizabeth because it was before we started our work.

ANALYST: Saying things to your father like what?

PATIENT: I'm being more directive to him. Here's what we're dealing with. For example, he *has* to tell his children. He can't leave it to me.

ANALYST: Like we've been discussing.

Commentary

Hearing about his father's metastatic spread, the analyst acknowledges "significant, ominous developments" since the last session. Brent responds with a mixture of psychological insight and strategy, saying, "What you and I need to work on is how this situation is replaying the things that I experienced with Elizabeth." He thinks of his analysis as a laboratory in which to use his father's imminent death as a chance to review and revise his reactions to his wife's death and "even to see the antecedents of my symptoms before even meeting Elizabeth." He detects a degree of cold-heartedness in this focused approach. He says that he could have had an intimate experience, and he knows that the analyst is "acquainted with this" but he does not really expect help with his emotions from her. He says that he does not think that "we can turn our sessions into an anticipation of death." By not feeling "emotions of love, loss or sadness" he defends himself against death anxiety.

We note that Brent describes his focused, detail-oriented, mechanical way of dealing with family demands as follows; "I am then and I am now, all business, and the steady, focused caregiver." Having collapsed after being so fully occupied caring for his wife, is he holding himself together now by caring for his parents?

The first session continued

PATIENT: Yes, when I called my father to tell him about Elizabeth, he offered to tell Donald and Ronald [older and younger brothers], and I agreed instead of telling them myself, and now I see myself moving into the caregiver role, taking the directive, the initiative. It's spinning. In all of this, you're not going to help me, except indirectly. Psychoanalysis will continue, and a peripheral benefit will be I'll handle things better. You're not going to help me directly.

ANALYST: So in a certain way, you feel dropped by me.

PATIENT: No, it's just a kookaburra dance. You're not going to help me directly. You do little things that are helpful. I was present when my father first told my mother. Dad was sugarcoating it for my mother. Dad gave *me* the report to tell my mother. The pain doctor was sugarcoating it. The CT scan showed an esophageal cancer and the nuclear bone scan showed "some things." He did not say, metastatic esophageal cancer, stage four, incurable.

Commentary

Brent hits the analyst with the full force of the cancer diagnosis as it was conveyed to him. Then, what does he mean by a kookaburra dance? The kookaburra bird is merrily laughing, eating greedily, and feeling on top of the world. Then he gets wounded by sitting on a rusty nail. Does he mean that his analyst will dance around the issues until the cancer has to be faced? Does he feel that she will not really prevent him from deep injury? Perhaps he feels that she is not in touch with the death threat that he is facing. Or might he be unconsciously referring to the rigmarole of connecting to her via VSee? Dr. Sehon recognizes the negative transference and speaks directly to it.

The analyst's description of the image on the screen

Sitting in my analytic chair, looking at the screen while Brent told the sad news with the echo of his experience of his wife's terminal illness, I was gripped by the recurrent image of him lying motionless on his bed, with his hands clasped firmly together around his waist. He lay on the left half of the bed, not straying over an imaginary line that seemed to divide the left from the right side of the bed. The room was minimalist, cold, austere, impoverished, devoid of a sense of life. Even the right side of the bed looked as if it was denuded of a cover. I thought I was seeing the bare mattress to the right of where he lay. I was thinking about how he lies in the same, fixed, frozen posture on the couch in my office when he is here, but that image is framed by a tree full of foliage beyond the window, and a multicolored picture at the end of the couch.

I was noticing how he had made no mention yet of the fact that we were meeting on VSee, a situation about which he had carried considerable anxiety before we successfully convened by video.

The first session continued

PATIENT: I don't have emotional feelings about my parents in general. I'm feeling this emotional distance, this shutting down, this quiescence, this clicking down into a businesslike, mental state, where I know what's coming, I know what I need to do, and to do what I have to do, and also to get past the resistance that my dad feels like the resistance that Elizabeth felt. I don't know the particulars of what I feel. I'll have to get in the way of my mother's care of him, because she's simply not strong enough to care for him. And I'll have to take care of the bills that my mother doesn't know how to deal with, and managing the medical administrative work that needs to be done and that I know how to do well. I'll need to go on over there, and to be there all the time.

ANALYST: It's like you're fully employed now.

PATIENT: Not now, but I can see I will be. I'm doing a scraping and painting job.

[I continue to think about him lying still, like a corpse.]

PATIENT: I see to heavy things like bottled water. I see things and I do things. I don't ask. I just do that. That's okay. I've done it before. There are things that I did wrong with Elizabeth that were harmful with her. There were conscious things and unconscious things. The cold-hearted and cynical thing is that what is going to happen is a laboratory for what happened to me and Elizabeth. It will be a laboratory, which I suppose is good for me, but to think that my father's death is going to be a clinical opportunity seems cold-hearted.

ANALYST: The "clinical opportunity" that you talk about, is also about the opportunity for you to become more aware of your feelings in here with me.

PATIENT: Yes, if I don't suppress them before I get in. Well, if you're in a dangerous situation, you don't have time to fear. You only have time to act. You get directive. I've clicked over into that place.

ANALYST: Clicked over, like a machine?

PATIENT: Yes, like a light switch, it's absolute. Yes, I think you've said that with my being like a machine, [I shuddered at his ascribing my having used this word "machine," to describe him previously. Did I really say that? I did not recall that] and my becoming detail-oriented [I did recall having said that], I missed an emotional opportunity, feelings. I could have had an intimate experience. I don't know—I think you're acquainted with this. I don't think we can turn our sessions into an anticipation of death.

Commentary

The analyst has again mentioned being struck by the recurrent image of him lying still, frozen on only the lightly covered left half of the bed with the bare mattress to the right of where he lay. We imagine his late wife no longer there beside him. The analyst also mentions being aware of irregular breathing, and Brent connects this to the suppressing of his emotions. He would not want to cry in his sessions, but only to report about any emotions that had occurred in private.

Brent is consciously referring to his parents' death in the near future and to his wife's death in the past. We wonder, is Brent feeling afraid that he would collapse after losing his father and mother? Unconsciously he is fearing his own death, and feels deadened unless he keeps busy. But perhaps his anxiety is not about the actual future. Perhaps he is rehearsing for a future event in reality that has already occurred early in his life but at a time when he "was not there for it to happen to", leaving him with an unconscious dread of its recurrence (Winnicott, 1963, p. 92).

The first session continued

ANALYST: Maybe you hope it might be possible to focus on your growth in the face of the imminent loss of your dad.

PATIENT: The thought that occurs to me is that the key to all of this is the new way of thinking. I said—you said—it's not all about emotions, it's about thinking in general with all things. Then it's going to help me with my mother, because she's next. Then it's going to help me with my brothers if I do it correctly this time without being damaged like I was last time, although it's tough not to be damaged when your wife dies.

ANALYST: [He was talking non-stop, with an urgency in his voice, afraid to stop, breathing in fits and starts, irregularly and with interrupted long sighs. His words began to wash over me, so that I could not track him any longer. Instead it was as if I were aware only of his irregular breathing.] I notice your breathing is more rapid, and more irregular today.

PATIENT: I guess it is. My breathing is a kind of oddity. I still think that the CPAP breathing machine is affecting my breathing. [He attributed his somatic responses to the CPAP machine but I believed that they correlated with his emotional experience localized in his body.] I think I'm suppressing emotions both consciously and unconsciously. I think the unconscious is primary. I don't feel emotions of love, loss, or sadness. I turned my back on my parents for twenty years. I made up things to be mad at them about. I resented them.

ANALYST: You made up things, you say?

PATIENT: Things I imagine they did to me, and they offended me, and I resented them. So I feel I should have emotions. I should have emotions of loss and love. I should have anticipatory emotions of loss instead of the suppression of emotion. What about the new way of thinking? I don't know what it's about.

ANALYST: I'm thinking how this is our first time we are meeting using distance technology, and I know you have put in a lot of work to set everything up to make it possible to work this way. I'm noticing you haven't said what that was like, or what it's like for you to be meeting this way.

PATIENT: I'm laughing, because you know how meticulous I would have been, going over every part of the set up. Wait a moment, I just lost my earplug. [He repositioned it in his left ear.] Yes, I was the typical me. But it worked!

ANALYST: Yes.

PATIENT: I didn't know it worked until you *clicked* in. [I thought about how he uses the word, clicked in, as if the teleanalytic setting brought to mind a machine-like part of me that might be resonating with the machine-like part of him.] So medical emergencies to some degree can be dealt with by this. The appointments can take place this way, though a problem is that I'm still trying to hide this from them, and I think I'll still be hiding this from them for a long time.

ANALYST: Well, there's a way in which hiding this from them is like hiding your feelings from yourself.

PATIENT: My father has very negative views about psychiatry. But I don't follow how hiding this from them is like hiding this from myself.

ANALYST: Hiding this from them inside yourself. There's something very powerful about the emotions that could come up in you, in here, emotions that you want to keep at bay. [I felt as though I might be losing him.]

PATIENT: I wouldn't want emotions to come up in here. I've worked on suppressing my emotional experience of sadness in here. Expressing my emotions is not something I want to do in here with you. I think I'll tell you *about* my emotions of sadness, about crying in here.

ANALYST: Like a reporter.

PATIENT: Yes, but I don't want to come in to *this* room and cry. That would be a waste of time.

ANALYST: The interesting thing is that your room and *this* room are contiguous today.

PATIENT: Well, we are in psychoanalysis, as far as you're concerned.

ANALYST: And as far as you're concerned?

PATIENT: I'm in psychoanalysis. When I walked behind the iPad, I could see the couch where I recline exactly the way it is when I am there. I tried to replicate it here. I'm in the room, metaphorically. I don't feel like I'm here. [He paused briefly for the first time in the session.] Well, where are we going? What are we talking about? [He sounded very panic-stricken.]

ANALYST: Well, right at this moment, you seem to be panicking about where to go.

PATIENT: I've told you that I need to focus on new ways of thinking. My father is going to die in weeks or months, maybe in a year or two. [His voice became quieter.] It's going to be really bad. I'd like to be able to say about my father that I've done my best, like I did with Elizabeth.

ANALYST: You're terribly frightened about what it's going to be like when your father dies. And you feel like you can cry when you're alone, in your room—not in here—because you think for some reason, that crying here would be a waste.

PATIENT: I can't say to you, "Here's the situation with my father. What are you going to do?" You're not going to tell me. I missed telling you the story. [He is tracing back to the part of the story about how he felt helped by me, a story that he wanted to tell me earlier in the session.] I missed finishing the story. I asked you what to do when my father told me not to tell anyone about his abnormal X-ray. What you did at that point—you said, let's examine your feelings, and I did, and then I realized I *could* tell my brothers. I can figure out what to do, but you're not telling me what to do. That will work. That will be useful, but you're not going to tell me explicitly what to do.

ANALYST: Hmm. Maybe that's how you also feel about me not telling you explicitly about how it would go for us to meet this way, today. I wonder if we could explore a bit more what it's been like for you. You had been feeling a lot of anxiety in anticipation of this video session.

PATIENT: The technology, it's okay. The technology has worked. [He laughed.] I would have described it better than it's described on the VSee website. That's the story of my life. This worked. I think it's fine. I read it somewhere, that teletherapy is effective, as opposed to in-person work. I think I've read it somewhere. I think there's something to be said for the drive-in and the drive-home, and getting outside of where you usually live.

ANALYST: Ah, that's an interesting way of putting it, of "getting outside of where you usually live". When you enter the world of emotions with me, that's in a sense like getting outside of the world, where you usually live.

PATIENT: Yes, except when I'm alone.

ANALYST: Yes, being alone is a different version of that world, isn't it?

PATIENT: I sense that is something you want me to do in your presence. Um, I don't want to do that. When I came in after I've cried about something, and I tell you about it more, I've figured it all out. I have to think about it before it's there.

ANALYST: You have it all worked out before you come in.

PATIENT: Yes, although you are able to work in nuances, and helping me with it, but crying on it by myself is part of working on it. All the handwringing emotionalism is done. Then in the forty-five minutes we have, I can tell you *about* it.

ANALYST: You were worried about exposing parts of your apartment that you didn't want me to see.

PATIENT: What I wanted you to see was what you ordinarily see. I wanted the camera to be set up properly, that's what I was worried about.

ANALYST: It's interesting, because I also remember your worrying about my seeing clutter in your apartment.

PATIENT: Yes, sometimes I get busy, and yes, there's clutter around here.

ANALYST: Yes, in a way, you don't want me to see the clutter of your emotions.

PATIENT: I get what I think you're saying. If we see the clutter in me, that's like me wandering, like letting my mind wander. It's more useful, so far, if I present you with clutter, so long that I present you with what the clutter was like when I was alone. I don't think I get insights if I cry in there. I can see where it gives you information though.

ANALYST: The feelings you're trying to keep out of here is what feels so untidy and messy for you, the clutter. So we're out of time for today, and I believe we'll be meeting in the office tomorrow.

PATIENT: Yes, at the usual time.

Brent remained in a reclined position on the couch. I turned off the video, and so ended the first teleanalysis session. I hesitated whether to wait for him to rise so as to greet him in the usual way after he has risen from the couch to leave the office.

Commentary

Brent wants to use the session as a laboratory in which to examine his feelings about his parents as a way to re-experience his feelings about losing his wife. The analyst understands that, but she is also concerned about his reactions to her and to the setting in the here and now. She tries to use the unusual set-up of the VTC to create a laboratory in which to examine feelings about the use of technology. Brent tells her that, while on VTC, he can imagine himself in the room with her, but then feels anxious about where the process is going. He seems to cling to technology to avoid feeling lost.

When the teleanalysis clinical research group members share our impression that Brent remains somewhat distant, the analyst explains that he is actually bringing more of himself in, and following this session has been more comfortable on the couch and has brought in a dream. This recalls a chapter in *Psychoanalysis Online 2* in which the argument is made that VTC is actually indicated in analysis of those who are emotionally withdrawn because the deprivation of bodily presence brings out the trauma of early lack of response while offering understanding that had been missing (Varela, 2015).

Work proceeding in the analyst's office

As analysis proceeded, Brent shared more detail of his personal history. His development was profoundly impacted by early loss and disrupted attachments. His father was a vice-admiral in the US coastguard, who traveled most of the time on dangerous combat missions, and uprooted the family every two to three years. At the age of twenty-two, Brent met his wife, Elizabeth (then twenty-nine years old) a captain in the Marines, where he was also employed as a second lieutenant. In a self-sacrificing way, he voluntarily left the US Marine Corps a few years later because his wife had chosen to leave. Over the next two decades, he took on administrative jobs each of which ended unsatisfactorily when he was fired or quit voluntarily. At thirty-nine, he felt overwhelmed by his long trail of occupational failures, and so resigned himself to being a house-husband who orbited around his wife's every want and need. After retiring, Brent severed his contact with his parents, feeling bitter and resentful for ways he felt mistreated by them. When his wife became ill with a progressive, systemic illness, he became her primary caregiver for the remaining five years of their life together. Upon Elizabeth's death, he relocated back to the Washington, DC area, to look after his parents, motivated by guilt at his silent treatment of them, and by a desire to repair his relationships with his brothers—Donald, the eldest, and Ronald, the younger, born when Brent was four years old—and Ronald's wife, Melissa.

Occasional sessions on VTC, when indicated

Typically, we continue to meet in the office, but, on occasion, we hold the session on video teleconference (VTC) not only in case of medical emergency as Brent had foreseen, but also when weather conditions make traveling to the office unsafe, when his parents require him to accompany them to medical appointments, or when he travels. Six months after the first video session, Brent had flown to see his brother Donald who lives in Colorado, and so we had rescheduled his Monday and Tuesday sessions to Thursday and Friday, and moved his Wednesday session to an hour later in the day when he would arrive back home for his first session of the week, to be held online from his home shortly after his plane landed, because his home is closer than my office is to the airport.

The VTC session I will describe is the first of three on this particular week, after a week's break, a longer separation than the typical four-day separation from Thursday to Monday each week. Prior to this session, we had been exploring Brent's resistance to establishing more autonomy in relation to his parents, his conflicts about dating again, and his fears that he would recapitulate the destructive patterns of his former intimate relationship with his late wife. It had been difficult to open a space in his mind to explore the possibility that maybe he would not have to remain trapped in his parents' house following their death, and that he would not have to be wedded forever to repairing their house, which they would leave for him in their will. In the transference, he projected his desires for new romantic possibilities into me, and experienced me as wanting him to enrich his intimate life rather than remaining single and beholden to his parents. He disowned both his own desires for this situation and the fears that he often had expressed in the past that he "would be scared to death" to develop a new, intimate relationship. The analysis was investigating his defenses against the anxiety of closeness with a woman with whom he could potentially establish a more symmetric, mutually gratifying relationship, rather than repeat the asymmetric situation in which he positioned himself as the other's caregiver.

Example: the second session on VTC six months later

I initiated the VTC session, and suddenly noticed that Brent was already lying down. I had anticipated that he would be facing me at the moment of greeting as usual on all prior VTC sessions. There he lay already on his bed, with his headset in place. He lay facing the bare wall at the head of the bed, with his head placed where his feet would typically lie. In the right-hand, front corner of the bed, a side-table was positioned without anything on it. Again I was struck by the bareness of the sparsely furnished room with no wall decoration.

PATIENT: Are we all set?

ANALYST: I can see and hear you. How about you?

PATIENT: I believe so. I can too. I guess we're all set. My efforts have worked out. Some things happened that might have made it impossible, but I mastered them, and I'm here to meet. [He was breathless, getting his words out quickly. I felt his sense of urgency as if something catastrophic had happened, feeling anxious myself as I listened.] We almost didn't meet.

ANALYST: Oh! My goodness.

PATIENT: Well, it was kind of intense, but here we are.

Commentary

At the beginning of the session patient and analyst connect by testing the adequacy of the connection, and appear to get it settled fairly easily. Brent conveys the vulnerability of the teleanalysis connection and Dr. Sehon responds with a spontaneous expression of affect. We soon realize that the technology is carrying a charge from another level of anxiety about connecting. Then Brent quickly glosses over it, and moves on to discuss what to do about his parents' house. As we listen we assume that what Brent is about to tell us will bear some relation to his anxiety about being with Dr. Sehon.

The second session continued

PATIENT: It's a wreck. I began to open up to Donald, how much work it would take to get that house into a livable system. I just don't want to do it. He said he and Ronald have been wanting to talk to me about it. They feared that I'd have some misplaced loyalty about our parents' townhouse, and I'd stay there for some misplaced loyalty towards them. I said, "I don't want to do it." He said, "Don't." I said, "It's an expensive place to live." If Mother and Dad are going to be gone, and if Ronald and Donald are not going to be there, it doesn't make sense for me to stay there. Am I going to be there all on my own? I need to talk about it with Ronald. Well, the three of us would each say how we thought the house was. I think it was important to Donald that the whole thing be talked about. I said to Donald, "I don't want to live there." He said, "Then get out of there, and go on with the rest of your life." Now Ronald is going to have more realistic things to say.

ANALYST: Did you say, Ronald or Donald?

The audio quality diminished appreciably so I could hear his voice, but his words were indistinguishable one from the other. I checked my audio controls, and I noticed that I had the sound up as high as possible. He said he could hear me, but I could not hear him clearly. The computer image continued to be clear and uninterrupted. Rather than his sitting up to assess the situation with his iPad, he remained motionless on his bed, using hand motions to signal with a thumbs up that he could hear me. I offered to change my headset, and as I was about to do so, the audio quality improved. At his suggestion, we also incorporated the use of the phone to provide good audio, and used his iPad and my computer with the sound muted to supply only the visual element.

Commentary

The analyst and patient accommodate to another technical challenge in which the patient cannot be heard by the analyst. By chance this happens as Brent is talking about fearing being left on his own.

The second session continued

PATIENT: Donald would say, "Get rid of the house, and don't do anything." I don't know what Ronald would say. I haven't talked to him in a while.

ANALYST: This is a radically new way of thinking, and it does relate to what we've been talking about more.

PATIENT: I'm going to rely on what I need to do. I can't explain why this is happening.

ANALYST: I think we could consider how this new opportunity relates to things you've said, things I've said, and things we've talked about together.

PATIENT: Both my brothers have given me permission to not live there. That does open things up. It kind of does give me permission to do some new things. That does open up the possibility that I may have a life beyond what I've been able to allow myself to think about. I might gut the kitchen. I don't know.

ANALYST: Can you keep going? [I was pleasantly surprised by his newfound sense of optimism that he could be released from the burden of residing at his parents' home. At the same time, I was taken aback by his attributing this forward movement simply to his brothers having given him permission. As Brent dodged my efforts to explore the link between his growth and our work, I realized he may have needed to defend against his dependency on me in the transference, by crediting his growth to other relationships outside the analysis.]

PATIENT: It was a disaster. The kitchen is a wreck, and things are not working there. There are leaks in the upstairs' plumbing that have been coming through the ceiling into the kitchen. That's been going on for forty years. It's really a terrible house, and the house there is not livable. The wiring is wrong and the bathroom would have to be completely gutted, because the fixtures are all gone. He thinks that the kitchen would need to be gutted, but then it wouldn't be livable.

Donald added something about Dad's financial situation. He had put all his assets into a trust account to protect my parents from my being a bad fellow. No one has said that but that's what I think. It's something that I made up. It makes perfect sense.

ANALYST: Your ideas about this is that they would do this to guard against your misbehavior. Your belief is very much aligned with the strong sense that you have that they would hold you in their mind in a disapproving way. You feel they've long disapproved of you, and at the same time, you have your own feelings of disapproval of them for feeling so unwanted by them.

PATIENT: Meanwhile, I had resolved to behave properly. They would not know that. It makes perfect sense that my father would make sure their assets were protected against me. I don't feel badly about it, because the fellow that I was deserved that kind of precautions.

ANALYST: Hmm, and that fellow has changed.

PATIENT: It's fair that the fellow I was ought to have penance. But I have the permission now from my brothers not to stay there, and that's a pretty good deal.

ANALYST: I wonder if what your brothers are saying seems aligned with my inviting you to think about the opportunity that you could exercise, not to feel trapped to live in that house, in a forced way as if you would be destined in an unchangeable way to have to live there.

PATIENT: It's a faulty house. It's an uncomfortable house. The heating, the ventilation, the wires don't work—just living there—the plumbing doesn't work. Just living there doesn't work. Both of my brothers recognize that it isn't a good house, and they would give me permission to move. I'm not sure. I'm going to go back and forth on that. So this predestination thing is kind of collapsing, and I don't know what to do, and you're not going to tell me because you don't know. But if my parents died tomorrow, and we sold all the contents of the house, I'm going to move north or west, and that would have an impact on our sessions. [Brent paused, and then surprised me by changing direction.]

There's a sense I'm having that you think our sessions are so extraordinarily important that I've become so dependent on them, that I would be extraordinarily distressed if I didn't have them, and it's kind of an extraordinary thing for us to have a video session when I've just flown back into town. Are you keeping the regular number of sessions by moving them around? It seems to me that you think that it's really,

really, really important for the continuity, for the sessions to occur. I don't know if you feel that there's a precariousness to me that requires me to have the session times you're out of town, or something.

Without skipping a beat, he stated in a matter-of-fact way that I required him to have the sessions when I traveled. I was stunned. I have never offered him sessions when I have been out of town, nor have I ever said I would do so. Rather, the sessions have occurred at times when *he* has been out of town, or stuck at home dealing with emergency care for his parents, and on this occasion because his plane landed in time for an online session from his home near the airport but not in time for an in-the-office visit. So, he misattributed his need to me, I thought, as a way of disowning his own desire, also possibly revealing his unconscious wish that we would not lose session time when the sessions would be cancelled if I should travel.

PATIENT: It doesn't bother me. I don't have afflictions. It occurs to me that extraordinary efforts …

ANALYST: Extraordinary, like a video session?

PATIENT: It happened that my travels meant I couldn't come in person.

ANALYST: Well, let's see if we can think about that. You have a lot of thoughts and some strong feelings.

PATIENT: Uh, I don't have strong feelings. I have thoughts. I feel it's coming from you that it's really important. They can move [referring to the sessions], as they have moved before. I wouldn't feel lost without a session.

ANALYST: Well, I noticed at the very start of the session, you mentioned a sense that there had been an imminent risk that the session would collapse, but you made it happen, and you said, "Well, anyway, you're here, and let's go on." Do you think that might be something to bring in?

PATIENT: I sort of wanted to protect you from the burdens of knowing about it. It was always going to be the case that a small delay might happen that would mean I'd miss a part of the session. If we were still doing psychotherapy, I would set up the VSee somewhere on my computer because we would be face-to-face, but we're in psychoanalysis, and the iPad works best for that.

In Colorado, I was playing around with my iPad, and the iPad hung up. [He sounded frantic as he relayed this story.] The iPad wanted me to go to my computer, plug it in, and open it up with iTunes, and I couldn't do it because Donald didn't have iTunes. I couldn't update my iPad. I went to the Apple Store, and they said, "Your iPad is ruined." I came up against time. They said, "We cannot unlock your iPad." The word is bricked. They said your iPad has become completely nonfunctional. I bought the iPad a year ago and I got the extended protection [I thought about how that approximated the time period of conversion from therapy to analysis]. All my data was lost!

ANALYST: Oh!

PATIENT: Including my VSee, and the email you sent me to set up the session was lost.

ANALYST: Everything was gone.

As he talked about the loss he had suffered, the connection over VSee was suddenly lost. We could not hear each other again. Without panic or complaint, he lifted up his phone to signal to me that he would be calling me. As the session continued, he spoke of the anxiety he had experienced about getting the technology set up to be on time for his session.

PATIENT: I had to get back home from the airport. I had to connect my iPad to the computer. It only took fifty minutes. I wondered, was the restore going to be effective? Was the VSee somehow going to be workable? Yesterday, my iPad became a brick. I learned that I can put backups on the cloud. I thought, Geez, I sure hope I can get home in time. The email you sent to set up VSee was not on my iPad. Then I realized I could link to it by sending an email to myself.

ANALYST: You felt a lot of worry, about whether we could make the connection.

PATIENT: Well, it wasn't that I was really worried. It was a situation, "You said, Well if it's delayed, we'll have as much of the session as is left, depending on when you arrive." I wasn't wringing my hands. My worry didn't make me nonfunctional. I took a taxi instead of a bus, so it took me fifty minutes instead of one-hour-and-fifty minutes. I got here with just under an hour to spare. I don't think it's a worry if you're thinking it's realistic. I was thinking—what are the things I need to do to make this happen?

ANALYST: You were quite creative and resourceful, and quite dedicated to preserving the session.

PATIENT: Yes, and I think maybe a lesser person couldn't have done that, and would make excuses. But I made it work!

ANALYST: Could we say that you made it work, both because you were capable to do it, and you made it work because you wanted to?

PATIENT: Yes, and also I was wanting to meet your expectations. I guess, pleasing you, I suppose. I thought you were working me a little bit. I have this feeling that you were setting me up to have this difficulty, to have this problem with this anxiety.

ANALYST: How does that follow?

PATIENT: You are not going to play into my time anxiety.

ANALYST: Time anxiety. Traffic anxiety.

PATIENT: I'm making this up: You're still going to impose on me the expectation that the session happens, despite the logistical issues, and my feelings about that will need to be discussed. That might not be true, but I made it up.

ANALYST: Well, we'll need to stop here for today. We'll continue tomorrow in the office.

PATIENT: Yes, 12:15 pm, in the office. Oh, very fine.

Brent remained lying on the couch, and I signed off.

There was a relentlessness to Brent's description of the problem with the parents' house as legacy, a wreck, and a reminder of his punishment for having rejected his parents. It also seems to represent his longing to return to his childhood, but this is outweighed by the description of disaster. It is a really terrible house. So perhaps he is talking about how nothing in his childhood was satisfactory. Perhaps he is talking about the disorder of his own mind, his parents' relationship, and its representation in his mind as an unsatisfactory internal couple.

Commentary

What happens with Brent's aggression? Is the condition of the house the proof of his destructiveness? Does it refer to the poor condition of relationships in the family? He does feel remorse about what he has done to his parents and his younger brother. Maybe there is some possibility of restoring the house and the relationships that it represents. He believes that he is deserving of punishment for his misdeeds. Why did his wife die and abandon him? He seems to be saying, "Look how I am left!" Why is he sentenced to be the caretaker of the disaster? He is protesting against his legacy and lack of care and the unfairness of his feeling guilty.

The house is a reminder of the death of his wife and his parents, and his own death. He feels cheated. He feels aggressive, and in the first part of the session he was hiding it. In the second part of the session his iPad is completely collapsed, like a personal collapse. He lost everything, perhaps as he felt when his wife died. He depends on his parents, his brothers, and especially his analyst, and his aggression is a reaction to his dependency and its frustration when the analyst will not tell him directly what to do. He protests that the analyst sees him as needy and he prefers to see her as needing him, while he sees himself as invulnerable. At the same time he thinks she should repair the house, the iPad, and everything else for him. Brent presents the internal object as one that will always frustrate, disappoint, neglect, and control him. Brent turns his dependency into a complaint against the analyst for creating that dependency by insisting on teleanalytic sessions for continuity.

This takes us to the second half of the session in which Brent explores the impact of technology. He takes a relaxed, passive attitude to the interruptions and loss of volume, in contrast to his highly active stance in relation to making the connection work, and his energy in making sure he got home in time to have the full value of his session. He enjoys the mastery of solving the technical glitch caused by his iPad. He makes a huge commitment to pleasing Dr. Sehon, but at the same time he likes to imagine that she is the one who needs the session. And yet his emphasis on the wreckage of his house and the ruin of his iPad speak symbolically of his dire need of personal repair.

This takes our discussion back to the sparse setting that Brent created for his teleanalytic sessions—he presented the ghostly image on the screen of the empty bed without lively, colorful accoutrements, and thus conveyed the bleakness of his abandonment by persons of significance, including his wife who died. Hence, Brent delivers to Dr. Sehon the inner devastation of his mind and the death constellation he lives with. We realize that this has become acute as a response to the trauma of losing his strong wife to illness, but we wonder if it predates that, perhaps because of his childhood deprivation by living in a family where the father was often away from home and the mother was left alone to take care of the children. Not only that they must all have lived with the anxiety of losing him when he was in harm's way.

So we ask, is Brent preoccupied with death since being so close to his wife's death, or has he been feeling dead before then? Is he making reparation for causing a death? If that is so, which death is he guilty of? The death of his wife, the emotional cut-off from his parents, or an earlier death? We wonder if Brent is rehearsing for a future death that has already occurred early in his life, leaving him with an unconscious dread of its recurrence (Winnicott, 1963). All these questions have been stimulated by our responses to the images on the screen. We learn from Dr. Sehon that indeed there was an earlier traumatic loss: Brent's mother suffered the awful loss of a stillborn daughter when Brent was a toddler. The aftermath of such a devastating loss could explain why Brent felt that his mother was not responsive to him. So Brent lost the mother he had known before, lost the anticipated baby sister, and joined them in a death constellation. This internal configuration, reactivated by his involvement with his dying wife and now his parents, was unconsciously conveyed through the choice of teleanalytic setting.

Conclusion

In traditional psychoanalysis the analyst provides a uniform setting for all patients, and the patient's unconscious is expressed in relation to the analyst, the frame, the analyst's office environment, and in the use of the couch. In teleanalysis, the patient provides a unique setting, and the patient's unconscious is expressed in relation to the analyst, the frame, the virtual environment, and the use of technology. But in teleanalysis, the patient's choice of setting conveys a vivid image on the screen that is a snapshot of the personal narrative and unconscious internal object relationships.

References

Varela, Y. (2015). Cyberspace as potential space. In: J. S. Scharff (Ed.), *Psychoanalysis Online 2: Impact of Technology on Development, Training, and Therapy* (pp. 233–238). London: Karnac.

Winnicott, D. W. (1963). Fear of breakdown. In: C. Winnicott, R. Shepherd & M. Davis (Eds.), *Psychoanalytic Explorations* (pp. 87–95). Cambridge, MA: Harvard University Press.

CHAPTER NINE

Technology: convenience and therapeutic leverage

Dina Oren (Israel and USA)

In recent decades, the world has become a global village and people move around within it frequently and over great distances. Alongside the distances crossed by people, technology has developed that allows us to maintain close contact. Texts and images get passed along in real time from one end of the world to the other. How do all these alter the meaning of closeness and distance? Intimacy? Do they open new options for therapy? Movement by therapists and clients around the world has created a need to keep tabs on the therapeutic relationship, and technology has made that possible, but is there really a need to carry on these existing relationships? Whose need is it? The client's? Or the therapist's? Perhaps it's our difficulty, as therapists, to separate from and frustrate our clients. Perhaps it's our feeling of omnipotence that we are irreplaceable? Complex and numerous questions surface, all of which relate in one or another way, to this issue: does the Internet provide sufficiently viable conditions for therapy in general, and analytical therapy in particular?

For two years, my husband and I had been thinking about realizing a long-held dream of ours to travel to be with our children in New York for three months and make a five-month journey in Africa. My thoughts about technology became acutely relevant. Technology could easily allow me to work consistently in New York and possibly even to slot some therapy hours into my leisure trip in Africa. We made the decision to travel, and I prepared my clients for my day of departure when I would temporarily close my clinic in Israel. Some of my clients completed their therapy, some were referred to other therapists, and some chose to stay in treatment with me via Internet contact, knowing that Skype would be our medium for conducting therapy sessions, and that there would inevitably be interruptions in our connection.

When I actively considered being involved with teletherapy, two main aspects came into focus. The first was technological: Is it partially or fully conducted via Skype or any other technology? What do we see? And what do we hear? Am I viewed on the screen at a reasonable size, or minimized to several centimeters on a cellular phone screen? Is the conversation protected and its confidentiality assured? The second was philosophical. How many hours will I spend online compared to being with clients in my consulting room? Will I think of this teletherapy as a routine part of my work or an exceptional circumstance? Is it a necessity for my client, or is it a necessity for me?

Having decided to undertake this long journey, I realized that using technology for continuity of care of some clients was a choice, a risk, and a responsibility. I took a warning from this quote from *Psychoanalysis Online*: "It's not sufficient to ask what technology does *for* us; we should also ask what it does *to* us" (Stadter in Scharff, 2013, p. 3, italics in original). I have to admit that my relationship with technology is highly complex, I don't trust it, I don't feel safe around it, and every fault that occurs arouses my anxiety, and causes me to lose my clear thinking. So before leaving on our trip, I made sure I was equipped with a new computer, high-quality broadband, and at each new location I would do everything I could to ensure the quality and stability of the Internet connection. With that in mind, I was able to use technology in individual and couple therapy in changing settings and in uncertain conditions. I began to think of technology as an electronic third object. How would it affect the analytic third, that space between, within, and beyond the dialectic of client and therapist? Would it be a helpful companion, or an interference? What would happen? What I could not know before I embarked on Internet-based therapy sessions was that I would learn to use the impact of technology for the benefit of therapy and that I would see my own situation reflected in my clients' therapy conversations.

I will present vignettes from a weekly couple therapy (Maya and Sam), a weekly individual therapy (Danny), and a twice-a-week couple therapy (Doreen and Oscar) as examples of technology's influence on psychotherapy and on the fulfilment of the therapist's desire and professional identity.

The meaning of cut-offs: Maya and Sam

When Maya and Sam came for their first couple therapy session seven years ago, their twins, a boy and a girl, were eighteen months of age. They came to explore the possibility of divorcing, or to be more precise, Sam was brought to therapy by Maya, since he was against divorcing. Sam said very little. After eighteen months of weekly meetings (about seventy-five sessions) therapy reached its conclusion. Sam and Maya remained together, and another little boy was born. Eighteen months ago, Maya once again approached me concerning therapy, saying that she wanted to improve their communication. She made the approach alone, saying that Sam refused to join therapy. Because I was on my journey, the only option I could offer them was to conduct therapy via Skype, and I asked if she would check whether Sam would agree to that. Sam, who had been reluctant about face to-face therapy, did agree to Skype. My hypothesis was that the distance and the space created by the Internet felt safer to him than face-to-face encounters.

Therapy began, and along with it came repeated technical problems that interfered with or even cancelled sessions. Our work in the first two months was in fits and starts, which led to Maya's blaming Sam for the Internet not working properly. She told him that he could easily have done something to fix it without much expense. It occurred to me that this was something that she could have done too without waiting for him to do it. My own relationship with technology is complicated, and everything I was doing was aimed at overcoming breakdowns, rather than focusing on them, and definitely not letting them take control of therapy. I wanted to provide the best therapy I could to my clients, who really needed my help, and so I had tried to overcome my own anxiety and present a confident, capable appearance. I ignored the technical faults and quickly got back to focusing on therapy itself. But technical problems kept happening. Therapy was going nowhere.

More than thirty percent of therapy time was wasted, so to speak, due to the many technical interruptions in our conversations.

Sometimes they could see but not hear me, and so my time to help them was reduced. Sometimes they could not see me on the computer, and so they connected via their cellphones, which meant my image was reduced to barely a few centimeters. Their excuses for Internet issues were countless, and I needed endless patience to continue holding these fragmented sessions. I knew that I must not give up on them; this fragmented technical communication was a "test of love and care." I also realized that the anger and blame cast on the husband for the poor Internet connection was part of the couple's pattern of relating.

It took me a lot longer, and a great deal more patience, until I realized that the online disconnections symbolized an entire world of meaning. Once I understood that, I realized that I had better not ignore the technical aspect but focus on it and comprehend what was being reconstructed through it. This moment of understanding enabled me to use technology for therapeutic leverage.

The fragmented conversation

This conversation took place some two months into the endlessly fragmented sessions. We had set the appointment for 9:00 pm. Ten minutes in advance of that, the couple called to request resetting the appointment to 9.15 pm since the children were not asleep yet.

At 9.15 pm they call for the session. I can hear, but not see, them. They try again and this time we can all see and hear one another.

ME: How difficult! How much uncertainty! Will we connect? Won't we? Will there be both sound and image?

Maya smiles in recognition and tries to answer but the connection drops. We reconnect.

MAYA: It's terrible. It is really hard for me, these cut-offs. Now we have a line, now we don't. Why? And how does this happen? I really hope it works. I wasn't here when the technical people came to check it. Sam spoke to them about the problem, and you understood it, right, Sam?

SAM: (pointing it out to me) The line needs to be moved from here to there, behind this wall, from top to bottom.

For several sequential sentences, which is a rare occurrence, Sam explains the technicalities of what he was told by the infrastructure provider. I don't fully understand but I am unwilling to halt him and ask him to explain it to me.

MAYA: (cutting him short) In short, there's no infrastructure here. The infrastructure here is in really bad shape.

ME: Sam, you say it's hard to build communication here, and Maya, you say there's no infrastructure.

MAYA: Right, there's no infrastructure.

ME: The infrastructure's shaky.

Maya laughs.

ME: You're laughing?

MAYA: That's so typical of what happens between us. There really is this uncertainty.

The connection breaks again. We reconnect.

ME: And what about the connection with me? How does it feel to be in touch with someone who disappears from you all the time? First I disappeared from Israel, and now I'm disappearing from the screen. There's an unstable figure who can't be depended on.

MAYA: No, I'm the unstable one. I should have made sure of the Internet. It shouldn't have been like this. I'm judging myself here.

ME: Familiar?

MAYA: A familiar and insufferable experience.

Silence.

ME: Can you say more?

MAYA: I feel that it really typifies our relationship, and the truth is that it typifies other relationships in my life, especially with my mother. The connection with her is very changeable, and unstable, and uncertain, and there are all kinds of factors influencing it. This is a mother who can't be relied on, who I can't get support from, or even an opinion. The house was great, always in tip-top shape, and there was always food. She was seemingly there, but she was never really there.

The line disconnects again. We reconnect.

MAYA: I asked Sam if he doesn't feel the uncertainty between us, and he answered that he doesn't feel any uncertainty in our relationship.

ME: You agree that there's difficulty with creating and maintaining communication, but Sam, you think that has nothing to do with the certainty of the relationship between you whereas you, Maya …

I do not get to finish my sentence because we are cut off again, and the session is over.

This was the last time we had to work with such a poor connection. After that, Maya made sure that the Internet would work well, and the connection was fine for the remaining four months of the treatment for a total of twenty-five sessions over the six months of online treatment. Once I had taken responsibility for my part in causing the difficulties in connection, Maya was able to take responsibility for her part. The technical problems showed that Sam was holding the certainty in the couple and Maya was questioning it all the time, and brought out the affective basis for Maya's dislike of her mother, a topic she had often complained about but could never explain. This example taught me how technology is in the service of therapy, in this case by embodying the couple dynamic and revealing the maternal void transference.

Discussion

The fear of disconnection is constantly there in a Skype call. Even when the Internet is working well at both ends, the prior experience of interruption and the constant expectation of it happening again arouses a range of thoughts, feelings, and anxieties. A frequent experience for patient and therapist is that of abandonment anxiety. Do I have everything I need in order to uphold my commitment to this relationship? Will we manage to reconnect successfully? Who should call whom? If both sides call simultaneously, no connection can be made. Repeated disconnects also introduce aggressive affect. The experience of the disconnect raises the question: Was the disconnect accidental, coincidental, or intentional? What was said prior to the disconnection? Does it have any unconscious link to the disconnection? What if we cannot reconnect? What if we never reconnect? Another anxiety is that therapy might come to a sudden end, beyond our control. Skype, then, raises issues of life and death.

Fear of acceptance: Danny

I am preparing for a meeting with Danny, a client I have been meeting at my private clinic in Israel face to face for two years. Danny has agreed to meet twice a week online while I am traveling. Knowing that Danny had to undergo surgery and that I would begin my journey before he was fit to return to sessions, we arranged in advance for the first teletherapy session to occur at an arranged time.

My journey has taken me to New York where I have an office in Manhattan and no worries about my Internet connection. At the appointed time, I sit down in front of the computer to await his call, only to see from the call record that he had rung through a minute earlier. Initially I'm flooded with guilt feelings. How can it be that I wasn't there when he contacted me? Immediately I check to see exactly what time he called. The call record on the screen shows me that he called a couple of minutes before our set time. My guilt feelings partially dissipate, and I call back on Skype. The computer shows me he's online, but I can't seem to make contact. What I hear is not the usual continuous ringing, but a call rejection sound. But hadn't he just called me? I know for sure that he's there on the other side, watching my attempts at communication, and not reacting to my calls—or more correctly, he is rejecting them.

I wonder why he didn't send a text explaining what was happening. Then I text him to ask him to call me again because I am there for our appointment but he hasn't called back and I can't seem to make contact with him. But that goes unanswered. I text again, saying that I'll be online until the end of our allotted time. More than half an hour later, I receive a text from him, as follows: "There was some technical problem which is unclear to me, but in any event it's late now, and I need to go. We'll meet next week."

It's completely clear to me that a technical problem is not the issue! I feel sure that Danny is trying to convey a message to me. I wait eagerly for our next meeting.

Conversation

ME: What happened last week?

DANNY: There was some technical thing I couldn't figure out.

ME: When I sat down at the computer I saw you'd already called. I tried to get back to you, but wasn't successful.

DANNY: I heard your ringing but I couldn't connect, and I also tried to connect to you but didn't manage.

I note to myself that the computer shows no attempt on his part to connect.

ME: What were you feeling?

DANNY: I don't remember anything in particular.

ME: We had arranged the online appointment after two weeks of not meeting. You call, and I'm not there.

DANNY: I was aware of calling too early, and it's legitimate that you're not there, so I waited, but I don't remember any particular thoughts going through my mind. I don't know. I don't know.

ME: I called again and again. Did you want the rings to stop? To continue?

DANNY: My behavior speaks for itself—that I didn't answer you for half an hour, and didn't send you a message for that half hour. Maybe *that's* what was going on back there.

ME: What is 'that'?

DANNY: I decided it suited me to forego the conversation at that time. I don't know how to explain to myself what hides behind that. Clearly I didn't decide in advance to forego the meeting because then I would simply have cancelled. I can't identify what happened there at the emotional level. I can't reconstruct it. Maybe there was some reaction at your not answering, which is entirely illogical, and it's clear to me you don't have to be seated at the computer in advance.

ME: We set a meeting time. You arrived, and I didn't.

I wait for his response. Silence.

DANNY: Look at what I just did. I remember something that I never mentioned before. One day, when you were still at your clinic in Israel, I came to see you at the wrong time, and you weren't there. I felt disappointed and frustrated, and helpless too because I couldn't reach you by phone either. But this time is different. I can't figure it out, because it was only a matter of half a minute's difference.

ME: (referring to both the online call and the mistaken appointment in Israel) You came to see me, and I wasn't there. The door was locked.

DANNY: Maybe there was some flash of emotion that I can't reconstruct now. It was so brief, I can't seem to see how it could happen.

ME: A flash of emotion …

DANNY: Yes, of course there are situations that are *casus belli* for me, situations where I have been completely turned away, and if you identify what happened a week ago as such, then I agree with you. But it's not quite the same thing. It's similar but not the same. If it was the same, I'd write you a check and say thank you and goodbye, like I do in *casus belli* situations.

ME: How is it different?

DANNY: I don't know, I can't even think why I got locked up because of half a minute.

ME: When you called me online, I wasn't there in advance of the time. When you arrived for your appointment on a day we had no appointment, I wasn't there. What's the fantasy?

DANNY: Ah. I think I know what you mean. I never behaved as expected in the social environment, and so I was really unpopular among my peers, and yet it was really important for me to be accepted. The frustration of not being accepted is always with me, and has been all these years. And if you're not there when I need you, then it means I'm not accepted.

We recovered from this incident, and Danny continued meeting with me online for another fifty-four sessions to complete his treatment over the next six months. The point is that Danny had not told me of his coming to see me at the wrong time, and so I didn't know of his vulnerability to rejection by me. When he made a similar, but very minor version of the same mistake in calling too early, the old story popped out. The stress of the half minute of waiting was amplified by the uncertainty of Internet connection. In the old story, I did not know he had come to see me. In the new story, I saw from the computer record of calls that he had indeed called me early, and that he was online but not picking up. This fruitful conversation would not have taken place if I had not known that he came to our online meeting when I wasn't supposed to be there. His need for acceptance was made available for work, thanks to the Internet. As with Maya and Sam, technology had provided me with an opportunity to find therapeutic leverage.

Holding in uncertain, shifting conditions

Here is a vignette from therapy with a couple who "accompanied" me through the whole journey.

* * *

Doreen and Oscar are in their late thirties. When they met, Doreen was in the process of seeking a gay male partner who would father a child for her, since she had not yet found anyone appropriate for marriage. She had not become pregnant, and so she felt her biological clock was ticking away and that her ability to create life was dissipating. Oscar, by contrast, had already been divorced for two years, and was the father of a seven-year-old boy. That child was preceded by a premature infant who died shortly after birth. The feeling of life and death accompanied therapy from its start to its end.

Oscar proposed to Doreen some six months after they met. He said he felt very sure of his choice. On a trip to Tuscany he plucked a flowering stalk, shaped it into a ring, and asked Doreen to marry him. From that moment on, he said, he considered himself married to her. On their return to Israel, Doreen wanted to hold a party for family and friends to tell everyone they knew of their marriage. Oscar preferred a small family gathering in the garden of Doreen's mother's home, which is what ultimately took place. Doreen said she was not able to invite even the closest of her friends.

Doreen, who at the time of meeting Oscar was in the process of trying to bring a child of her own into the world, understandably wanted to become pregnant as quickly as possible. Oscar, by contrast, was in no hurry. "A child," Oscar said, "is a real commitment." Doreen pressured until Oscar capitulated, but all their efforts to conceive led to nothing. They finally met with a trusted gynecologist who told Doreen that she needed artificial insemination but that he, an orthodox Jew, could do this only for couples who were married by an orthodox rabbi, a ceremony that had not taken place. A deep conflict arose between Doreen who accepted the gynecologist's conditions, and Oscar who defines himself as atheist and is resentful towards the institution of religion.

He completely refused to comply with "that doctor's request" and felt they should change doctors. Slowly we clarified the need for an official marriage in a religious ceremony, as Doreen revealed her sense of insult over the way Oscar had married her and Oscar confirmed his commitment towards her and their future children.

Doreen

Doreen is the baby of the family. She had to tune in to her mom's needs and contain her emotions, and not the other way around. Doreen's mother turned her into her confidante. Doreen's father comes from a family of Holocaust survivors. He passed away in his sixties from severe lung disease. He spent a good deal of his life depressed, and he drank heavily. Doreen had experienced a serious depressive crisis during her military service.

Oscar

Oscar grew up in a "rational home" where the father, who was the be-all and end-all in the family, once said, "Emotions are extraneous and don't bring any benefit." His mother, a school principal, was demeaned by the father but never tried to stand up to him.

Oscar's marriage to his first wife, Mimi, was his first ever relationship with a woman. The crisis between them began with the tragedy that befell them when their firstborn, a son, was born prematurely and died days afterwards. Mimi fell into a deep depression. Oscar on the other hand put the catastrophe "behind him" and moved on. From this point on, a gaping abyss opened between them, into which their second son, Nate, was born. Mimi was barely able to care for the infant, and the entire burden of both providing a livelihood and raising the child fell to Oscar. Currently, Nate spends two days a week with Oscar, as well as every other weekend. His presence in Doreen and Oscar's home creates strong tension, and is an endless source of conflict.

The couple treatment

The couple treatment had three phases.

The first phase was conducted weekly for seventy meetings over eighteen months in my private clinic in Israel. Our meetings dealt with their marriage and Doreen's attempts at getting pregnant. Towards the end of this phase Oscar and Doreen tied the knot beneath the religious wedding canopy. Not long afterwards, Doreen became pregnant, and against all odds gave birth to twins, a boy and a girl.

The second phase started not long after the birth of the twins, and was conducted via Skype twice a week for thirty sessions over three months in New York City where it was part of my routine working life.

The third phase was conducted on Skype approximately twice a week for fifty-five hours during the trip, where it was a small, but significant, commitment during my leisure.

So for Doreen and Oscar, the setting was changed from face to face in my private clinic in Israel to Skype, first in New York City, a new but stable setting for three months, and then in uncertain and ever changing settings for five months while on our journey. At first, it seems to me that the switch from "face to face" to Skype was smooth, and I did not notice any difference in the therapeutic process. Oscar is a techie, fully fluent with all things computerized, and could even help me out when I got stuck. Later on it seemed different.

I will now give three vignettes from three different online sessions using Skype.

Vignette one (in New York before my trip)

OSCAR: I would like to talk today about the place of Nate in our family. No way can I agree with this as a Cinderella and stepmother story.

DOREEN: (crying) I feel the opposite, I feel an injustice has been done to me.

OSCAR: What injustice??!! Is it anything other than things being difficult for you with Nate?

DOREEN: They're not difficult for me with Nate. They're difficult for me with you.

OSCAR: So. They're difficult for you with me too.

DOREEN: They're not difficult for me with you TOO, they're difficult for me with YOU. I feel that you put things on me that you should be doing, not me. I can't take care of him twice a week for hours when you're at work—with two tiny babies. He's not a nice person. So yes, I'm not nice to him, I don't want him, and he feels unwanted.

[I noticed that while Doreen focused her words on Oscar, he chose to shift the center of gravity to Nate. I noticed, but did not say anything just yet.]

OSCAR: I understand that right now you're not capable of coping with him and you need some separation from him until it's easier for you. Right now I feel like I'm walking on eggshells, because the twins arrived before you and Nate had enough time to connect with each other.

DOREEN: He hasn't connected with himself. It has nothing to do with me. And anyhow, he's not a pleasant person, and that has nothing to do with me. He's a burden to everyone around him. He demands that a lot of attention and energy be directed towards him.

ME: He's a child. He needs a lot of attention.

[I repeat her emphasis on the need for attention but I change her word "person" to "child." I am fully aware that the change contains an element of criticism but I'm anxious over this rejected child, which makes it harder for me to be fully empathetic towards Doreen.]

DOREEN: I understand what you're saying, but unfortunately that's not my experience with him. He's an unusual child, and not only this, but also he's a very expensive child. The amount of money spent on him is very high.

OSCAR: Expenses for the twins are also very high.

DOREEN: That's not true!!! I'm not prepared to work harder for him. I think he lives very well. I think the sums spent on him are too high, and Oscar behaves this way because he's doing it to spite me. (To Oscar) You have no boundaries on anything except love. Love is the only thing that isn't there. Everything is an act of material compensation, and I'm not prepared to be a partner to this endless compensation, and especially not now when I have *children of my own*, and when everything Nate gets is at their expense. I don't allow myself more help with the twins, but he goes off to study playing the drum.

ME: (repeating her words) Doing it to spite …

DOREEN: (interrupting) That's the place that Oscar defines as his territory, his area, and he's not willing for me to interfere. It indicates his independence. Nate and everything to do with him belong to Oscar, and the rest is external to him.

ME: You and the children are external to him?

DOREEN: Yes, that's what I feel. (Pause) I've never spoken that way about any other child, and if I'd hear someone else talking that way I'd go nuts. These feelings are extreme. Nate is the only child I've ever actually lived with. I'm a youngest child and didn't grow up with other children around, and my greatest fear is that my own children will grow up to be like him.

[Now I hear the "Cinderella experience" of Doreen and her twins.]

ME: Doreen, you're saying that Oscar shows more concern for Nate than for you and the children, and Oscar, you're saying that Doreen tries to distance Nate from your home. Both these feelings are very harsh, and turn Nate into the center of the problem and the absorber of the hostility. In your way of thinking, if there's space for Nate, there's no space for you, Doreen, and the children, and so in order for it to be good for you and the children, Nate needs to be distanced from the home. It's an either-or situation.

[This split place, the schizoid situation in which they find themselves, leaves room for only one of them, for just one truth. It's a place without the space to clarify and talk and negotiate needs. It also leaves me with the feeling of an either-or situation. On the one hand, I am dealing with a husband and wife who alternate roles between being the "wicked parent" and being the "rejected child." Both of them grew up as children with their emotional life negated and unrecognized, and they need me to acknowledge it. On the other hand, I am dealing with worry about Nate who has become the center of Oscar and Doreen's fight. We are nearing the end of this session.]

ME: Both of you are undergoing a highly complicated experience. You Doreen, who've never spoken that way about a child, suddenly have such strong feelings, which aren't familiar to you, against your husband's child. And you, Oscar, see Doreen's distress and inability to contain Nate, but you can't acknowledge it because, you can't bear the thought of losing your son since you have already lost one child.

Both nod their heads, and I have the impression that they feel understood.

[I could see Doreen and Oscar alternating the role of the "wicked" mother but I couldn't see myself as their "wicked mother." I preferred them as my "own" children at home in Israel more than as the New York "step-children" who I "forced" to connect to me by Skype, and who I "dragged" with me around the world. It definitely was not the next way for them to have therapy. But at the time I recommended it, I could see only the benefits of not interrupting their sessions but not the price.]

This dialogue of a "wicked" parent and "second best" "deprived" child went on for a very long time, with various emphases each time, both before my trip and after setting out, as Doreen sank even further into depression, lost her appetite for life, stared into space, and became so sad that she could not play with her children, to the point that Oscar was sure she constituted a danger to them. Oscar was increasingly withdrawing into anger at her, denied her feelings, and definitely conditioned his love for her on her acceptance of Nate as part of their family. The more he closed his heart against her, the more she rejected Nate. The more she rejected Nate, the more Oscar closed his heart, feeling that her mental state was tainting their reality.

So it happened that, on the evening of my departure on my trip to Africa, Doreen and Oscar's therapeutic process was at a critical point. Having informed my other clients of a break of some five months, I found myself unable to tell Doreen and Oscar that I was leaving for such a long time, while they were in such a deep crisis. So "I took them with me," meaning that I maintained continuous contact with them twice a week for the five months of the trip. I had a lot of doubts, and I was struggling to reconcile the benefits of uninterrupted treatment with the problems of interruption due to uncertain conditions for therapy that we would have to face because of my wishes to fulfill my dreams and travel the world. I did suggest that they approach another therapist but in a spirit of full disclosure I must admit that I wanted to have them continue in couple therapy with me. In addition to the obvious fact that they were very dear to me, it was important for me to keep up the therapeutic aspect of my life. I did not want to lose my professional identity, while fulfilling my dreams. So, I would take them with me on my journey, not before speaking and processing the difficulties that may arise along the way.

Now I have left New York and I'm at "the end of the world" and moving around, not always with a precise estimate of how long it will take to get from one location to another, which does not always depend on me. The time differences between Israel and Africa, though, actually work in our favor but Internet access is often poor and usually available only in public areas rather than private rooms. Sometimes I receive permission to use offices at the places where we are staying. Sometimes, I look for a quiet spot in a public area, without people too close by so that we can talk. I create a closed corner there, and make sure that no Hebrew speakers are in the vicinity (The language creates the privacy). Sometimes I am in our room, having asked my husband to wait in the lobby. It's difficult to arrange conditions to ensure full client confidentiality. I am particular about getting to our lodgings on time, do not drink alcohol on evenings I hold meetings with the couple, and am very committed to their therapy. But I am very worried about Doreen's deep depression. Without my professional community, far from colleagues with whom I could consult, without supervision, without my professional literature, I have nothing but myself. I think back on their history.

I remember the crisis of depression Doreen experienced in the army, and her statement, "Only when I hit bottom could I turn and rise up." I understand that the current depression must reach its maximum before she can let it go. I also recall her father, a Holocaust survivor, who suffered from depression most of his life. Doreen heard his Holocaust narrative as he was dying in hospital, and it sounded like a myth, a legend or fable. His story comes back to me.

When Doreen's father was an eight-month-old infant, his parents and extended family left their home in Poland, understanding that the earth was shaking beneath their feet, and that war was about to erupt. The family moved from country to country until exhausted with this fleeing. Near one of the borders, a family decision was made to stop wandering and return to their home in Poland. Doreen's father, who was at the "crawling age," crawled about and crossed the border. His parents crossed over to fetch him and stayed there, while the rest of the members of their extended family returned to Poland, where they were exterminated. Doreen's father's family survived, had another baby during the war, and eventually immigrated to Israel. I understand that in such a family, with no small amount of depression, the drive to live is eventually victorious, which encourages me.

Several months into the deep crisis, during which I hear them and give space to anything surfacing in them, I feel upset that I don't have the right conditions for therapy and that I am taking a risk, continuing treatment but at the expense of in-depth therapy. I feel like I am working in a field hospital, doing open heart surgery without the most basic of suitable conditions.

Then the "outburst" moment arrives. It breaks over the issue of the infant caregiver they hired to help with the twins. Doreen has claimed for weeks and months that she does not trust her. I must explain that in Hebrew we use the same word *metapelet* for caregiver and therapist. Oscar said that the problem was Doreen's difficult mental state and that no infant caregiver would earn her trust, and so there was no point in letting her go, especially now that the children had become attached to her and love her. Doreen was fiercely insulted by this, and said that Oscar criticizes her constantly, does not support her, and negates her feelings.

Vignette two

OSCAR: The metapelet [infant caregiver] quit.

DOREEN: Oscar fired her! That's absurd, that in the end Oscar fired her.

ME: Who was fired?

doreen: The metapelet quit after a tough talk with Oscar.

ME: The metapelet [infant caregiver] left. And your metapelet [therapist] left too.

DOREEN: I'm saying that it's absurd, how in the end Oscar fired her.

[I invite them to speak about the relationship between them and me but they don't bite. Yet I listen to what they say about the metapelet and try to see how it relates to me.]

DOREEN: Until now Oscar has sided with her, and thought I was nuts. This has been part of his criticism of me as a mother, ever since the children were born. I needed support and all I got was criticism.

[I hear Doreen talking about collusion between Oscar/Nate and me that resulted in a lot of criticism towards her. I have to admit that being worried about Nate's situation in Doreen and Oscar's home made it difficult for me to be fully empathetic to Doreen. That's a good reason to want to dismiss me.]

DOREEN: It restores my confidence in my reality checking. Oscar now sees that I wasn't just crazy when I said she's not okay. My maternal instincts were right, and Oscar needed to rely on them and affirm them, rather than cast doubt on my feelings.

OSCAR: (in a warm, intimate pampering tone) You see, you can rely on me. You see that I'm attentive to you.

[I sense that Doreen and Oscar have reached the same place from two different directions: Doreen wanted to fire the caregiver because she felt that she was not caring for the babies properly, and so she was afraid of leaving her alone with them; Oscar fired her because she often came late, which kept him from leaving for work on time. Regardless, Doreen viewed Oscar's dismissing the caregiver as Oscar recognizing Doreen and legitimizing her feelings, which switched the negative dynamic between them to a positive one.

A thought crosses my mind about the "wicked step-mother" that the children in the story want rid of, but it remains an unspoken thought, probably because it is difficult to accept my responsibility for all the discomfort I am causing them. I am having trouble facing my guilty feelings about not being empathetic enough to Doreen. Seeing a rejected child is too difficult for me.]

ME: Doreen, you say, Oscar needed to rely on and affirm your feelings. What about your feelings?

DOREEN: I have a lot of feelings of regret.

ME: Anxiety? Regret? [In Hebrew these two words are almost identical—*kharada*—*kharata*.]

DOREEN: Both, actually. I regret this motherhood which I wanted so much, since it's taken myself from me, my freedom. It changed my whole life. Nothing is like it used to be.

ME: Regret over motherhood? Or over motherhood to the twins?

DOREEN: Both, actually. I didn't really understand what I was getting into. [Brief silence.] Still, I wouldn't change a thing. Even though it's clear to me that being a mother of twins is completely different to being the mother of one child. Those mothers carry on with their lives, but I've completely come apart.

ME: Completely different?

DOREEN: It's hard to contain two completely different creatures, each of them arousing something completely different in me. Let's start with their gender, with the fact that one's a boy and the other's a girl, which arouses different things. I really wanted a girl, and I really didn't want a boy. It's very connected with Nate. He's the closest thing to a son that I know, and I don't want one like that.

[Oscar responds to this rejection of Nate, (and actually, all males) but not reactively.]

OSCAR: I feel that Doreen's watching a color television and I'm watching a black and white one. I see it more simply: I have plenty of love for all of them, Nate, the twins and Doreen.

[I sense a movement in their dynamic: Oscar is not reacting with a direct attack on Doreen, and she is open and honest.]

DOREEN: Is it really so easy to love everyone? Two or three weeks ago you said it was hard for you to contain everyone and give to everyone.

OSCAR: True, it continues being hard and demanding but there's something calmer about it now. I don't know exactly what.

DOREEN: I do know exactly what, and that's what worries me. I'm more relaxed, and then the whole household's calmer, and then it's easier for you to contain me and love me, but when I'm in a bad place you hate me, and reject me.

OSCAR: It's true that the past few months have been really difficult for me. I've never been in such a tough place in my whole life. I didn't understand what was happening to me. Everything seems so complex, one thing on top of another, that I can't seem to find the beginning and end of things. I was already so uncertain about whether I was reading reality right that I needed to check with other people. It required a lot of faith in couple-hood from me, a lot of thinking, being considerate, seeing what to do and how to do it. But I didn't throw in the towel.

ME: Oscar, you said you see things in black and white, but I hear that you see how complex it is to be a father to everyone, and at the same time be Doreen's husband. And you, Doreen, describe how complex motherhood is for you, particularly as a mother of twins, and how alone you feel with that. You're both talking about difficult emotions, which are hard to contain. But they're very human.

[At the end of this session, I feel we're no longer on a thin line between oppositional poles towards either of which we might slip at any moment. Rather, a space has opened where it is possible to observe, talk, share, and reflect. I feel that their collusion against me has helped them to unite.]

The next meeting takes place less than two months later.

Vignette three

OSCAR: We've decided our lives are too boring, calm, and easy. So, we've become pregnant.

ME: (smiling) And how does that feel?

DOREEN: We're confused. I hadn't thought of that option so I didn't notice any signs, and then one day I checked, and the physician confirmed that I'm in my fourth month. Mostly, I'm confused. I need to take a really tough decision, one way or the other. I don't know how to make such decisions. I don't know how to extricate a decision of this kind out of myself. Something inside me that will tell me what's right for me.

[I close my eyes and very loudly hear how this developing pregnancy is being ignored. This kind of ostrich-head-in-the-sand attitude by enlightened, aware people in the twenty-first century surprises me. They are splitting off from a reality that is difficult to acknowledge and sequestering it in the unconscious. In this case, I feel that the reality of the impact of the pregnancy is ignored not because it's unwanted, but in order to preserve and protect it, and this feeling of mine is reinforced by the word "extricate." The phrase "extricate a decision out of myself" is not a common one, and in addition the word "extricate" can be interpreted in Hebrew as to "save from danger of death." My feeling is that discovering the pregnancy at such a late stage, one in which Doreen, due to her gynecological history, can neither abort nor continue to term without endangering her life, is an act of the unconscious in the service of life. It's Doreen's way of saving her baby from rational decisions that face her.]

The conversation continues.

DOREEN: I'd already glimpsed the light at the end of the tunnel. The twins would go to nursery school in September, and I'd have time for myself again. Suddenly in September I'll have a new baby, probably a girl, so we'll have three children a year apart, each with the same financial needs. It won't be easy, and tomorrow registration closes for the studies I wanted to start. What should I do?

OSCAR: You register for the studies. Of course you do!

DOREEN: And I'm scared that life won't wait for me. I'm afraid of being left a Mother Goose. It doesn't match my worldview of myself, and I'm confused, I don't know what to do.

OSCAR: I want another child, but not at any price. All the considerations need to be taken into account, but I'll stand with you and back you up on any decision you make, with great love.

DOREEN: When you say that, you remain neutral and leave me alone with the decision, and that's really hard for me.

OSCAR: OK, I lean to not continuing this pregnancy. I want another child but not right now.

DOREEN: I'm at the other extreme, I lean more towards keeping the child. First of all, because I'm carrying this pregnancy, and slowly it's becoming part of me. Both of us ignored it, so now we need to cope with it. I always suffered from being the baby of the family to older parents, and have no siblings close to me in age. I always longed for siblings close to me. My fantasy is of a life with close connections. That's very present for me, and maybe this is how my fantasy surfaced, to show that I can become pregnant.

OSCAR: That's not logical.

DOREEN: True, but not everything is logical in life.

ME: Together you're raising the voices of logic and fantasy, and both of you are asking if there's room for your lives alongside those of a new baby, or whether you need to forego the pleasure of having another child to have a life of your own.

[I feel that despite the weight of the issue, and the depth of its impact on their lives, they are managing to conduct a conversation and give room to the different voices. There is another expansion of the space between them, with room for complexity and lack of perfection. What choice would they make? In the final run, the choice is in favor of life. "We've decided to keep the baby," they tell me at the beginning of the next session.

The new baby was born about six weeks prior to the due date. The birth was difficult as before. During it, Doreen lost a lot of blood, and her life was at risk. When our sessions resumed, I said to Doreen, "You almost lost your life in order to give life to this little girl," and she answered, "That little girl brought me back to life. She brought balance and smiles back into my life."]

In one of the African villages we visited, we stopped to send a package to our grandchildren. A mother carrying her baby walked past our car; this golden curly-haired child in the hands of a white mother in an African village was striking in this area, and my gaze followed them. The phrase going through my mind was: "A mother carries her child with her everywhere." My thoughts went a step further: "Just as my mother took me to a nursery school, where she used to work since I was a baby."

This sentence has changed its hue over the years. For a long part of my life I heard it in positive connotations: What could be more positive than a mother taking her child with her everywhere? Later in life I realized that most of the time, my mother was taking care of other children and not being uniquely available for me, since she was working there. That new observation brought me great sadness over something I had lost, something that had gotten ruined, but which explained the phenomena and processes shaping my personality.

And so I'm listening to the radio in a car in a faraway African village, and letting my tears flow. "Just missing home," I reassure myself, and continue watching the mother and her child. Some moments later I tell myself that I, too, carry my therapy clients with me all over the world. On the one hand, it means that I did not give up on them, even though the conditions for therapy were difficult. I did not "abort" them. On the other hand, I dragged them all over the world under difficult conditions for therapy, which was not the ideal situation for them.

I realize that I did my best, just as my mother did. This image of the infant needing its mother and receiving her care only partially softens inside me and brings me one more step toward acceptance. It helped me to encounter my mother and accept her with her limitations, and that helped me accept the mother that I am, with my limitations, all of which helped me to help Doreen and Oscar to accept their parenthood and to make room for a new baby.

Back home when I read the vignettes, I think that they could have taken place in a conventional setting rather than on the move in Africa, and nonetheless, I can feel the footprints of my journey on the therapy. I can see the parallel processes between them and myself. My accepting complexity and imperfection by allowing myself to wander through the world and realize my dreams without completely foregoing my professional life, helped the clients to make room for complexity and lack of perfection in their lives.

Not once throughout my trip did the couple ask where I was, or question the setting's discretionary aspect. I did not identify any curiosity or concern, which seemed a little odd to me. Later on, when this subject was raised they said that they were very curious but tried to respect my privacy, being very appreciative that their therapy was not interrupted.

Conclusion

My weekly couple therapy with Maya and Sam relates to the impact and unconscious significance of cut-offs in the line of connection. The second vignette from weekly therapy with Danny concerns the fear of acceptance revealed by difficulty in switching from in-the-room sessions to online sessions. The intensive couple therapy with Doreen and Oscar raises the issue of transference, and no less of countertransference; for I had as many issues as the couple. That case in particular reflects my own experience with the difficulties, the doubts and sensations, accompanying me throughout my journey as I attempted to fulfil my dream and yet, thanks to technology, maintain continuity of care for a couple in need.

The therapy sessions that took place while I was traveling became linked to certain sights and events occurring at each time and place. The therapy sessions—the tension of preparing for them, the excitement as they took place, and the processing afterwards—became an integral part of my journey. Just as I prepared albums with notes and photos, which are my personal diary of my journey, I also felt the need to write about my professional experience during the trip. I wouldn't suggest turning my personal situation into any generalized insights, but my experience may open our eyes to the growing practice of teletherapy in our open world, and the world of modern-style wanderers.

Reference

Stadter, M. (2013). The influence of social media and communications technology on self and relationships. In: J. S. Scharff (Ed.) *Psychoanalysis Online: Mental Health, Teletherapy, and Training*, pp. 3–13. London: Karnac.

CHAPTER TEN

Screen images: transitional and defensive internet use among LGBTQ adolescents and adults

Andi Pilecki (USA)

The internet can be relationally adaptive when it is used as a transitional space (Balick, 2014; Dryer & Lijtmae, 2007; Naso, 2011; Pilecki, 2015). Within this transitional space, individuals from marginalized communities can access otherwise unavailable and much needed recognition and support; those who suffer from impaired self-esteem can develop greater social and sexual confidence; adolescents can find expansive opportunities to explore and experiment with identity; and socially isolated individuals can begin to build bridges to the outside world and toward a more flexible, empathic sense of self and other. Furthermore, the internet might be used as a relational venue in which to negotiate tensions between closeness and distance, schizoid and depressive modes of relating (Klein, 1946), and false and true blends of self-expression (Winnicott, 1956). Of course, internet use can also be defensive, characterized by idealized or false self-presentation, psychic splits and disembodiment, social isolation, and the derailment of authentic relational engagement in real life. The quality of internet use, whether transitional or defensive, is informed by the internal object relations of the user and by how that world is enacted online. These enactments invariably emerge in our consulting rooms as screen images or vignettes described by patients, and we use them as grist to the therapeutic mill. For now, let us look at some possibilities for relationally adaptive forms of internet use.

Before I go on, I would like to offer one caveat. As the title suggests, I will be focusing on transitional and defensive internet use among LGBTQ (lesbian, gay, bisexual, transgender, queer) adolescents and adults. I happen to work primarily with LGBTQ patients, and as a queer therapist myself, am concerned by the paucity of LGBTQ narratives, especially from the perspective of LGBTQ people themselves, within the analytic literature. My hope is that this chapter will contribute to the growing conversation of Internet-age dynamics within the analytic community, as well as to a discussion of working analytically with LGBTQ patients in ways that move beyond binary and heteronormative assumptions regarding gender and sexuality. This topic, however, relates to a broad demographic scope and can be applied to any patient who uses the internet, which at this point in time would be most patients.

Transitional aspects of internet use

When asking the question of whether internet use is transitional or defensive, we must first consider what qualifies an object or space as transitional. Citing Winnicott, Joy Dryer and Ruth Lijtmae (2007) suggest that internet use serves a transitional role in the degree to which such use helps a person to "repair and rework an empathic connection with the primary object" (p. 52). In their paper, "Cybersex as twilight zone between virtual reality and virtual fantasy: Creative play space or destructive addiction," the authors present case material in which a patient's use of cybersex helps him to integrate previously split aspects of self and develop a positive internal self-image that buffers against the deleterious effects of an unrelenting superego.

Next we must consider what qualifies a relationship as real. Ronald Naso (2011) encourages us to avoid dichotomous thinking when it comes to this consideration. Online relationships can embody a vitality and authenticity, Naso asserts, that make them just as real as relationships offline, and they serve a transitional role in the degree to which they "transform linkages between one's past and one's present in an enriching way" (p. 30). Naso presents case material of an adolescent who, through a relationship formed within the cyber walls of the RPG (role-playing game) *Second Life*, becomes attuned to previously inaccessible capacities for empathy, compassion, and commitment.

Indeed, when teens speak for themselves about their experiences online, they often refer to this potential, and to the ways in which they find and support one another through social media sites, blogs, and other internet venues. These "digital natives" (Prensky, 2001) challenge the assumptions of generally well-meaning adults, those "digital immigrants" who often have understandable concerns about the dangers of meeting people online. Dreams of Hope, a performing arts troupe led by queer youth and allies (dreamsofhope.org) explore the transformative (and transitional) nature of online relationships in their musical play, *Webs*. Disillusioned and frustrated by the lack of representation of, and resonance with, their own life experiences in school lessons and subjects, these young people "struggle to make a narrative that includes their whole selves, through a post, a story, a selfie, a song" (Kruse, 2016). The transformative quality of this narrative and the transitional nature of the relationship between the two main characters, which is formed online, is conveyed through the following lyrics from the *Webs* song, "Arachne":

> You weave your lies
> Caught up in your own disguise
> You weave your lies
> And I'll open up their eyes
> I'll make you something so passionate
> So mercurial
> I'll use my will
> You use your spite
> I forgive you
> I forgive you

These lyrics speak to the characters' sharp, and observant criticism of a school curriculum that fails to incorporate the voices, mythology, and history of LGBTQ people and people of color. They sing of how they will tell their own truths, write their own narratives, many of which will be posted online for others to find and relate to. Through these experiences, they will transform one another and be transformed by one other, becoming, as they say, "passionate" and "mercurial." In the transitional space of their relationship, forged online, these characters will use their "will" and their "spite" to "transform linkages between past and present" and "repair and rework empathic connections" through the alchemy of mutual recognition and forgiveness.

Another defining feature of the transitional object is that it supports the individual's psychological progression toward acknowledging and accepting both similarities and differences in the other (Winnicott, 1953). Those generations that would be considered digital natives, from Millennials to the most recent Generation Z, have grown up with the overlapping trappings and advantages of the internet age. The internet offers unprecedented access to the endless spectrum of human identity and experience. Barriers that once separated people by class, race, nationality, sexual orientation, and religion are being broken down by this online window into the great human well of hopes, dreams, suffering, stories, songs, geopolitical landscapes, daily realities, similarities, and differences. While one can easily point to the ways in which life online promotes narcissistic modes of relating, I would argue that connections made via the World Wide Web might also promote empathy, compassion, and a broader understanding of and appreciation for diverse human experience.

In my interactions with adolescents, which have primarily been with those who identity as LGBTQ and have a special link to the cultural experiences and heritage of this community, I have been struck by the apparent values of this demographic. Certainly, as adolescents they can interact from within the bounds of the normal narcissism characteristic of this age, but I also note the following values: a shared agreement to be sensitive toward one another's vulnerabilities and challenges; a prohibition against "othering" one another or making fun of differences; a respect for and desire to understand one another's particular circumstances and identity experiences; and a keen attunement to power dynamics around privilege and oppression that benefit some while disadvantaging others. This is seen in internet campaigns such as #IllGoWithYou (2016), which was organized by young queer people with "passing privilege" (the ability to fly under the radar when it comes to gender expression and avoid potential social ire and discrimination). They took a pledge to support transgender and gender-expansive friends by accompanying them to bathrooms or other gender specific facilities that could feel unsafe or threatening. This emphasis placed by the Millennial and Z generations on the role of ally speaks to the value of seeing beyond the limits of their own lives, and can also be found in movements such as Black Lives Matter and Immigration Justice.

Elaborating on the democratizing element of social and digital media, Carol Leader (2014) states that these new platforms "create an increasing challenge to old hierarchies and foster new forms of collaboration, closeness and global connectedness" (p. 5). While family is still the primary carrier of culture (Scharff & Scharff, 1998), the growing accessibility of the internet, particularly through hand-held devices, gives the "old hierarchy" of the family system a run for its money when it comes to the role of culture carrier. If those of us working as analysts and psychotherapists want to remain attuned to the field that impacts the inner lives of patients, as well as ourselves, we would do well to follow the lead of the Millennial and Z generations, and widen our lens to explicitly include cultural considerations beyond the family, such as race, class, sexuality, and gender identity. To the aphorism "There is no such thing as an infant" (Winnicott, 1960) I would add, there is no such thing as a mother. Every mother lives and cares for the infant within the broader context of family, community, and culture (which includes the internet). The pressures, supports, influences, and problems of this context have an inextricable impact on the infant/mother dyad and the developmental process that shapes the internal world and sense of self.

Distinguishing transitional from defensive internet use: clinical considerations

In describing the qualities of the transitional object, Winnicott (1953) said that eventually the object becomes decathected, that is, it "loses meaning ... because the transitional phenomena have become diffused, have become spread out over the whole intermediate territory between 'inner psychic reality' and 'the external world as perceived by two persons in common', that is to say, over the whole cultural field" (p. 91). This speaks to one of the primary points of distinction between relationally adaptive and defensive internet use. A person may use the internet as a transitional space, eventually internalizing the experience and branching out toward broader relational and social contact offline, or may remain entombed within what Yolanda de Varela (2015) calls a "*desmentida*, a place of disavowal that negates reality and at the same time accepts its own reality as *the* reality" (p. 234). I will explore each potential by comparing two case examples.

Case material: J

J is a twenty-two-year-old transgender woman. She has been in once-weekly therapy for three years. When J was twelve years old, she lost a parent to cancer. As she moved further into adolescence, she experienced increasing gender dysphoria and depression, and turned increasingly inward and away from the world. By the time she was sixteen, her depression and anxiety had debilitated her to the point where she was missing significant amounts of school. As is the case for a growing number of adolescents, J decided to leave behind the social pressure she experienced within brick and mortar public school for the relative insulation of cyber-school. While such a decision can further isolate some teens who already struggle with profound feelings of alienation, this transition gave J the adolescent moratorium (Erikson, 1956) she needed to explore and experiment with her own identity in the relative anonymity of the internet (Lev, 2004), build meaningful connections that helped to buffer her developing sense of self against a harsh internal object world (Naso, 2011), and work through characterological difficulties toward achieving interpersonal resolutions (Turkle, 2004). In these ways, J had made use of the internet as a primarily transitional space toward greater connection with self and others.

J was able to begin the process of coming out with the support of relationships forged online in chat rooms, blogs, and RPGs. As is the case for many transgender and gender expansive individuals, these relationships provided the mirroring, validation, guidance, and support crucial to positive identity formation (Devor, 2004; Lev, 2004; Pilecki, 2015). From a developmental perspective, such connections are essential to the successful navigation of the adolescent psychosocial crisis of identity *vs.* role confusion, an achievement that paves the way for adaptive maneuvering of the next crisis, intimacy *vs.* isolation (Erikson, 1984). Furthermore, these relationships create a kind of container (Bion, 1965) in which relationally toxic experiences brought about by bullying, prejudice, and invisibility, can be detoxified and transformed. As the aforementioned *Webs* song suggests, within this process of detoxification, socially alienated teens use their "will" and their "spite" to make themselves and one another "something so passionate, so mercurial." In other words, through one another, they come back to life.

Certainly, J did. She went from barely leaving her house, to building friendships online that she extended into real life, initiating the transition process with family support, becoming involved with local community events and organizations, and eventually enrolling at a local university as a full-time student. She is also in a committed relationship with someone she initially met online, where she is fairly successfully navigating the terrain of intimacy *vs.* isolation, as well as negotiating and developing insight into characterological features and relational patterns.

It is doubtful that without the facilitating environment provided by the internet, J would have had access to this kind of transitional space. I do not want to paint a completely rose-colored image, however. J's internet experiences have not been free from problematic encounters. For example, early on in treatment, J spoke in wistful ways about a lover she had met online. While one of the apparent safety features of contemporary online relationships is that one can actually see the person with whom one is talking, J's lover said she was not ready to be seen. My suspicion increased as J continued to report that her lover kept putting off visual contact. Then one day, she came into session looking distraught, and explained that her online lover had apparently staged her own death in an attempt to cut off communication with J. This dealt a harsh blow to J's somewhat naive vision of the world and other people. Not only was she sad, but also she was embarrassed and angry that she'd been played for a fool. While the specifics of this situation are unique to the internet age, the experiences of wisdom gleaned through mistakes and betrayals are not. J emerged from this lesson with a greater appreciation for the process of discernment, a savvier sense of the world, and a more finely tuned understanding of the fundamental links between trust and intimacy.

Case material: S

S is a twenty-five-year-old transgender woman. She has been in once-weekly psychotherapy for about two years. S first came to therapy to address ongoing depression, anxiety, and problems related to attention and motivation. S's depression hit a level of severity during her first year of college, a year that she was unable to complete. She is highly intelligent, and did very well in school up until this point. My sense is that despite her intelligence, she has lacked social, emotional, and relational skills for some time but that this did not interfere significantly enough with school performance to demand intervention until she entered college.

S herself identifies with the term "sociopath," saying that she relates primarily to the anti-social, and shallow emotional and empathic, features of this disordered personality type. My diagnostic impression is more of an autism spectrum disorder, on the higher functioning end, which inhibits S's affective range, interferes with her capacity to understand and respond empathically to social and emotional cues, and leads to restricted and repetitive behaviors and interests. She also fits into what de Varela describes as the "schizoid generation" (2015, p. 234), that is, a generation of people who are reporting record-breaking levels of depression, which de Varela links to the object loss brought about by rapidly developing technology that replaces and distracts from actual human contact.

The degree to which internet use is harmful or defensive is generally associated with its addictive or dependent qualities (Dryer & Lijtmae, 2007). While she does not see it this way, S's internet use certainly qualifies as dependent, particularly in the extent to which it interferes with her engagement in other areas of life, such as school, work, and relationships. During her first and only year away from home at University, S sank into a deep depression and barely left her dorm room, missed almost all of her classes, and spent the majority of her time online. While she currently reports decreased depression and anxiety, S continues to spend most of her time online, playing RPGs (role playing games). She is particularly drawn to the multiplayer online battle arena genre, which, I believe, enables her to engage socially at a tolerable level, and offers a venue in which she can act out aggressive drives within a tightly controlled, and disembodied, environment. Her sleep patterns are inconsistent and out of synch with the regular operating of the world outside: she often stays up into the early morning hours playing RPGs and surfing the web, then sleeps until the mid- to late-afternoon. She also forgets to eat, which demonstrates another disconnect from her most foundational physical needs.

Discussing the relationship between schizoid states and over-reliance on technology, specifically RPGs, Naso (2011) explains, "RPGs attract individuals who struggle profoundly in the social sphere. They feel isolated from others, but, more significantly, from themselves-from their most basic wants, needs, and capacities" (p. 28). This resonates with the thesis of the final installment of Sherry Turkle's (2011) trilogy of analytically focused books on the impact of the internet on human relating, *Alone Together: Why We Expect More from Technology and Less from Each*

Other, in which she claims that while we are lonely, we are afraid of intimacy. Certainly, S's compulsive engagement in the world of RPGs speaks to both her need for connection and profound fears of intimacy. Unlike J, who eventually moved out of the confines of her bedroom into the wider world, S continues to live at home with her parents, on whom she is completely financially dependent because her avoidance of the outside world inhibits her from becoming gainfully employed. She has recently started taking classes at a local college, however, and we continue to consider the implications of excessive internet use in her life.

Summary of case material: J and S

These case examples highlight some of the primary differences between transitional and defensive internet use. For J, the internet provided a transitional space where she explored her identity and made progress toward a greater expression of true self (Winnicott, 1956), built relationships that helped her to effectively modify her internal object world (Scharff & Scharff, 2005), integrate previously split self-states (Dryer & Lijtmae, 2007), develop greater capacities for empathy, compassion, and commitment (Naso, 2011), shift from a more or less schizoid to depressive position (Klein, 1946), and fairly successfully navigate the psychosocial crisis of identity *vs.* role confusion (Erikson, 1984).

Conversely, S's internet use keeps her more tightly entombed within a schizoid state, or *desmentida*, where she denies the reality that her use is addictive and it further exacerbates problems she has with engaging in real life. Relationships developed online remain within the tightly controlled and fantasy-based atmosphere of the multi-player battle RPG, and while she reports that gaming helps her to develop problem-solving abilities, it does little to increase her capacity for empathy, compassion, or commitment. Her life is primarily lived online, and while voracious internet use is often an aspect of early transgender identity development, S stays frozen in place there, likely still grappling with issues related to identity, which prevents her from successfully approaching intimacy. This arrested development relates to significant, and paralyzing, anxiety linked to avoidance of separation/individuation. On an unconscious level, it seems she is terrified of leaving the safety and security of home, and therefore remains in a state of extended dependency. Linda Cundy (2015) discusses this state of suspension in adolescents addicted to online fantasy games, in a way that resonates with de Varela's description of *desmentida*, saying that they, "lose all relationship to real others and to time, cut off from contact with the rational world" (pp. 16–17).

Internet use as defensive

The case of S encapsulates some of the primary indicators of defensive, or non-transitional, internet use: dependency, isolation, and social withdrawal, encasement within a schizoid mode of relating, limited insight, and a severe disconnect from one's own physical and emotional needs. The use of internet and other digital technology may also reveal a kind of manic flight from vulnerability and the limitations imposed by time and space. Never before have we been able to be in so many places at once, or to be reached by the desires and demands of so many others. In her study of internet use, Turkle (2011) notes that one interviewee described feeling like a "Master of the Universe" as a result of the unprecedented multitasking abilities afforded to her through modern technology. Such a fantasy of transcending the boundaries of time and space is not unusual, and can often be heard in narratives of frustration, disappointment, and longing encountered in our consulting rooms. It is also embodied by the character "Samantha," in the film *Her* (2013). Samantha is a futuristic operating system (OS) designed to meet the complex relational needs of human beings. When she begins to recognize her own capacities as an OS, especially as compared to the human being with whom she is in a relationship, Samantha gloats that she is able to be everywhere and anywhere, and can grow in a way she could not if she were tethered in time and space by a body destined to perish.

Like Samantha, Turkle's interviewees seek to overcome the real limitations of being human, most notably, mortality. Thinking of this race to split oneself up into so many places and personae at once, I can't help but associate to Lord Voldemort, the super villain of J. K. Rowling's (1997) incredibly successful Harry Potter series. In his attempt to cheat death, Voldemort fractures his soul into multiple pieces and stores them in magical objects called "horcruxes." Turkle documents the tension in her interviewees between, on the one hand, wanting to master the universe, and on the other, feeling completely overwhelmed by and unable to keep up with the unrelenting demands of schedules without boundaries or breaks.

Whether a person feels integrated or further fractured depends on the degree to which they present a true, or false self, online (Balick, 2014). As discussed earlier in the case of J, some internet use can promote experimentation with, and eventual embodiment of, a self that more closely resembles the true end of the true-/false-self continuum. Conversely, more defensive internet use can rely on false self, or idealized self-expression, and a compulsive focus on pedaling a perfect presentation. One could argue that for as many opportunities for genuine engagement and expression that the internet affords, there are as many invitations to engage in narcissistically defensive self-branding and marketing, even in the pictures casually posted on social media outlets such as Facebook.

A patient once quipped that Facebook must be making therapists rich all over the world. At first glance this just seemed a pithy comment, but upon further consideration I realized how insightful and layered an observation this was. Over the years, I have had many patients bring up, often in somewhat sheepish or embarrassed tones, the real pain they have experienced while in the halls of social media sites, especially Facebook. One patient, who suffered from major depression and opioid addiction, and operated primarily from a false self-orientation (which, of course, contributed significantly to her depression), found confirmation through Facebook of her distorted perception that everyone else was perfectly happy, popular, and surrounded constantly by loving family and friends, while she suffered alone and completely unloved. These Facebook encounters triggered such painful transference experiences that she would be driven into suicidal states. Such perceptions arise from internal world dynamics projected out into the screen, which might be thought of as screen images that can be explored and made use of within the containment of therapy or analysis. I will now present more detailed case material that further illustrates the transferential power of social media experiences, particularly when used defensively in the service of promoting what is false in order to mask one's actual feelings of shame, inadequacy, and dread.

Case material: V

V is a thirty-two-year-old, queer-identified, cisgender woman. She has been in twice-weekly therapy for around four years. V is fairly successful in her vocation, and is always on the move, juggling multiple obligations at once. She acknowledges that she is reluctant to take time to relax because she can become uncomfortable with herself in the absence of external distractions and demands. V's internal object world is significantly influenced by childhood trauma, by her relationship with a depressed mother, and by the relational trauma she experienced among peers throughout primary and secondary school where she generally felt like an outsider and was frequently bullied. She is particularly avoidant of acknowledging and experiencing her own vulnerability, associating this with what she sees as the weakness that made her susceptible to abuse, and resists slowing her pace and relaxing because she is afraid she will sink into a depressive state where she will get lost like her mother. She seems to use constant activity as a way to rise above vulnerability, avoid contact with her own limitations, and drown out the voice of a harsh superego that, in a tone that echoes the voices of peers from childhood and adolescence, admonishes her for being inadequate, lazy, selfish, and weak. Through the process of therapy, V has made good progress toward modifying these internal object sets, and developing a more integrated sense of self. She can still find herself in triggering moments, however, when these harsh internal objects rise up and overwhelm her ego functioning.

In a recent session, we realized that such a chain of events was set in motion by her engagement with social media. She mentioned that she sometimes finds herself using social media compulsively. When I asked her what she meant by "compulsively," she said there are times when she initially goes online to post information about events, and ends up spending much more time than intended. With limited consciousness in the moment of the dynamics being provoked, she describes vignettes in which she finds herself caught in a web of enactments, which betray traces of her internal world and early relational experiences. First, she finds herself posting scenes from her life on social media sites, such as Facebook, and waiting in anxious anticipation to see how others respond. On a conscious level, she believes she wants positive feedback, and indeed, this is what she gets. People like, admire, and support her, and are undoubtedly impressed by her. Why wouldn't they be? She's incredibly talented and devoted to her craft. Unfortunately for V, this just isn't enough. Paradoxically, this feedback, while initially gratifying, fuels her belief that people only like her because she's successfully hidden her true self behind an idealized veneer. If they could really see how afraid, inadequate, and inferior she feels, they would inevitably laugh at and reject her, just as peers throughout childhood and adolescence did.

As V described her experience, I associated to a recent episode of the HBO series *Girls* (2016), in which Hannah, the protagonist played by the show's creator Lena Dunham, is having a conversation with Tally, an old friend from college, played by Jenny Slate. Hannah feels jealous of Tally because she has become a successful writer and, in a moment of truth, reveals her true feelings. Tally registers this statement on a level unanticipated by Hannah and goes on to tell her how incredibly isolated and lost she feels. She Googles herself on a daily basis to see if people are being complimentary or snarky because, she explains, seeing herself through their eyes is the only way she can see herself.

When I mentioned this association to V, her eyes widened as she immediately related to this reference. Furthermore, V explains that when she sees what friends and colleagues are doing through their posts on Facebook, she is overcome with envy and insecurity, and pervasive associations to feeling like an outsider. While V's initial motivation to engage in social media seems to be rooted in her longing for connection, the actual experience leaves her feeling alienated, insecure, and anxious, and it activates enactments informed by a childhood and adolescence defined by a persistent sense of estrangement and of not belonging.

Internet use as grist for the mill

Tiffany Schlain (2016), a filmmaker who is "committed to reframing technology as an expression of the best of what humanity is capable," insists that the internet is not something that is happening *to* us, but rather, that the internet *is* us (Schlain, 2016). For those of us tuned in to the internal lives of patients in our consulting rooms, this is a powerful, and deeply relevant idea. Balick (2014) asserts that the degree to which destructive patterns of social media use will be found, relates directly to the environmental failures experienced early on as defined by interruptions to what Winnicott called "good enough" mothering. These past failures are internalized, and will be enacted in the transference, and until then are experienced through contemporary relationships, including those online.

Do we, like J, experience the internet and those we meet online as primarily friendly and caring, using it as a transitional space through which to experiment with and embody true self? Do we, like S, use the internet as a psychic retreat in which to escape the relational and real life demands offline? Or do we, like V, intend to use the internet for primary functional reasons, but get caught up in a web of enactments that stir deep insecurities and reliance on false self-presentation? Of course, these are just three possibilities, and within each one there is the potential for divergence, variability, and modification. V, for example, upon becoming aware of the deleterious effects of her online persona, said that she was going to work on presenting a more honest depiction of herself on social media sites, essentially turning toward a more transitional use of internet space. J, while generally using the internet transitionally, can at times use it defensively and compulsively as a means of escape from grief-related anxiety and feelings of loneliness. Through internet gaming, S has developed problem-solving skills that could potentially be applied in life offline, such as in the career in computer programming she is considering. The key is that, as clinicians, we continuously hold in our minds a level of curiosity for the spectrum and contours of internet use, with a particular attunement to what this use tells us about the intrapsychic and relational dynamics at play in the lives of our patients.

As I hope the case material presented here demonstrates, online engagement can be thought of in much the same way as any other form of relating. Namely, this level of relationship and the enactments therein are reflective of internal world dynamics, and object relation sets informed by early attachment experiences. I hope that I have weaved together the literature, my observations, and case material in such a way as to promote flexible thinking about both the transitional and defensive aspects of internet use, and to contribute to the growing body of work on how to use internet experiences as grist to the therapeutic mill.

References

#IllGoWithYou (2016). An Ally Response to #WeJustNeedToPee (n.d.). Retrieved 23 May 2016 from http://www.illgowithyou.org/

Balick, A. (2014). *The Psychodynamics of Social Networking: Connected-up Instantaneous Culture and the Self*. London: Karnac.

Bion, W. R. (1965). *Transformations: Change from Learning to Growth*. London: Tavistock.

Cundy, L. (2015). *Love in the Age of the Internet: Attachment in the Digital Era*. London: Karnac.

De Varela, Y. (2015). Cyberspace as potential space. In: J. S. Scharff (Ed.), *Psychoanalysis Online 2: Impact of Technology on Development, Training, and Therapy* (pp. 233–238). London: Karnac.

Devor, A. (2004). Witnessing and mirroring: A fourteen stage model of transsexual identity formation. In: U. Leli & J. Drescher (Eds.), *Transgender Subjectivities: A Clinician's Guide* (pp. 41–67). Binghamton, NY: Hawthorn Medical Press.

Dryer, J. A., & Lijtmae, R. M. (2007). Cyber-Sex as twilight zone between virtual reality and virtual fantasy: Creative play space or destructive addiction? *The Psychoanalytic Review, 94*: 39–61.

Girls (2016). Love Stories (Television series, April 17 episode). L. Dunham, M. Brockman, & J. Kim (Writers). New York, NY: HBO.

Erikson, E. H. (1956). The problem of ego identity. *Journal of the American Psychoanalytic Association, 4*: 56–121.

Erikson, E. H. (1984). Reflections on the last stage—and the first. *Psychoanalytic Study of the Child, 39*: 155–165.

Her (2013). (Motion picture, Director, S. Jonze.) USA: Annapurna Pictures.

Klein, M. (1946). Notes on some schizoid mechanisms. *International Journal of Psycho-Analysis, 27*: 99–110.

Kruse, P. (Playwright) (2016). *Webs* (Musical). Pittsburgh, PA: Dreams of Hope. Retrieved 21 May 2016 from http://www.vimeo.com

Leader, C. (2014). Turned on: Romantic love, psychoanalysis and our attachments to new and social media. *Free Associations, 15*: 67–87.

Lev, A. I. (2004). *Transgender Emergence: Therapeutic Guidelines for Working with Gender-Variant People and Their Families*. New York: Routledge.

Naso, R. C. (2011). Role-playing games: Bridge or barrier to object relationships in socially isolated teens? *PsycEXTRA Dataset*.

Pilecki, A. (2015). Transitional space: The role of Internet community for transgender and gender non-conforming patients. In J. S. Scharff (Ed.), *Psychoanalysis Online 2: Impact of Technology on Development, Training, and Therapy* (pp. 53–66). London: Karnac.

Prensky, M. (2001). Digital natives, digital immigrants, Part 1. *On the Horizon, 9*: 1–6.

Rowling, J. K. (1998). *Harry Potter and the Sorcerer's Stone*. New York, NY: A.A. Levine Books.

Scharff, J. S., & Scharff, D. E. (1998). *Object Relations Individual Therapy*. Northvale, NJ: Jason Aronson.

Scharff, J. S., & Scharff, D. E. (2005). *The Primer of Object Relations*. Lanham, MD: Jason Aronson.

Schlain, T. (2016). Growing up the Internet. In: K. Tippett (Producer), *On Being* (audio podcast). Retrieved May 21, 2016 from http://www.onbeing.org

Turkle, S. (2004). Whither psychoanalysis in computer culture? *Psychoanalytic Psychology, 21*: 16–30.

Turkle, S. (2011). *Alone Together: Why We Expect More from Technology and Less from Each Other*. New York, NY: Basic Books.

Winnicott, D. W. (1953). Transitional objects and transitional phenomena—a study of the first not-me possession. *International Journal of Psycho-Analysis, 34*: 89–97.

Winnicott, D. W. (1956). On transference. *International Journal of Psycho-Analysis, 37*: 89–97.

Winnicott, D. W. (1960). The theory of the parent–infant relationship. *International Journal of Psycho-Analysis, 41*: 585–595.

CHAPTER ELEVEN

Couple psychotherapy settings and change in the digital age

Amita Sehgal (UK)

Electronic communication has a powerful impact on the way we conduct our daily lives. In this chapter I explore the influence of the digital revolution on our professional lives, in particular on the provision and practice of psychoanalytic couple psychotherapy. I attend to the importance of the setting within which psychotherapy is delivered over the internet and illustrate circumstances in which couple therapy was provided online. I discuss the advantages and disadvantages of providing psychotherapy online versus the traditional analytic setting. I conclude with my ideas on how transformational change occurs in couple therapy in which sessions are conducted in cyberspace.

Innovations in digital information technology represent a revolution that has fundamentally changed the way people think, behave, communicate, and work. Digital technology has made it possible to digitize information thus enabling words and images to be recorded in binary combinations of the digits 0 and 1, also called bits (Compaine, 2001). Digitizing information in this way has two advantages: large amounts of data can be compressed and preserved on small portable storage devices; and data transmission is speeded up. Through creating innovative ways of storing and disseminating information, the digital revolution has forged new ways of connecting people across geographical locations and time zones. Advances in mobile telephone technology, for instance, have now made it possible to use the cellphone to send and receive text messages and emails, make voice calls, and connect to the internet for activities ranging from accessing social media websites to online banking.

In the field of psychotherapy, clinicians have increasingly begun to use digital media to exchange information and communicate with one another, in addition to using its various forms for supervision and for working with clients (Caparrotta & Lemma, 2014). A recent preliminary survey carried out by the British Psychoanalytic Society revealed that thirty-one percent of respondents had conducted analysis over the telephone or via Skype (Fornari-Spoto, 2011). Skype is a type of software application of the Voice over Internet Protocol (VoIP) technology, specializing in providing voice calls and video conferencing online. It allows registered users to communicate by voice using a microphone, video by using a webcam, and instant messaging over the internet. Much of the service is free of cost (www.skype.com/en/about).

In addition to this, in our clinical practice we find ourselves increasingly working with the psychic significance on clients of cyberspace and digitally mediated communication (Balick, 2014; Scharff, 2015). This includes a range of Internet-mediated activities such as online addictive gaming, gambling, shopping, and pornography; social networking and internet dating; and staying in touch with loved ones around the globe through the use of videoconferencing software such as Skype (Cundy, 2015).

VoIP-mediated psychotherapy alters the conventional way in which psychotherapy takes place. In this chapter I explore whether videoconferencing technology interferes with, and intrudes upon, the traditional practice of couple psychotherapy, in which the couple and the therapist are physically present together in a consulting room; or whether it might be possible to regard digital technology as an aid to the provision of couple psychotherapy in certain circumstances, provided it remains grounded in theory and adheres to professional practice guidelines. I draw upon my experience of using VoIP software to conduct therapy with couples in order to explore some of the implications for the analytic setting of practicing in this way. Attachment and object relations theories form the framework within which I explore the difficulties encountered during this process to arrive at understanding. I hope that, in doing so, I contribute to a broader discussion on whether training and professional bodies might now need to consider training and develop guidelines for practitioners using VoIP software in clinical practice.

The setting in couple psychotherapy

Couple psychotherapists are currently trained to provide psychotherapy to clients where therapist and clients sit together in the same space, typically in the therapist's consulting room, across from and facing one another. The sessions are generally an hour in duration and take place at the same day and time every week. At the end of each calendar month clients are presented with an invoice for sessions delivered during that month. The transaction of presenting the bill and receiving payment is made in person between client and therapist.

Psychoanalytic couple psychotherapy training emphasizes the importance of setting, maintaining and preserving the framework within which psychotherapy takes place. Couple psychotherapists understand this as a vital part of the therapeutic work that enables the transference/countertransference processes to develop. But not all couples can get to the office of a competent couple therapist. The conventional practice of face-to-face couple psychotherapy is limited by geography.

Technological innovations present clinicians with the opportunity of circumventing the geographic restrictions of psychotherapy, thereby expanding its accessibility to clients around the world (Bouchard et al., 2004; Manhal-Baugus, 2001). Some practitioners have responded to the digital revolution by saying that "the present state of modern telecommunications … must be taken as a new opportunity to allow for the implementation of analysis beyond the walls of the psychoanalyst's office" (Carlino, 2010, p. 3) thus expanding access to individual treatment. Others have found it "difficult to accept the argument that psychoanalysis, or we psychoanalysts, have to chase after the changing times and society. Our task," they argue, "is to understand and interpret change" (Argentieri & Amati Mehler, 2003, p. 18). Though some resist harnessing technology to the therapeutic task, others increasingly embrace it.

Psychotherapy via videoconferencing is on the rise (Drum & Littleton, 2004). It has been found to be both an effective alternative to face-to-face work (Maheu & Gordon, 2000) and a way to provide access to therapy for clients who may otherwise not receive it (Nelson & Bui, 2010). The increasing availability of high-speed internet connections and the advent of new technologies such as VoIP offer an opportunity to simulate face-to-face therapy, not only in individual therapy. I have found that couples request therapy over the internet for a variety of reasons and I present some of these differing circumstances below. But first, an introduction to the technology that couple therapists are using.

VoIP software

Voice over Internet Protocol (VoIP) is a term that refers to Internet-based software applications that allow registered users to make cost-free calls via the internet, enabling audio/video calls between two computers irrespective of their geographical location. Two well-known VoIP applications are Skype and VSee. They work similarly, but there are some differences between the two.

Skype is a market-dominant, free, consumer-grade platform from Skype Communications, a division of Microsoft Corporation (www.skype.com/en/about). It is widely used by families and friends for keeping in touch, and has been applied in clinical work with false confidence in its encryption. In 2013 Glenn Greenwald, an American lawyer and columnist for *The Guardian* US newspaper, published documents that were provided to him by Edward Snowden, a former contractor of the US National Security Agency. This event formed part of what is now termed the 2013 mass surveillance disclosures. In a follow-up article written in the week following the 2013 mass surveillance disclosures, Greenwald revealed "Microsoft has granted intelligence agencies unfettered access to … Skype communication content" (Greenwald, Ackerman, Laura, MacAskill, & Rushe, 2013).

VSee is another major software application, but unlike Skype, VSee is a medical-grade platform. VSee is compliant with the Health Insurance Portability and Accountability Act (HIPAA). HIPAA works to keep patients' medical information private by setting minimum standards for the protection of the confidentiality of all electronic health information (Fitzgerald, Hunter, Hadjistavropoulos, & Koocher, 2010). Communication via VSee is securely encrypted during transmission from endpoint to endpoint. Information is not stored on any VSee servers and VSee does not have access to the decryption keys. This adds a layer of security to the use of videoconference in clinical practice because information leakage during transmission is prevented (http://www.VSee.com/blog) and so clinical conversations remain confidential.

For VoIP-mediated psychotherapeutic work with couples I use the VSee software application in preference to Skype.

VoIP-mediated psychotherapy for couples

Living abroad

Some couples have approached me because they live in areas that are quite remote and so would have to travel long distances to see a qualified couple psychotherapist. For these couples the effort involved in accessing help in this way felt strenuous and the expense would become prohibitive to the process.

Two elderly partners sought couple therapy to help them communicate more effectively with each other. They requested "Skype therapy" because they were not fluent in the language of the country in which they currently resided, and were seeking an English-speaking therapist. I told them I could not work on Skype but that they could just as easily download VSee and I would work with them using that software. Before committing to working with this couple, however, I suggested they travel to meet me for two in-person consultations where we were all physically present, and they agreed. Following the two assessment meetings that took place in my consulting room in London, I formed the view that embarking on couple therapy was probably not necessary for the couple at that point in time. The partners were advanced in age and living four hours' drive away from each other. Each suffered from loneliness and wanted a closer relationship with the other but they were too frightened to reveal this vulnerable side of themselves for fear of scaring the other off. Through the two assessment consultations we uncovered their hope of treatment was that a couple therapist might form a conduit through which they could safely express their desire for each other without fear of being abandoned. Once this shared anxiety had been voiced during the two consultations, both partners felt reassured and confident that they could progress in their relationship on their own, and that couple therapy was not necessary going forward. But they knew that, should they have need for it going forward, they could have therapy with me using VSee.

In a war-torn zone with poor internet connection

On another occasion partners who resided in a war-torn zone contacted me via email explaining that the ongoing long-term difficulties in their relationship had recently reached a crisis point for which they now needed professional help unavailable locally. As in the previous case, we agreed that the initial consultation would take place during their upcoming trip to London. During this meeting the couple explained that whilst VoIP-mediated therapy was the most viable option for them to access psychological help, the process would not be straightforward. They were mindful that frequent fluctuations in the signal strength of Wi-Fi at their end would inevitably affect the quality of the Internet-based connection. Running alongside this, they highlighted, was the threat of unpredictable and unplanned electricity cuts that could result in a total loss of connection for a few moments, at least until the temporary electricity generators switched on. With this in mind we jointly agreed to embark upon an extended assessment period where a further four sessions would take place via VSee upon their return home. We felt this arrangement provided us with an opportunity to assess the viability of working through this modality.

At the end of this assessment period, which had largely gone well, we agreed to continue working together on the understanding that they would travel to London periodically for sessions in my consulting room. The couple accepted this flexible work schedule, of switching between VSee-mediated sessions and in-the-office therapy, and over the course of their treatment this arrangement worked well.

There were technical drawback, however. When the Wi-Fi signal strength wavered, the sound of the couple's voices became distorted and asynchronous with the image on the screen. Sometimes the image on the screen froze mid-sentence and the couple was unable to hear or see me. In these moments the train of thought quickly shifted to re-establishing the lost connection. Re-establishment of contact resulted in palpable relief on both sides, often signaled by a brief smile or laugh by them and me. We accepted the possibility of interruptions as part of the treatment contract. In this treatment, the frozen-screen interruptions were largely infrequent, but when session time was lost due to disruptions in the internet connection, it was not made up.

The temporarily dysregulating experience of technical interruptions reminded me of the emotional disturbance observed in the "still-face paradigm," an experiment that involved filming mothers playing with their three-month-old infants (Tronick, Brazelton, & Als, 1978). Tronick's test consists of two minutes of play between mother and child, followed by two minutes where mothers maintain a still, non-responsive facial stance, and then a final two minutes where mothers resume normal playful interaction with their infants. The researchers found that during the maternal still-face period the infants "attempted to solicit the mother's attention, and when their efforts failed they looked away, withdrew, and expressed sad and angry effect" (Tronick, 2007, p. 11). Some infants appeared to become confused and found it difficult to re-engage with mother following the maternal still-face phase.

Some couples with early histories of misattunement might be thrown off by technical difficulties and experience them as empathic failures. In this example, the commitment displayed by both parties to re-establishing contact appeared to strengthen the therapeutic alliance. This is in keeping with Tronick's observation that "infants who experience frequent repairs of minor interactive errors (e.g., misreading of cues) during mother–infant face-to-face play were likely to elicit their mothers' attention using smiles and vocalizations during the still face. Infants who experienced fewer repairs were more likely to become distressed" (Tronick, 2007, pp. 312–313). Tronick concluded that infants who regularly experience the ability to repair a rupture in relationships develop a sense of effectiveness, and of the "mother as responsive and sensitive" (Tronick, 2007, p. 313).

Reeves (2015) reports VoIP technology has given her the opportunity to better understand and strengthen the therapeutic alliance by continuing the therapy through this medium as a way of navigating a break in therapy that would have been detrimental to the work. Under these circumstances she has found it helpful, and integral to the therapeutic process, to discuss the rupture-repair cycle and the clients' experience of physical distance versus the access to the therapist, which bridges the distance. Here the client's distress at becoming separated from the therapist is alleviated by the comforting provision of contact with the therapist.

Another drawback of working via VoIP is that the visual sensory information available for analysis is limited, resulting in the therapist inevitably missing the subtle nonverbal interactions that pass between partners. In thinking about working with the restricted view of the client and therapist on the screen, Bayles (2012) asks, "Is seeing the physical presence of the patient/analyst different from being in their physical presence? Or, is actual physical presence an intrinsic element of the analytic process" (Bayles, 2012, p. 572). This is an important factor to consider, one that I found affected the overall richness of the therapeutic encounter. For example, in a session that took place during this couple's visits to London, I noticed the wife was touching the husband's knee whilst talking about a long-standing grievance in the marriage. I have no doubt that this gesture would have gone unnoticed by me during a VSee session where the camera generally only captures an image of the couple's head and shoulders. However, during the in-person session I was able to notice and comment on this visual information and, in turn, engage the couple in exploring the meaning of this nonverbal gesture in the context of their relationship. This led to us opening up a hitherto unexplored area in the couple dynamic of the anxiety inherent in expressing discontent to an object perceived as psychically fragile.

Relocating to live and work overseas

There have been instances where couples in regular, ongoing psychotherapeutic work have had to relocate. Instead of losing their therapeutic relationship, they have asked to continue the weekly work via VoIP-mediated software. In one case the husband of a couple in weekly psychotherapy explained that the company he worked for now required him to relocate to another continent for a period of two to four years. The request to move had come unexpectedly and with some urgency. Although the move symbolized a promotion in salary and status within the firm, it involved a great upheaval of their lives and that of their relatively young children. Both partners expressed their need for therapy to continue during this period of transition, and felt strongly opposed to its premature termination. Here VoIP-mediated therapy presented a kind of "therapeutic compromise" (Scharff, 2014, p. 48). For a couple settling in to a new life abroad, VSee presented an opportunity to maintain an already established couple analytic relationship that otherwise was threatened by premature termination.

With this particular couple, a move to working via VSee introduced a layer of complexity to the setting that felt harder to manage remotely. For example, the importance of establishing the therapeutic space virtually came early on in the move abroad. During one of the first cyber-sessions the husband began the session by chatting as if he was on a social call. I quickly realized that both partners had begun to use VoIP-mediated software to keep in touch with their family and friends back home, and my demeanor was the only trigger that rekindled the couple's memory of the therapeutic space within which our contact was now taking place.

An added complexity to working in this way was that when the couple were in conflict, the tensions already present in the relationship became heightened and enacted between the partners, as they were artificially forced to sit almost touching each other so that their computer's in-built camera could capture their images within the frame of the screen.

During one such cyber-session the couple placed their call at their appointed time. As I accepted the call, the screen revealed the couple sitting close together with the husband's eyes cast downwards and the wife looking firmly into the camera. The stony silence between them felt palpable. Within seconds the wife launched into a description of how he had let her down and had not kept her needs in mind because he was always preoccupied with, and prioritizing, work. She understood he had a lot to do in this new job but she too was struggling to adjust to their lives overseas in unfamiliar surroundings. She felt he didn't know how hard it was for her, and often she felt he didn't care. She spoke with an uninterruptable intensity for about ten minutes, maybe more. During this time I noticed her husband had begun to stir in his seat. He lifted his head and turned to look away from both the computer screen/camera and his wife. As his wife continued to speak he sat back in his chair, still looking away, and his body began to jiggle in a way that made me think he might have been impatiently shaking one or both legs. Then he leant back in his chair, yawned, and stretched himself. All this while his wife, undistracted by her husband's physical agitation, continued to relay a string of incidents that had occurred in the week that illustrated how he did not notice her or take her feelings into account.

After she stopped speaking, there was silence between the partners. Neither spoke. Addressing the husband I asked what was going on inside him in response to what his wife had been saying. He said she had gone on for far too long. He wished her boring speech had been shorter. Then he looked at me and smiled as if to reduce the impact of what he had just said. I suggested that perhaps he was conveying a wish that her list of complaints against him were shorter. He fell silent again.

I wondered if he found it hard to talk about his emotional response to what she had been saying even though he had physically conveyed discomfort and impatience whilst she had been speaking. He said he thought her negative experiences of their interaction were excessive and over-inflated but he also wondered if she had a point, that perhaps he was being inattentive to her.

His response stumped me, and I fell silent. He seemed to be offering his view of her response alongside being self-reflective—it sounded balanced—but something felt missing. I noticed his wife staring expectantly at me, not him. He too was looking at me, smiling. It was as if the space was now mine, to fill. Internally I went over the session so far: she had spoken, laying out her thoughts in a way that did not invite or encourage discussion. Then he had done similarly. My attempt to engage him in conversation about his feelings had failed. Now I was also left wondering what she felt observing me talking to her husband about her. Emotional intercourse between the partners, and between couple and myself, did not seem possible. In wanting more emotional contact with each of them I became filled with a desire to bore into them with my curiosity. My frustrated attempts at engaging this couple in being curious about themselves and about each other's experiences filled me with hopelessness.

I addressed the husband once more. I asked if he recognized times when he needed his wife but she was unavailable to him either because she was away or engaged with their children. He said yes, there were plenty of such occasions on a weekly basis but he understood she was busy setting up their home in this new country as well as settling their children at new schools and also at home. He felt bad that he wasn't able to help her more but he had work pressures of his own which he didn't want to burden her with, so he managed without her. What he found difficult was she didn't offer him the same kind of understanding that he offered her, but instead angrily highlighted his shortcomings. I wondered whether in the moments he wanted time with his wife but found her occupied with other things, could he let her know that he needed her? He seemed both surprised and interested by my question. Indeed the idea that he might tell her when he needed her to be more attentive to him was a novel one that had never previously occurred to him. At this point his wife his wife interrupted him saying this was nonsense because he frequently asked her to do things for him. Over the years they have been together this had irritated her as she felt she did a lot for him but got little in return. But now she had so much to do with relocating their lives, that his demands were not only unwelcome but maddeningly insensitive. She complained that he rarely called or texted her during the day to see how she was managing, and at night he returned home exhausted with little energy for conversation. She would tell him about their children's day over dinner but he seemed so preoccupied that if she stopped speaking they would eat in silence. This is why recently she had taken to leaving his dinner in the oven to eat on his own when he returned home. She reasoned he could have a taste of his own medicine, after all he excluded her from his life, behaving as if she didn't exist yet he gave her a list of chores to do for him. This infuriated her and inflamed her ongoing dissatisfaction with him. She agreed that she expressed this harshly and critically, but that was because she felt he took no notice of her complaints.

Internally I went back to the start of the session. I thought of my becoming flooded with detail as the wife spoke but not quite remembering what she had been talking about, and my observing his seeming disengagement. I noticed that my countertransference response stemmed not from a wish to exclude her from my mind, but to protect my mind from being invaded by her thoughts that were coming in fast and furious and were threatening to fragment my thinking. I linked this with feeling utterly hopeless following my frustration of not being able to engage in any meaningful way with either partner.

I offered my impression that each of them struggled to separate out their requirement for some individual space in which they attended to things significant to them individually but in the service of their family, like his going to work and her current focus on homemaking, from a shared couple space in which they needed the other to be attentive to them as they transitioned through life-altering changes together. I drew a mental image of a Venn diagram, a mathematical representation of two circles placed side-by-side but with a central area of overlap, the circles symbolizing each partner and the clearly demarcated area of overlap signifying their shared couple space. The partners found this image helpful and began to use it to talk about what they needed from each other.

The husband expressed experiencing great happiness, contentment even, when he felt her attention was on him. He explained that hearing her talk of her own and their children's struggles as they worked to settle into a new life abroad often left him wondering if the move had been worth it. He had felt unable to share this with her, fearful of inviting more criticism. He explained that all he wanted was to have that lovely feeling between them again, and that it was his search to recreate this lovely feeling that fueled his requests to her to do things for him. But it seemed to have backfired and her criticisms wounded him so he kept his distance. The wife said that when he showed interest in her day and the activities within it, and similarly shared his day with her, she felt close to him and cared for by him. We were now nearing the end of the session and as I called it to a close I voiced my observation that the partners seemed to be listening attentively and with interest to each other's struggles but that both were expressing a shared need for closeness with the other. Both agreed and laughingly contrasted the way they had begun the session with not speaking to each other—indeed he had not wanted to attend at all—to the way they were now ending the session—engaged and keen to carry on talking with each other.

This clinical example illustrates the value of providing therapy via VSee to a couple who faced premature termination to their ongoing therapy. VSee enabled the therapeutic work to continue as the couple adapted themselves and their family to their new life in unfamiliar surroundings. The act of sitting in front of the camera at the start of this session seemed to latch onto the couple's dynamic struggles. Having to physically sit close to each other in order to fit in front of the computer's camera highlighted how angry and how divided they were. Sitting together seemed to echo the sense of being thrown together in a foreign land and not having enough resources to cope. Each partner heavily depended upon the other to navigate this transition for the couple, particularly at the beginning of the move. However, as each struggled with trying to do their best in managing the disruptions to their family's routine, it came at the cost of their ability to openly express their need for each other. Each felt deprived of attentive care from the other, leaving both partners feeling uncared for. Here continuing therapy via VSee provided the opportunity of maintaining continuity with a familiar therapist seated in a familiar consulting room (the background being visible to the couple) and enabled them to reconnect with each other in a meaningful way.

Traveling for work

Some couples that travel extensively for work have requested VoIP-mediated therapy in preference to missing a week's session. One such couple described how the constancy of the therapeutic contact within their jet-setting lifestyle seemed to settle them somehow, especially as during business trips abroad they would often wake up and work in one city, then in the evenings travel to another city to sleep in preparation for the following day's appointments. For this couple it seemed as if the therapeutic contact symbolized a secure base (Bowlby, 1993) in which the couple felt safe and held. To miss a session felt too disturbing. The internal sense of disorientation was compounded by the effects of jet lag as they traversed multiple time zones often within the same week. In addition to enabling them to circumvent feelings of loss and abandonment as they travelled, it seemed as if maintaining continuity with the therapeutic encounter via VoIP provided some kind of umbilical connection for each of the partners, from which they appeared to draw the resources needed to stabilize them as they operated in an ever-changing external environment.

Discussion

The internet alters the traditional therapeutic relationship in a myriad ways. For a start, in VoIP-mediated therapy the image on the computer screen replaces as well as represents the therapist or the couple. This inevitably affects the intimacy and privacy of the analytic relationship till the therapist and clients become accustomed to its presence (Sabbadini, 2015). Another difference is that, unlike therapy taking place in the analytic consulting room, VoIP-mediated therapy requires that the therapist and client share a virtual space, the cyberspace. This has implications for the formalities surrounding the analytic contact where, for example, instead of going to the consulting room and announcing one's arrival clients now must go online and make a VoIP-mediated call from their computer. Handling of payment for sessions, too, becomes altered as the clients are emailed their invoices and payment is directly credited to the therapist's bank account (in preference to a check in the post).

Sabbadini (2015) points out that conducting an analysis in cyberspace does away with the physical body of the therapist and the client, and that this inevitably will have repercussions on the transference and countertransference phenomenon of the analytic process. In her paper "Transference: The total situation" Betty Joseph (1985) develops Klein's (1952) idea that the analytic encounter is the stage upon which everything the client brings into the analytic relationship might be viewed as being part of the transference. This raises the question of how this relates to VoIP-mediated therapy. For instance, what do transference enactments in VoIP-mediated therapy look like? My experience of working with couples echoes Scharff's observation that "[a]s the sessions continue over time … [t]ransference flourishes … as in real life, evokes a countertransference response from the analyst, and the transference–countertransference dialectic is analysed as it would be in in-person sessions" (Scharff, 2014, p. 53).

I have encountered resistance being expressed through the couple forgetting to call or calling late because one partner got held up elsewhere. Sometimes one or both partners have begun the session chatting as if on a social call. One of them may move away from the camera so the face is hidden or partially visible (possibly reflecting a wish to hide distress or not be seen by the therapist, or sit far from the partner and avoid the therapist). Late payment or non-payment of fees is another area where enactments can occur. For instance, as we were coming up to my two-week break over Christmas, one couple cleared December's invoice via bank transfer but held back twenty-five percent of the full amount. Upon resuming our work together we were able to understand this within the context of the themes the couple were struggling with, namely painful feelings associated with experiencing abandonment, exclusion, and a lack of control within their relationship with each other and also with me.

Theory of change in online couple therapy

These examples raise the question of how transformational change occurs in couple psychotherapy conducted using VoIP software. Is change effected by the couple therapist working in the transference, or by her providing a containing framework so that the couple can work at their difficulties in an ongoing way? From an object relations perspective, we would say that the dynamic intersubjective relationship generated between the therapist and the couple presents the opportunity to work in the transference and for transference interpretations to be made (Baranger, 1993). From an attachment perspective we might emphasize the setting over the transference–countertransference dimension. Bowlby's attachment theory focuses upon the importance of the therapeutic process presenting a secure and reliable base from which individuals can freely explore themselves and their relationships. He viewed the therapeutic encounter as providing the environment within which change might occur. We can think of the cyber-session as one that extends the secure base and protects against loss and abandonment.

Winnicott (1971) looked beyond the provision of a secure base for going on being, to the provision of the "play area" for doing and imagining. Extending Winnicott's idea of the "play area" to the cyber-session, we can think of the cyber-session as a space for creative thought, one that belongs neither wholly to the therapist nor to the couple, but one that arises from their relatedness. The cyber-session provides the room for something different to develop and grow.

Bion's concept of containment (Bion, 1962) underpins the psychoanalytic approach to couple psychotherapy where the therapist's capacity to take in the couple's projections and think about the feelings being communicated, and then return it in a "transformed condition" (Bion, 1965), gradually enables the couple to make sense of what is going on in their relationship. It is hoped that over time as the partners become more able to internalize this capacity for themselves, their relationship functions more effectively.

The couple therapist's role, therefore, of thinking with couples about how each partner tries to communicate their affective experience to each other remains, irrespective of the setting. Is the traditional setting in which couple and therapist are in the same room a prerequisite for the analytic process to unfold and for effective therapeutic work to occur? The intersubjective encounter between the therapist and the couple involves the therapist's ability to be attuned to his or her own internal emotional states as well as to that of each of the partners. Provided the basic ethical and technical parameters are maintained, planned alterations to the psychoanalytic setting "can be advantageous to both analysts and patients, should be welcome whenever their enforcement improves the quality of the work and are anyway inevitable as the external environment … Evolves" (Sabbadini, 2015, p. 29). However, he stresses that for distance analysis to work in ways similar to classic analysis, the constancy and consistency of the setting needs to be rigorously preserved, that is to say, the sessions take place at regular times and intervals, each party calling in from a constant location. The same holds for couple analysis and couple psychotherapy.

Conclusion

The human instinct to reach out to another in times of potential danger, anxiety, or illness persists throughout life. Technological advances enable communication across geographical space and time zones, offering the possibility of maintaining emotional connections with significant others. It can promote psychic survival by making others readily accessible and can engender feelings of security. Equally, if mismanaged, where for example, boundaries become blurred and contact arrangements are not firmly adhered to, it can equally accentuate anxieties associated with insecure patterns of attachment.

Clearly not all couples can accept psychotherapy in these modified forms of analytic couple psychotherapy, but it may not just be that some couples are unsuitable, but also that some couple analysts cannot make good use of these new media (Caparrotta & Lemma, 2014). Sabbadini warns that "psychoanalysis in its traditional form might soon become a curiosity from the past" (Sabbadini, 2015, p. 32). The psychoanalytic community is urged to respond proactively to the electronic revolution to ensure the continual survival and relevance of the profession in the rapidly advancing digital age. With practice, analytic couple therapists who become comfortable with technology can offer effective treatment with couples who respect the setting of cyberspace.

References

Argentieri, S., & Amati Mehler, J. (2003). Telephone analysis: "Hello, who's speaking?" *Insight, 12*: 17–19.

Balick, A. (2014). *The Psychodynamics of Social Networking: Connected-Up Instantaneous Culture and the Self*. London: Karnac.

Baranger, M. (1993). The mind of the analyst: From listening to interpretation. *International Journal of Psychoanalysis, 74*: 15–24.

Bayles, M. (2012). Is physical proximity essential to the psychoanalytic process? An exploration through the lens of skype. *Psychoanalytic Dialogues: The International Journal of Relational Perspectives, 5*: 569–585.

Bion, W. R. (1962). *Learning from Experience*. London: Heinemann.

Bion, W. R. (1965). *Transformations*. London: Heinemann.

Bouchard, S., Paquin, B., Payeur, R., Allard, M., Rivard, V., Fournier, T., Renaud, P., & Lapierre, J. (2004). Delivering cognitive-behaviour therapy for panic disorder with agoraphobia in videoconference. *Telemedicine Journal and e-Health: the official journal of the American Telemedicine Association, 10*: 13–24.

Bowlby, J. (1993). *A Secure Base: Clinical Applications of Attachment Theory*. London: Routledge.

Caparrotta, L., & Lemma, A. (2014). Introduction. In: A. Lemma & L. Caparrotta (Eds.), *Psychoanalysis in the Technoculture Era* (pp. 1–21). Routledge: Hove.

Carlino, R. (2011). *Distance Psychoanalysis*. London: Karnac.

Compaine, Benjamin M. (Ed.) (2001). *The Digital Divide: Facing a Crisis or Creating a Myth*. Cambridge, MA: MIT Press.

Cundy, L. (2015). Attachment, self-experience, and communication technology. In: L. Cundy (Ed.), *Love in the Age of the Internet: Attachment in the Digital Era* (pp. 1–29). London: Karnac.

Drum, K., & Littleton, H. (2014). Therapeutic boundaries in telepsychology: Unique issues and best practice recommendations. *Professional Psychology: Research and Practice*, *45*: 309–315.

Fitzgerald, T., Hunter, P., Hadjistavropoulos, T., & Koocher, G. (2010). Ethical and legal considerations for internet-based psychotherapy. *Cognitive Behaviour Therapy*, *39*: 173–187.

Fornari-Spoto, G. (2011). Feasibility study of a psychodynamic online group intervention for depression. *The Bulletin of the British Psychoanalytical Society*, *47*: 7–11.

Greenwald, G., Ackerman, S., Laura, P., MacAskill, E., & Rushe, D. (2013). How Microsoft handed the NSA access to encrypted messages. *The Guardian* (London). 11 July 2013.

Joseph, B. (1985). Transference: The total situation. In: E. Bott Spillius & M. Feldman (Eds.), *Psychic Equilibrium and Psychic Change: Selected Papers of Betty Joseph*. London: Routledge.

Klein, M. (1952). The origins of transference In: *The Writings of Melanie Klein, Vol. 3* (pp. 48–56). London: Hogarth, 1975.

Lemma, A., & Caparrotta, L. (Eds.) (2014). *Psychoanalysis in the Technoculture Era*. Hove: Routledge.

Maheu, M., & Gordon, B. (2000). Counseling and therapy on the Internet. *Professional Psychology: Research and Practice*, *31*: 484–489.

Manhal-Baugus (2001). E-therapy: Practical, ethical, and legal issues. *CyberPsychology & Behavior*, *4*: 551–563.

Nelson, E. T., & Bui, T. (2010). Rural telepsychology services for children and adolescents. *Journal of Clinical Psychology*, *66*: 490–501.

Reeves, N. (2015). The use of telephone and Skype in psychotherapy: Reflections of an attachment therapist. In: *Love in the Age of the Internet: Attachment in the Digital Era* (pp. 125–152). London: Karnac.

Sabbadini, A. (2015). New technologies and the psychoanalytic setting. In: A. Lemma & L. Caparrotta (Eds.), *Psychoanalysis in the Technoculture Era* (pp. 23–32). Hove, Sussex: Routledge.

Scharff, J. S. (2014). Clinical issues in analyses over the telephone and internet. In: A. Lemma & L. Caparrotta (Eds.), *Psychoanalysis in the Technoculture Era* (pp. 47–61). Hove, Sussex: Routledge.

Scharff, J. S. (Ed.) (2015). *Psychoanalysis Online 2: Impact of Technology on Development, Training, and Therapy*. London: Karnac.

Tronick, E. (2007). *The Neurobehavioral and Social-Emotional Development of Infants and Children*. New York: Norton.

Tronick, E., Brazelton, T., & Als, H. (1978). The structure of face-to-face interaction and its developmental functions. *Sign Language Studies, 18*: 1–16.

Winnicott, D. W. (1971). *Playing and Reality*. London: Tavistock.

CHAPTER TWELVE

Listening and therapeutic alliance online

Lea S. de Setton (Panama)

This paper discusses the importance of listening in the analytic process. My purpose is to stress the effectiveness of teleanalysis as an alternative frame that is as valuable as in-person treatment. To support this idea, I review some research about human listening.

The auditory system develops very early, prior to the other senses. Babies can hear before they can see. Voices are sounds produced by the vibration of the vocal cords, and are internalized from the beginning of life. The word *voice* stems from the Latin *vox*, "voice" or *vocare*, "to call" (Merriam-Webster Dictionary). In traditional Ancient Greek, the voice was called "arrangement" or "condition." The voice is the condition for the production of verbal communication. Sounds give voice to feelings and ideas. The tone of voice conveys a message about how the person is doing. The voice calls for a response.

Research has shown that learning begins in utero when the fetus is able to recognize sounds and speech patterns, mainly of the mother's voice. Babies are linked to their parents through a real audio-phonic communication system (Herren, 1971; Oleron, 1976 qtd. Anzieu, 1979, p. 27). New studies suggest that babies start to assimilate language inside the womb, primarily during the last ten weeks of pregnancy.

They can listen, learn, and remember (Kuhl et al., 2013). Interestingly, they can hear the mother's voice because her body amplifies it.

Infants learn to recognize the mother's voice as she speaks. Moon and Lagercrantz (2012) studied how exposure to ambient language in the womb can alter phonetic perception once the child is born. They measured differences in babies' response to familiar *vs.* unfamiliar vowels. According to these authors, it has been proven that hearing begins at the onset of the third trimester of pregnancy through bone conduction—from the amniotic fluid through the fetal skull and into the inner ear. Neonates' perception of speech sounds reflects some degree of learning. Mother's voice can calm a two-week-old baby. It is more effective than other sounds or the presence of other faces (Wolf, 1969).

Anzieu (1979) corroborates this idea. He describes that at five weeks an infant distinguishes his mother's voice from other sounds, and at approximately three months it reaches for her voice. This author agrees with Freud that prior to language learning, the ego develops an autonomous structure, using the skin as a boundary. Freud (1950a) stated that children identify with the mother on the basis of a phenomenological corporeality, and connected the articulation of sounds with perceptions. For Anzieu, in turn, the self emerges as an envelope of sounds that originate both in the environment and in the baby, an envelope that appears before the skin self. This author considers that the auditory environment is very important during the early evolution of the self; the mother provides a mirror for the baby's sounds.

Regarding language development, Vygotsky (1962) refers to the relationship between thought and word as a process, a movement from thought to word and from word to thought—a verbal relatedness. Stern (1985) also emphasizes that language provides a way to relate with others. He considers it a space where connections, associations, and intimacy can take place.

The research described above recognizes the importance of sounds and language in children's lives. Listening is also pivotal to the analytic process. It is a skill that analysts develop during their training. Hearing, the perception of sound, of distinctive tones of voice, offers information concerning how the person is doing. Listening and trying to understand meaningful material precedes any intervention. The listening process becomes an important tool for analytic treatment (Adams-Silvan, 1993).

Sound arouses immediate feelings. According to Knapp (1953), the ear plays a decisive role in psychic life; it is an emotional instrument. Unlike the eyes, the ears never close. The most vital function of the ear is to offer the possibility of developing an emotional link with the external world (Ramsdell, 1947). In turn Isakower (1939) refers to the "auditory sphere" as the nucleus of the superego. Language reaches us through this sphere.

The auditory system guides human behavior. Baranger (1993) states that analytic listening constitutes an attempt to listen to the unconscious. For this author, the analytic process is governed by the analyst's desire to know, understand, help, or discover. She considers that "above all, the histories of the analytic relationship and of the process are present in the analyst's mind with the analytic situation in its totality, in its planned and spontaneous (unconscious) dynamism" (Baranger, 1993, p. 18).

Another important aspect of analytic listening is empathy. Freud alludes to the establishment of a "proper rapport" (1913c, p. 139). Aragno (2008), for her part, states that "'affective resonance' and 'cognitive referents' are two operative strains that converge in the deliberate conscious use of empathy" (Aragno, 2008, p. 720). Aragno analyzes the nature of this feeling. She considers that empathy provides access to unspoken emotional dimensions of another person's experience. An empathic attitude is more than a stance. It conveys a disposition to establish nonverbal channels that depend on the transmission of affect (Basch, 1983). In the psychoanalytic process, listening with empathic attunement helps analysts gain access to the emotional meanings conveyed by patients beyond the surface.

As shown in the studies discussed above, the nervous system allows us to learn, connect with the world, and protect ourselves. Sensory integration makes it possible to use the body effectively in our interactions with the environment. Anzieu (1979) is one of the main authors to stress the importance of the auditory environment in the earliest development of the self. If this environment is pathogenic, it will affect the child's narcissistic integrity through dissonance, abruptness, and impersonality. From the beginning of life, the nervous system prepares us to respond to affect signals from other humans. Empathy originates in affect mirroring.

Clinical empathy makes it possible to perceive special qualities and types of nonverbal information. Teleanalysis provides an adequate environment for empathy to develop. Patient and analyst feel that their voices are very close to each other. We can hear patients' breathing, even during their silences. Analysands can perceive analysts' attentiveness to every word; they can receive analysts' empathy and understanding. Teleanalysis, therefore, promotes the strengthening of the therapeutic alliance. I would like to illustrate this thesis with some clinical material—three short vignettes to set the stage for the more detailed process report of a longer session, and finally a short vignette draws the clinical example to a conclusion.

Clinical example

Alana is a thirty-year-old married woman. She has been in analysis for five years at three times a week, and had previously had a year and a half of psychotherapy. She is a victim of incest by the father. This abuse lasted until her adolescence. She has a borderline personality and suffers frequent cycles of depression. A year ago she stopped taking her medication, arguing that she wants to "clean" her body for a future pregnancy.

Alana graduated from college and is now back in school for a second degree (she is in her junior year). It is very hard for her to stay committed to a job and to her studies. This struggle is very upsetting to her. In her own words, "I'm enthusiastic at first, but I can't finish." At the same time, it should be noted that she is self-destructive, and when she is doing well, she sabotages herself. Her mother has always been intrusive and invasive, while her father remains distant and hardly speaks to her.

For the last five years Alana has had occasional telephone sessions. Over the course of her analysis she has preferred to have these sessions on the days she feels very depressed. In my opinion, the main factor in analysis is the therapeutic alliance, and the importance of teleanalysis is that it offers the possibility of avoiding discontinuity in that alliance when patients are not able to come to the office or when they are out of town. The following vignettes have been drawn from different moments over the last three years of the analysis and show how analytic work unfolds within the alliance supported by this frame.

Winter, 2013

P: "Sometimes it's hard to go to your office, but I know it's important. [Silence]."

A: "What are you thinking?"

P: "That it's true that sometimes I don't want to go. You know, B. resembles P. physically, but not in personality. I don't answer P.'s calls anymore. B. wants to get engaged in June. I want to marry him, but we need to have a more solid foundation. We've only been dating for a few months. [Pause] I haven't dared to tell him that I'm in analysis; I don't know how he'll react, maybe it's me …"

A: "What's your fantasy?"

P: "That he will ask me a lot of questions."

A: "Will he leave you?"

P: "I don't think so. I thought of talking to him about it, but it's hard."

A: "Maybe that's why you don't want to come to analysis to talk about these things."

P: "Yes. I think I should talk to him, the sooner the better. [Pause]."

Alana still thinks about her previous boyfriend, P., who mistreated her. She feels that she deserves to be punished and has no right to be happy.

Fall, 2013

P: "At the beginning of the relationship with B. everything was great. Now I worry about the responsibilities. I don't think I'm ready for this. I do things to delay the wedding."

A: "You're running the risk that the wedding won't happen."

P: "Yes, I can see that. I feel I don't have the personality to manage a house. But when I'm in his house, I'm different. I clean, I organize things …"

A: "Are you afraid you won't be a good wife and won't do things well?"

P: "I have a huge fear that I won't be able to have children."

A: "Maybe you're afraid of replicating with your child the relationship you have with your mother."

P: "Yeah … Sometimes I feel aggression toward her, and sometimes hate. I miss my dog. I would bring her to my bed and tell her what was happening to me …"

A: "You would talk to her more than to me."

P: "More than to anyone …"

A: "Because she wouldn't answer?"

P: "Yes, I don't like it when you say these kinds of things to me … It's hard for me. There's a failure in the connection between my brain and my mouth. I think something and then can't say exactly what I'm thinking …"

A: "I think it's rather a failure in trust."

P: "It happens with everyone. But I do trust you, believe me."

Alana doesn't feel she's in love with B., and is acting out so as to delay the wedding or trigger a break-up. She has always had a symbiotic relationship with her mother and feels incapable of being independent.

Spring, 2014

P: "I'm feeling really bad about the wedding. I feel I'm flying on autopilot. I'm not enjoying planning the party. Everything is a fight with my mother. Maybe I'm not handling things well. I feel that at some point I'm going to explode, and I won't be able to keep going. I try to tell her. I need for someone to intervene. My father also explodes. I have so much anger."

A: "You're angry that she's doing this to you during the wedding preparations."

P: "Yes … [She cries.]"

A: "What are the fights about?"

P: "The guest list, the shower, the invitations. We've made the list maybe twenty times. I chose certain songs for the church choir to sing. She wants to change them and says, 'Don't walk in with that song, you'll regret it.' She insists, and insists … I get so angry. I will not regret it! That's the song I want. Why does she have to force me? It's not her wedding! My anger doesn't let me sleep at night. B. says I'm right; she shouldn't interfere."

A: "It's difficult for your mother to let you be independent and make decisions."

P: "I told my mother that when she's stressed she's very rude, like my grandmother. And that's why I'm in analysis; I don't want to take this to the next generation."

Alana keeps fighting with her mother in order to differentiate herself from her.

Telephone session: winter, 2015

P: "I haven't been to your office in the last two weeks. I don't feel like talking. I'm tired, I feel blah. I just go to school and back home. School ends tomorrow."

A: "You haven't been up to coming to analysis and talking. And you're not enjoying your work."

P: "Not at all. A friend advised me to apply for tutoring at the Met School. Very few hours, but good pay. There were other applicants. The money issue is stressful."

A: "Are you stressed about having to pay me?"

P: "You know my mother pays for my analysis."

A: "But maybe you feel you could use the money for something else."

P: "I'm angry with myself; I'm not independent or productive. My parents still help me every month. I want everything right now. This is one of the reasons why I get aggressive. The new apartment, we have spent a lot of money and got into debt ..."

A: "What makes you so angry is not having things right away ..."

P: "I'm like a small child. It's immature. I want to buy things for the house, clothes. It's hard to control myself. Sometimes I tell myself I don't need it, and then I don't buy it."

A: "Maybe this is related to your not wanting to have boundaries."

P: "Yes, it's difficult to have boundaries. If I can't have something I get angry and fight with B. or with my mother."

A: "It sounds like a tantrum."

P: "Yeah ... It's anger toward myself, because at my age I should be independent, and work. I also want to finish my second degree."

A: "You think you'll feel better about yourself if you can work and pay for your things ..."

P: "Yes, I'm emotionally unstable, and I think I should have worked this week to earn some more money. I have my new apartment, and I think I should have waited to buy a house. B. says I'm never happy."

A: "I have the impression that you feel empty inside and that nothing from the outside can fill the void."

P: "I don't know; I feel an emptiness that I can't fill. Maybe it's my immaturity."

A: "What causes the feeling of emptiness?"

P: "I don't know, goals that I can't meet, and they accumulate."

A: "I have the feeling it's something deeper. Maybe you haven't felt loved enough since your childhood."

P: "I don't know; I'm sad and angry with my aunt. She sees me and looks the other way. And my grandma also made a fuss about Christmas dinner. My mother supports me in this. Also, I haven't been eating properly. I went to the doctor and my hemoglobin is low. He prescribed supplements. I lost thirty pounds. I'm happy, but I thought it would be faster. The doctor says I'm doing well, but I feel frustrated."

A: "You want everything at once."

P: "I know it's wrong. I remember at school when the kids wanted to use the bike and didn't want to wait for their turn. I'm like that. It's hard for me to wait for my turn. I can't tolerate feeling frustrated. I don't want to blame my mother, but I've felt like this since I was a child. My mother would solve everything right away. She would speak to the teacher. She made me switch schools twice, she was like that …"

A: "She couldn't calm you down? Do you feel this also happens with me in analysis?

P: "No … It's like today: they called me from the bank. I forgot to cancel the account and they charged me for 2016. I told my mother and she got angry. I was only three days late … I wish she would talk to me calmly …"

A: "You feel she doesn't understand you."

P: "No … And she tells me I'll be in debt … And she makes this into a huge catastrophe …"

A: "It's the catastrophe that you feel when something doesn't turn out the way you wanted."

P: "It's the same with B. I thought I was going to feel butterflies in my stomach, but I don't feel in love …"

A: "You don't let him express his affection and his sexuality. You distance yourself from him."

P: "I know sometimes I'm better. I don't want to talk; I don't want to have my session. I scold B. and tell him what to do and what not to do …"

A: "You're sabotaging yourself."

P: "Yes, it's wrong, and I withdraw."

A: "Maybe you don't want to feel good; you think you don't deserve it. You distance yourself with fights to avoid sex."

P: "That's possible. B. gets angry and tells me not to scold him."

A: "This kind of relationship, where you criticize him and tell him off, is like your relationship with your mother. It creates emptiness—no love, no empathy or understanding."

P: "[Silence.] Yes … I have to improve many things."

A: "And understand why you do this to yourself."

Alana struggles with her ambivalence. She cannot decide whether she wants to grow and be independent or to continue to be childish and immature.

Telephone session: Spring, 2016

P: "I asked for an earlier appointment because I'm feeling very depressed, without a clear path to follow. I don't want to do anything. I've been crying a lot. I don't know if I want to go on … Next week I only have a class on Wednesday. I don't want to tie myself to a job. My head is a mess."

A: "When you were crying, what were you thinking?"

P: "That I wanted to die. I feel I have no reason to go on."

A: "Where's B. in all this?"

P: "I don't know, I don't feel I'm in love. I'm not giving enough to the relationship. Responsibilities are difficult for me; it's the same with the jobs I've had. Sometimes I think it would have been better just to continue dating. Responsibilities kill love. And that's wrong."

A: "What's the effect of having responsibilities?"

P: "I don't want to do things. When I go to other people's houses, I compare myself to them; I look at how they manage their house. I think I do everything wrong. I don't feel calm or happy or satisfied. I let others deal with things. I prefer it that way. Not having all the money I want is upsetting to me. The other day we were with some friends, and I had an argument with B. I made a scene. The next day I felt ashamed."

A: "You had a tantrum."

P: "Yes, I've been functioning like that. I don't want to be that way. But I don't know if I should run away from my marriage or keep going and do things myself."

A: "You don't know if you should destroy your marriage, or force yourself to grow."

P: "I don't know if I should have a child; I don't have enough money."

A: "I think it's important for us to go more deeply into your ambivalence."

P: "My head is a mess … I get all confused and don't do what I should do."

A: "I feel that your self-destructiveness is like a negative force that pulls you back from loving yourself, from being independent and successful in your life and in your marriage."

P: "I don't know what to say … It's fear."

Conclusion

Voices are very significant to human beings from before birth. Language conveys messages, and tone of voice elicits feelings in the listener. In the transitional space of dialogue, patient and analyst are emotionally connected in an alliance that allows them to work in depth on the patient's history. The analyst acts as a sound mirror that helps the patient metabolize the material brought to the session. Teleanalysis provides a space where this exchange may take place. If an emotional link and trust have developed between the two members of the analytic couple, patients are able to use this frame to engage in the analytic process as they do in in-person sessions.

References

Adams-Silvan, A. (1993). "To learn the noble game ..." The transformation of the listening process into a therapeutic instrument with special reference to analytic memory. *Journal of Clinical Psychoanalysis*, 2: 513–527.

Anzieu, D. (1979). The sound image of the self. *International Review of Psychoanalysis*, *6*: 23–36.

Aragno, A. (2008). The language of empathy: an analysis of its constitution, development, and role in psychoanalytic listening. *Journal of the American Psychoanalytic Association*, *56*: 713–740.

Baranger, M. (1993). The mind of the analyst: from listening to interpretation *International Journal of Psycho-Analysis*, *74*: 15–24.

Basch, M. F. (1983). Empathic understanding: A review of the concept and some theoretical considerations. *Journal of the American Psychoanalytic Association*, *31*: 101–126.

Freud, S. (1913c). On beginning the treatment (Recommendations for physicians on the technique of psycho-analysis I). *S. E.*, *12*: 121–144. London: Hogarth.

Freud, S. (1950a). Project for a scientific psychology. *S. E.*, *1*: 238–391. London: Hogarth.

Herren, H. (1971). La voix dans le development psychosomatique de l'enfant. *Journal Francais d'Otorhino-Laryngologie*, *20*: 429–435.

Isakower, O. (1939). On the exceptional position of the auditory sphere. *International Journal of Psychoanalysis*, *20*: 340–348.

Knapp, P. H. (1953). The ear, listening and hearing. *Journal of the American Psychoanalytic Association*, *1*: 672–689.

Kuhl, P., Bosseler A. N., Taulu, S., Pihko, E., Mäkelä, J. P., Imada, T., & Ahonen, A. (2013). Theta brain rhythms index perceptual narrowing in infant speech perception. *Frontiers in Psychology*, 4: 690, 11 October 2013. http://dx.doi.org/10.3389/fpsyg.2013.00690

Moon, C., & Lagercrantz, H. (2012). Language experience in utero affects vowel perception after birth: a two country study. *Acta Paedriatica, 102*: 156–160.

Oléron, P. (1976). L'acquisition du langage. In: H. Gratiot-Alphandery & R. Zazzo (Eds.), *Traité de Psychologie de l'Enfant, 6*. Paris: Presses Universitaires de France.

Ramsdell, D. A. (1947). The psychology of the hard of hearing and the deafened adult. In: H. Davis (Ed.), *Hearing and Deafness*. New York: Murray Hill.

Stern, D. N. (1985). *The Interpersonal World of the Infant*. New York: Basic.

Vygotsky, L. S. (1962). *Thought and Language* (E. Haufmann & G. Vaker, Eds. & Trans.). Cambridge, MA: MIT Press.

Wolf, P. (1969). The natural history of crying and other vocalizations in early infancy. *Determinants of Infant Behaviour, 4*: 81–109.

Commentary

Caroline Sehon

We are given privileged access to the analytic journey between Alana, a thirty-year-old woman and Lea Setton, Ph.D., which began as a psychotherapy and transitioned eighteen months later into an ongoing psychoanalysis (three-times-weekly over five years). Usually, the analytic couple meets in the analyst's office. When the patient feels too incapacitated by depression to commute to the office, Dr. Setton offers Alana the option of telephone psychoanalysis.

Dr. Setton was dually trained at the International Institute for Psychoanalytic Training (IIPT) at the International Psychotherapy Institute and at Instituto Latinoamericano de Psicanàlisis (ILAP) in Panama. In the latter, she gathered an extensive repertoire of knowledge and skills in the fields of infant observation, neuroscience, and early development, applied to adult analytic practice, and, at the former, she is an ongoing participant in the IIPT teleanalysis research group. We learn that Dr. Setton values the therapeutic relationship as the primary agent of therapeutic action. In building this relationship, she is particularly interested in studying the way the body enters the consultation room through communicative language, including not only the spoken word, but also prosody of speech (rhythm, tone), vocal utterances, and silences. Dr. Setton is especially equipped to engage in attuned listening to the many dimensions of voice conveyed through analytic encounters on the telephone, and thus build a strong therapeutic relationship.

Alana was severely traumatized by both parents. Her father allegedly sexually abused her throughout her childhood until adolescence. Portrayed as "intrusive and invasive," her mother colluded with Alana's father by failing to shield her from the protracted abuse while turning to her daughter to meet her own needs. A description of the parents' own relationship is missing, likely echoing the void of an internal parental couple. In the here-and-now, Alana relates to an absent father who rarely speaks to her, and to an over-involved mother with whom she quarrels incessantly. We encounter other characters in Alana's mind—her maternal grandmother who mistreated her mother, her neglectful aunt, her abusive former boyfriend, her fiancé with whom she cannot *tie the knot*, and her lost dog whom she grieves as a bed companion and whom she trusted even more than her analyst. Alana's interior world is populated by *exciting and rejecting relationships* that impoverish her *central self*, which inadequately equips her to function independently (Fairbairn, 1963).

Tragically, such a history of trauma and maltreatment has complicated her development. Now, she has compromised capacities to engage in self-care, to regulate her affect, and to function reflectively at times of distress. Although capable to succeed academically at times—even to pursue a second degree—all too often, she sabotages herself. We are told that she has a borderline personality organization and that she finds herself often overtaken by depressive and aggressive feelings, suicidal despair, and outbursts of rage towards her mother and fiancé. Ridden by profound shame, she cannot disclose to her fiancé that she is in analysis. Terrified of intimacy, she feels too paralyzed to marry and conceive a family. Untrusting of most persons of significance in her life, she nevertheless feels differently about her analyst. Alana assures her, "I do trust you, believe me."

Many traumatized persons experience a range of failed outcomes when they seek help. Not uncommonly, treatments are complicated by premature endings, or by frequent missed appointments when patients dial down the intensity of the work amidst unbearable pain. Rather than absenting herself entirely from the analysis when immobilized to her home, Alana preserves the tie to Dr. Setton by the link of the phone. She is motivated to interrupt the intergenerational transmission of trauma, and to address her self-destructive patterns wherein she feels "enthusiastic at first, but can't finish." While she recognizes that her analysis is essential to address these problems, and to launch her own life, she is also frightened by the psychological demands of the analysis. She expresses such conflicts in the transference, by her unique relationship to the telephone as the vehicle for maintaining continuity of her analysis. Offered a flexible therapeutic relationship adapted to her needs, Alana is able to develop in a few years from being a faltering student to an educated woman planning her wedding.

Distance-mediated analysis

Over the course of the analytic treatment of a survivor of childhood sexual abuse, the trauma is recapitulated within the analytic relationship, and expressed in the form of a split positive- and negative-focused transference (Scharff, 1992). In order for the patient's central conflicts and trauma to be worked through successfully, the analyst offers a secure, arms-around holding—a *positive contextual transference*—within which the *negative-focused transference* will be delivered. In the context of a distance-mediated analysis, significant elements of the transference may be illuminated by the ways the patient makes particular unconscious use of the technology. Hence, aspects of the personality and its internal conflicts may become more immediately discernable and analyzable in those analyses that combine teleanalysis with in-office sessions, because of the ways the patient reveals different self-states in the separate settings, and because of the potentially enriched data set from which the analytic couple can address the integrative task.

In the case of Alana, who meets with Dr. Setton mainly in the office, we would want to be alert to her defensive use of the phone to titrate the dose of the analytic relationship. After a more intimate exchange with Dr. Setton, does Alana opt for a phone session as a distancing maneuver? Does she use her depression as a kind of passport to access a telephone session as a way to avoid a close-in encounter with the analyst in the office? Telephone analysis must therefore be integrated judiciously with a traditional, in-office analysis, to protect against the patient's steering clear of difficult issues by acting out instead of symbolizing her conflicts. The analyst is thus tasked with carrying a secure internal setting in her mind and with analyzing the patient's potential misuse of the technology as an avoidant strategy rather than as a vehicle to sustain and grow the analytic project.

Alana's interior world is fragmented by separate self-states without her having achieved an integrated personality. Severely traumatic influences have become installed in the mind of the patient. In the adult survivor of childhood sexual abuse, we often find a shattered psychic structure, expressed in the form of a split transference to the analyst. When that analyst offers both teleanalytic and in-office settings, facets of the internal world and of the transference may be split from one another and expressed either in the phone or the in-office settings. The combination of contexts invites Alana to give voice to some parts of her mind when the analytic pair meets by phone, while muting other elements of the transference when the analytic pair meets in the office.

Dr. Setton holds the view that analytic change is determined by the therapeutic relationship, and makes the case that teleanalysis in particular "promotes the strengthening of the therapeutic alliance."

I will discuss the nature of the analytic relationship between Alana and Dr. Setton with reference to five clinical vignettes selected over a span of three years. This commentary will offer reflections of the analytic process, and on the way that Alana uses the telephone adaptively and defensively in relation to the in-office sessions.

Vignette 1—Winter 2013

It's been "hard" for Alana to go to her analyst's office, just as it's been "hard" for her to disclose her analytic relationship to her boyfriend. When Dr. Setton invites Alana to think and speak about her fantasies of how her boyfriend would respond were she to tell him of the analysis, we learn that she is frightened he will probe her with questions (like her invasive parents and unlike the gentler version that she finds in Dr. Setton). In the teleanalytic setting, the analytic pair continue their work in the transference–countertransference. Dr. Setton interprets that Alana may be using a phone session to dodge having to confront these issues head-on in the office. Avoiding the transference aspect of Dr. Setton's comment, Alana replies that she should talk about it, but she is thinking of talking to her boyfriend, not to Dr. Setton. This suggests that Alana is defending against exploring her unbearable affect with Dr. Setton in the office.

We might ask whether the analyst is colluding with the patient's defensive avoidance of the work by conducting the session by phone. On the other hand, the teleanalysis amplifies the challenges that may be relatively hidden from view when the analysis takes place only within a traditional office setting. From this perspective, the teleanalysis session may advance the forward progress of the work.

Alana's associations in this phone session lend particular value to studying the splits in her psychic structure. Initially, she expresses her conflicted feelings about needing to go to the office while wanting to stay away. On the heels of this statement, she contrasts the personality attributes of her fiancé with those of her former boyfriend, and comments on their physical resemblance to one another. This passage suggests that Alana may be describing ways that dissonant parts of her personality emerge in each setting, while at the same time the analytic relationship remains a constant. After telling Dr. Setton that she ignores her former boyfriend's calls, Alana states, "We need to have a more solid foundation," again referring consciously to her relationship to her fiancé. Unconsciously, however, might she not be longing to stabilize the link to her analyst? In other words, could she be expressing her desire to find ways to bring all of her self into the in-office setting, and thereby construct a more integrated, solid sense of self?

Vignette 2—Fall 2013

During this analytic session, Alana expresses her fears and insecurities about marrying and bearing children. She feels so ashamed to reveal these vulnerabilities to her future husband, but finds a way to confide her worries to her analyst. She says, "*... when I'm in his house, I'm different. I clean, I organize things ...*," raising the possibility that she hides her internal messiness when *in the analyst's house (office)*, not yet able to have her analyst see her mental disarray, except over the telephone.

Alana tells us she misses her beloved dog, longing for his comfort and relief from the demands of ordinary, adult intimacy. She wishes her dog were available to listen unconditionally to her, giving her the reprieve of difficult feelings evoked in human conversation. Her dog may be speaking for infantile parts of her mind that are calling out to be honored and shielded from others' impositions, at long last. This passage may also open a window onto the focused, parental transference wherein she finds it so much easier to talk to her dog than to her analyst.

Alana states that there's a faulty connection between her brain and her mouth, as she can't say exactly what she's thinking. In this way, she seems to communicate a primitive oral need for taking in analytic nurturance and containment. Perhaps she feels it is too advanced a developmental step to use her mouth to symbolically transform her distress into words. In keeping with this hypothesis, she says that she doesn't think she is ready for this. Therefore, we may wonder if she is revealing her unconscious motivation to elect a telephone session as a way to retreat from the anxieties inherent to working within *this* relationship dedicated to the task of analysis, out of a desire to assume a more infantile, dependent posture in relation to her analyst.

Vignette 3—Spring 2014

In this vignette, we learn of Alana's explosive rage towards her mother, which she fears may stop her from keeping going. It may also stop the symbiotic relationship with her mother if Alana wins her independence. Instead, she goes on autopilot. It seems apropos to consider that she may have utilized a telephone session as a kind of autopilot rather than encounter her rage in the office in relation to her co-pilot/analyst. In other words, does the phone session represent an acting out of her anger towards the analyst/mother in a relatively risk-free territory of the phone, as an alternative to taking the chance of endangering the treatment by expressing herself with her own song and then regretting it? Alana fights with her mother as to which guests will be invited to the wedding, but we might wonder if she is actually speaking to the struggle as to which internal characters she can bring forward and onto which analytic stage—the phone or in the analyst's office.

Vignette 4—Winter 2014

This passage lends further strength to the idea that Alana feels safer to express her rage towards her mother and fiancé instead of taking up these feelings in relation to her analyst. Dr. Setton investigates Alana's anger in the transference, asking if she is worried about paying her. Quickly, Alana denies feeling any anger or disappointment in her analyst, reminding Dr. Setton that her mother pays the fee and insisting that she is angry not at her analyst but at herself. Later, Dr. Setton notes that Alana's mother couldn't calm her down, and asks directly about the transference: "*Do you feel this also happens with me in the analysis?*" Initially launching back to attack her mother, eventually Alana admits, *"I don't want to talk; I don't want to have my session."* We notice Dr. Setton's analytic interventions aimed at confronting the patient's self-destructiveness and her retreat from owning responsibility in relation to her fiancé and family. Importantly, Dr. Setton does not collude with Alana's avoidance of the negative transference.

Vignette 5—Spring 2016

Alana turns to her analyst to ask for an earlier session when unable to manage disorganized, depressed, and despairing feelings to the point of feeling suicidal. Dr. Setton interprets Alana's dilemma: Will she claim a sense of agency and cultivate new growth in her life, or will she collapse under the weight of her destructive rage? In the throes of Alana's suicidal fantasy, Dr. Setton fortifies the therapeutic alliance and sets the course: *"I think it's important for us to go more deeply into your ambivalence."* The analyst demonstrates her commitment to steady analytic work with the patient, holding a firm yet flexible frame, and accommodating the need for occasional phone sessions at times of crisis while also analyzing their potential defensive use.

Conclusion

Traumatized patients like Alana have been *"lifting their silent voices to us, hoping we would hear, accept, validate and understand, as they simultaneously concealed and conveyed their experience"* (Scharff & Scharff, 1994, p. 337). The theory that informs Dr. Setton's technique, and the ensuing analytic process illustrated in these phone sessions, reflects the principles of treating traumatized patients (Scharff & Scharff, 1994, p. 332). We see Dr. Setton welcome the *going-on-being* of Alana, listening to her concerns, and monitoring the holding environment, and refraining from pushing her to analyze her trauma. We see Dr. Setton translate the bodily communication of silence into the verbalization of affect. We see the splits in Alana's mind delivered into the treatment as Dr. Setton works to reveal the transference. We see Alana progress to create nuclei of genera around which to refind her self and rebuild her life. We also see much that remains to be done.

We have borne witness to the unfolding of the contextual and focused transferences within a several-year treatment of a traumatized woman, fortunate to have found an analyst skillful in teleanalysis, who agreed to provide a combination of in-office and occasional telephone analytic sessions when warranted by the patient's condition. This material lends support to the idea that the functional setting is one held by the analyst–patient couple as an internal setting, and not defined intrinsically by the external reality where they meet. The sample of five clinical vignettes was selected entirely from phone sessions over a three-year period, so this commentary has been limited to the study of the analytic couple's use of this technology medium without any available comparison to in-office transcripts. Thoughts about Alana's transference have been exclusively inferred from process material, without access to Dr. Setton's explicit countertransference responses.

It would be very interesting to learn more about the ways the negative transference was analyzed, and particularly whether there was any divergence in the interpretative approach utilized between distance-mediated sessions and the in-office setting. From the selected material, it appears that Alana is not shy in bringing forward her aggression, at least in the displacement. We would like to see more work on her self-destructiveness and aggression toward her fiancé and mother. In these sessions, Dr. Setton does not bypass interpretations of the patient's anger towards her, but we are not told whether Alana misses any sessions, or whether she acts out in other ways to sabotage the treatment. But we do know that the analytic discourse and therapeutic link has been sturdy and sustained over several years. Psychic change in this traumatized population requires a great deal of dedication, patience, and time, as shown by Alana and Dr. Setton as they soldier forward along this uphill journey.

In the one-hundred-year trajectory that our field has taken since Freud's invention of psychoanalysis, we lost opportunities for dynamic understanding and recovery from abuse when psychoanalysis moved away from the study of trauma to neurosis, and from dissociation to repression. In an analogous way, teleanalysis affords us a novel way of listening to the silent voices of patients who cannot always come to our offices. Fortunately, Dr. Setton refuses to turn away from Alana as she *conceals and conveys her experience,* while Alana continues to find and refind her way to Dr. Setton, to *lift her hitherto silent voice to her analyst to be heard, accepted, validated, and understood.* In conclusion, here's hoping we do not make the same mistake of letting yet another century go by before we recognize that remote analysis deserves to be systematically studied and offered judiciously to those in need, now.

References

Fairbairn, W. R. D. (1963). Synopsis of an object relations theory of the personality. *International Journal of Psychoanalysis 44*: 224–225.

Scharff, D. E. (1992). *Refinding the Object and Reclaiming the Self.* New Jersey: Jason Aronson.

Scharff, D. E. & Scharff, J. S. (1994). *Object Relations Therapy of Physical and Sexual Trauma.* New Jersey: Jason Aronson.

CHAPTER THIRTEEN

Thinking ethically about terminating therapy after trying new technologies

Ernest Wallwork (USA)

As psychodynamic therapists have become increasingly comfortable technically and ethically with using online technologies for treating patients from afar, new ethical problems have surfaced that were obscured when such treatments were relatively rare. One of the most troubling of these emerging ethical issues arises when neither the therapist nor the patient realize that online treatment is causing more harm than benefit or that better alternative treatments are available than those being pursued.

Ethically, the therapist is the member of the dyad with primary moral responsibility for identifying and addressing problems with how well the therapy is succeeding. But online treatment offers so many advantages to both parties in terms of convenience, continuity of care, provision of services when nothing equivalent is available—and, for the analyst, maintaining a full practice—that the therapeutic dyad can end up colluding to avoid addressing the limitations of this way of working. Ethical problems arise when the convenience of jumping on a computer rather than going to an office or avoiding the difficulties of terminating and beginning again with a local provider prevent better treatment alternatives from being pursued vigorously.

Two clinical examples will illustrate the development of an analytic stance when contemplating terminating a teleanalysis. To protect patient privacy, identifying details have been omitted or falsified.

Brittany: paying a costly price for maintaining continuity of treatment

A recent consultation about treatment options for a nineteen-year-old college student who was receiving therapy by phone and Skype from her hometown psychiatrist for disabling anxieties crystalizes the complex network of technical and ethical issues that may arise with distant therapies. I learned about the case from the student's parents who contacted me for a second opinion about their daughter's treatment at the end of her sophomore year.

Brittany's anxieties had become noteworthy during her freshman year in high school. But her anxiety then had been confined mostly to stressful social situations. Anxiety had not affected her academic work, except during oral presentations. She had an outstanding academic record when she applied to college. But academic performance anxiety became an increasingly serious problem during her freshman year at Georgetown University. Despite an impressive IQ and high SAT scores, Brittany failed two courses during her freshman year, placing her on academic probation. Her dismal academic performance continued into her sophomore year, and now she was facing the possibility of being suspended before enrolling for her junior year.

After listening to Brittany's parent's concerns, I made it clear that I could not proceed without first talking with their daughter and obtaining her informed consent and, if she concurred, consulting with her therapist. I agreed under these conditions to work with Brittany, her parents, and her therapist to evaluate the full range of treatment options, including continuing or terminating the therapy she was receiving as well as arranging for a psychopharmacological review. I also made it clear that to avoid any hint of self-interested bias I would not be considering taking Brittany as a patient, if a referral to a local therapist in Washington DC seemed desirable. However, I promised to help Brittany find a suitable local therapist, if she decided to pursue that option.

When I met with Brittany and talked with her psychiatrist, I was dismayed to learn that neither of them had considered, much less talked about, any of the pros and cons of online therapy. Brittany clearly did not know enough about her therapeutic options to even broach the matter without being prompted. Dr. Smith, her psychiatrist, just assumed that continuing therapy via the Internet was better than any alternative, a position that may have been justified at the outset of her patient's freshman year, but hardly during the entirety of a two-year period during which Brittany's anxieties had become increasingly more pronounced and pervasive.

Dr. Smith had been ethically derelict, I eventually concluded, in not thinking about the issues covered by the ethical principles of beneficence and non-maleficence (doing good and not doing harm). That is to say, she was not thinking of her patient's best interests (see Wallwork, 2012, 2013, 2015). While a therapist's reluctance to transfer a patient to a less qualified therapist in an underserved area, such as a rural college town, is understandable, this was not the case in the nation's capital, with its large and vital community of therapists. In fact, several excellent therapists were within easy walking distance of Brittany's dorm.

By not talking with Brittany about other treatment options and about the privacy risks of the phone and Skype, Dr. Smith also disrespected her patient's autonomy by preventing genuine informed consent. Dr Smith had offered the possibility of continuing therapy online before Brittany left her hometown for college and Brittany had accepted the offer immediately, without thought or discussion, largely because she was anxious about starting college and continuing their contact seemed reassuring. She liked Dr. Smith a lot, and found her warm supportive presence comforting. Dr. Smith liked her too, and did not want to lose Brittany as a patient. Unfortunately, Brittany was not offered an opportunity to ponder and evaluate the desirability of working in-person with a Washington therapist.

Neither Dr. Smith nor Brittany considered the possibility that working at a distance might be different in ways that would warrant a periodical review to assess how well this mode of relating was working for them. Unfortunately, failure to periodically reassess their new therapeutic relationship contributed to the formation of a collusive defensive avoidance in which Brittany used their sessions primarily to feel comfortable with her therapist "friend" rather than to honestly confront the multiple unconscious sources of her mounting anxieties.

Working by phone and Skype made it easy for Brittany to hide not only her severe academic anxieties but also her repeated inability to finish and submit assignments on time and to function well during examinations. Dr. Smith's limited access to Brittany's nonverbal affective communications made it difficult for her to pick up on Brittany's underlying affective distress, which she might have had more opportunities to notice if she had been seen in the office setting. And so Dr. Smith was blindsided at the end of each of four semesters when she learned belatedly that Brittany had been using their therapy defensively, as a resistance to jointly exploring the depths of her subjective distress.

Ignoring the problems with the frame that they had co-constructed, Dr. Smith and Brittany kept trudging along for four semesters over two years, with Dr. Smith trying unsuccessfully to monitor Brittany's academic work and Brittany avoiding Dr. Smith's disapproval by pretending she was doing fine, even though she was not. Dr. Smith's attempts to keep tabs on Brittany's academic performance were experienced in the transference as too much like her critical mom's intrusiveness, leading her to retaliate rebelliously by acting out her unconscious anger by lying about how she was doing and stubbornly refusing to go along with Dr. Smith's treatment goals. Acting out her transference anger eventually found expression in missing and being late for sessions that were explained away with bogus excuses, such as that she had competing academic commitments.

From an ethical perspective, the stalemate within the Brittany/Smith dyad was more than a technical shortcoming, though it was certainly that insofar as Dr. Smith failed to address adequately transference/countertransference dynamics. Brittany not only did not receive the full benefits of treatment, she was actually harmed by continuing non-effective therapy for two full years. Although Brittany was obviously smart enough to have excelled at Georgetown, her academic work suffered and, with it, her career prospects, because her dismal transcript—with numerous Fs, Ds, and Ws—precluded pursuit of graduate work in her chosen career.

This is not to say that Brittany received nothing from treatment. The acute social anxiety she experienced during the early part of her freshman year was tempered somewhat by continuation of her supportive relationship with Dr. Smith. It would be naive to expect that Brittany could have made greater progress in understanding and ameliorating the sources of her anxiety without considerable affective disorganization. Her grades may well have suffered to some extent anyway. The main ethical and technical problem with Brittany's treatment was that the severe anxiety disorder that underlay her failing grades was not addressed and, as a result, she suffered very real, lifelong harms.

Dr. Smith was not unaware that her therapeutic intentions were being thwarted. Unfortunately, she was too swayed by the allure of continuing Brittany's treatment by utilizing new technologies, and by the arguments that many of us have been making about successful online work, that she failed to give enough weight to the disadvantages of online therapy, such as being deprived of full access to the range of a patient's affects that are available during in-person work.

Eventually, Dr. Smith felt relieved of a burden when the weight of continuing ineffective treatment was lifted by Brittany's decision to transfer to a Washington therapist.

As of this writing, Brittany is much improved. Her anxiety has diminished after shifting to an experienced local therapist and her grades have improved dramatically.

What is sad is that Brittany was working at a distance not because no competent therapists existed locally, but because her therapist assumed she was the best person to treat Brittany's anxiety, even when it meant doing so at a distance. There was hubris in this judgment that led to a failure of due diligence, in reassessing the effectiveness of online treatment and checking possible referral sources locally. By not talking with Brittany about her options, Dr. Smith implicitly both disrespected her patient's autonomy and put her in harm's way—not only by delaying better treatment, but by continuing an ineffective process for two years as the real-world consequences mounted.

Chris: creatively reshaping therapy online before terminating good enough work for ethical reasons

Chris's online therapy, unlike Brittany's, was by most standards, a remarkable success. The opportunities made possible by new distance-shrinking technologies to reach patients whose lifestyles preclude standard in-patient sessions made successful psychodynamic work possible with this otherwise unreachable patient. Paradoxically, Chris's therapy also demonstrates the importance of frankly acknowledging the limitations of online treatment and the value of shifting to in-person work when appropriate.

Chris had seen seven different psychotherapists and had been an inpatient at two rehab facilities before he reached my door at age twenty-six for yet another try, vowing that "this time" he had the "mojo" to commit to three sessions a week. Suspicious of this newfound motivation in light of Chris's history of proving adept at scuttling what he learned in therapy, even though his mojo this time stemmed from an uncommonly painful withdrawal from his most recent bout with heroin, I explained that he would need to commit to being brutally honest about himself with me and to working on the affective triggers that had led him to return to drugs repeatedly, even when he had been clean for months and was trying not to relapse.

In the end, I agreed to work with him, despite my many reservations, partly because we made some modest headway during evaluation sessions in exploring some of the deep-seated motivations fueling his addiction. He was so desperate and desirous of change, I found myself wanting very much to help him, if I could, while keeping in mind that the rescue fantasies Chris evoked were still just fantasies.

So Chris and I made a pact that he would try with every fiber of his being to remain clean and to replace the actions involved in using with talk, not only during regularly scheduled appointments, but whenever he was thinking about using again. We agreed on the importance of trying to understand at the time it was happening why and how he was beginning to undermine his desire to change. I explained that he needed to be transparent about even trivial, passing thoughts and plans to use again, most especially when everything in him resisted talking about them. Otherwise we would both be wasting our time and his money.

I was agreeably surprised by how easily Chris established a therapeutic alliance. Chris noticed it too: "You're different from the others," he remarked at the end of one early session. I was impressed, too, by the candid, self-probing and soberly reflective way Chris took to exploring the multiple sources of the anger, anxieties, loneliness, rebelliousness, and longing for recognition, respect, and maternal comfort that had continuously fueled his addiction.

I was just beginning to feel cautiously hopeful when Chris suddenly scuttled what I thought we had achieved by disappearing, leaving me worrying about whether he had overdosed. Several days of silence ended abruptly when Chris resurfaced with a text: "Gotta talk."

He had used again, lost his job, and left town on what turned into a year-long search for ways to relaunch his life. When we connected by phone, Chris was going through a painful withdrawal while holed up alone in a seedy motel room several hundred miles away. Despite powerful wishes to isolate himself as he usually did for the duration of a withdrawal, Chris wanted a session. So we talked, as he shivered and shook, about some of the specific thoughts, affects, and fantasies that had gotten him to this place, overwhelming his conscious efforts to stay clean, and landing him with the truly awful physiological and psychological miseries of withdrawal that I could see in the haggard brown eyes and wizened facial features that filled my iPhone screen.

Using my anxious worrying during his absence, I interpreted the retaliatory anger at his loved ones implicit in dropping totally out of sight and leaving everyone else feeling "helplessly alone in the dark," as he had told me he often felt. Chris reacted by recounting a terrifying memory of when his parents forgot about him, leaving him alone as a three- or four-year-old at a gas station at a busy highway intersection that he was trying to cross in his pajamas when the police picked him up. These and other memories helped Chris dig deeper into the role played by anger, rebellion, and retaliation against his parents (and, in this case, against his analyst) in turning to drugs. We also talked about how using drugs provided a way of reversing the shameful dependency Chris experienced with his authoritarian father, by giving Chris the power to make his Dad feel helpless too. Unfortunately, I observed, in an effort to help him envision a different sense of agency, addiction was another form of dependency that robbed him of the truly effective agency he was seeking.

With Chris on the road, continuing therapy became possible only by shifting to FaceTime on our iPhones and, occasionally, Skype. My efforts to move sessions to safer technologies were rebuffed by Chris's understandable contention that the easy availability of sessions on FaceTime was far more important than his privacy, which he did not feel strongly about and would not count for much if he were to relapse.

Chris was subsequently continuously on the move, crisscrossing the country, restlessly looking for a fresh start, as he crashed for a few days at a time with his many geographically dispersed friends. The unfortunate downside for our goal of getting him clean was that Chris's newfound itinerant lifestyle exposed him to an increased array of triggers for substance abuse—as "friends" pushed him to drink, smoke, and use drugs. However, for the first time, thanks to the therapeutic possibilities opened up by Apple's FaceTime, Chris was exposed simultaneously to opportunities to explore and to understand the many conflicting motivations that endowed particular triggers with so much affective power.

Because I believe the keystone of the therapeutic frame lies in the quality of the relationship, I chose to abandon most conventional standards for constituting the frame. Endeavoring to be empathic and responsive to Chris's constantly changing circumstances, I tried to be as flexible as possible in arranging and changing appointment times, making up missed sessions, and billing. I did insist that we find the time to talk at least four times a week to preserve the continuity and intensity of treatment, but I reduced my fee several times and varied it frequently in accordance with his changing financial fortunes and needs. If he forgot an appointment or could not talk at the last minute, I did not charge him, if we could make up the session. But I did insist that we talk openly and often about the transference significance of all these interactions. And I encouraged Chris to supplement our four times a week schedule with calls to my private cellphone number at any time of day or night, if he were tempted to use drugs.

Chris responded appreciatively to my availability, by taking advantage of my offer by reaching out for help at odd times by ducking into a lavatory, alley, closet, or back seat of a car to talk when temptations loomed. We had sessions in toilet stalls, truck-beds, stairwells, rooftops, and bedrooms, where I was sometimes introduced to Chris's friends, including several sleeping partners, some of whom told me they wanted to get their act together as Chris was doing. The frequency of our sessions escalated to eight or nine times a week, where they plateaued for months, before Chris began to get himself under control.

I felt like a mother with a needy infant who was available on demand to meet basic needs, whenever they arose, for comfort, care, nourishment, and safety. And that, of course, is exactly what Chris needed, as evidenced by what he sought in heroin: the warm comforting maternal care he felt he lacked growing up. Because it met some of the same desires, the therapeutic alliance we co-constructed gradually became an alternative to heroin. The alliance was thus empowered to play a significant role in helping Chris gradually wean himself. It also provided a space within which we could explore unconscious and preconscious fantasies and motivations as they were in the process of ascending, making it possible for Chris to make immediate use of new insights about his motivations to resist currently active temptations.

As expected, Chris was at times incredibly provocative and sadistic with me. I often found myself struggling to put in practice the analytic virtue of holding in check retaliatory countertransference affects (Wallwork, 2012). Sudden absences were a frequently used weapon of choice that expressed simultaneously both Chris's anger at his caretaker's shortcomings and hope that he would care enough to be upset about Chris's absence.

A typical texting sequence of the cat-and-mouse, domination-subordination, love-hate scenario that played out in the transference/countertransference went like this:

ANALYST: (after waiting five minutes for a text, phone call, or Internet contact) Where are you?

Silence.

ANALYST: (several minutes later) We have an appointment.

Silence.

ANALYST: (fifteen minutes later) Are you all right?

Five minutes later.

CHRIS: Oh Shit. I forgot again. Sorry, man. Could we reschedule?
ANALYST: What's wrong with now? It's your time and dime whether we talk or not.
CHRIS: Okay. Let's talk until I get to someplace private where I can see you on FaceTime. I'll try the closet here. Must be quiet and private—and black as shit. Wow. Tight squeeze. Actually, I really need to talk.
ANALYST: Haven't heard from you, and it's past two pm.
CHRIS: (a few minutes later) I thought we said four.
ANALYST: No. We agreed on two.
CHRIS: I'm doing a terrible job of remembering these appointments. I'm not at Tom's place yet. Give me fifteen.
ANALYST: I'm here when you're ready.
CHRIS: Let's do Skype. I have a lot on my mind … Could you give me another session today?
ANALYST: Sorry. Not at two fifty.

CHRIS: Anything later—I need extra time?
ANALYST: Would eight pm work?

Silence.

Ten minutes later.

ANALYST: Need to know whether eight works before we start.

Ten minutes later.

CHRIS: Running. Almost there. Eight works.

Obviously, I am more actively engaged in maintaining the frame in these exchanges than my patient. It seemed necessary at the time for me to take the lead because Chris lacked the ego/superego strength and experienced too much psychic conflict to get himself to online treatment consistently, even when he needed to.

Continuity of treatment is always important but rarely more so than with the addicted patient whose mind is so easily hijacked by the overwhelming need for substances, such as opioids, that replace the pleasures of realizing normal motivations. It was absolutely essential for Chris to be continuously engaged in developing a firmer sense of self-security and self-continuity as well as self-reflective capacities to thwart impulses to self-medicate when faced with stressors. Without his therapist's presence and help, Chris was at risk of suffering any number of serious real harms, including killing himself with an overdose. Chris knew this intellectually, but he faced tremendous intrapsychic conflicts and neurochemical needs connected to addiction that made it tough for him to keep to scheduled plans, promises, and agreements.

As exchanges like those above were repeated and explored psychodynamically, Chris found ways of using insights to resist temptations. He developed somewhat stronger psychic muscles that enabled him to maintain the frame himself with significantly less monitoring by his analyst.

After two years of gradually diminishing drug use, Chris was able to stay clean because he had achieved a degree of psychic stability that allowed him to resist temptations with less ongoing support. More confident that he could be an active agent in the world and do something with his life, Chris settled down in his favorite West Coast city, where he found a job with an up-and-coming start-up that seemed ideally suited to his unique talents.

As Chris took decisive steps towards developing self-maintenance capacities along with a sounder sense of self-worth and even occasional glimmers of love of himself, I found myself thinking that the real work of analysis could begin (see Buie, 2013). I wanted very much to deepen the treatment with him, because we worked well together and we had become cognizant of some of the unconscious dynamics that fed his addiction and played into other conflicts. However, we had had to spend so much time putting out fires surrounding his addiction, our predominant transference/countertransference dynamics were configured around the supportive care he required to survive, not the limits and deprivations that Chris also needed to confront and explore analytically.

In time, I came to realize, reluctantly, as Chris repeatedly sabotaged my efforts to reset the frame, that we were stuck in an online relationship that was not conducive to settling into a stable psychoanalytic partnership, with the usual limitations that go along with a consistent, reliable, resistant frame. Our relationship remained too vulnerable to Chris's narcissistic neediness and fantasies of omnipotent control.

It was not that I doubted that reasonably good analytic work could be done online with Chris. But I became convinced that he would do better, faster, work and dig deeper, and derive greater benefits if he were regularly exposed to the real corporeal and affective presence of an analytic Other with whom he felt sufficiently contained to explore the full range of infantile and toxic affects stirred up by transference/countertransference dynamics that would be more accessible in the office than online.

Our loose, freewheeling, ever-changing frame had provided the kind of safe container that Chris needed to develop the self-maintenance capacities that are presupposed by conventional psychoanalysis. But this initial frame now needed to be set aside for Chris to enter into a potentially more mature analytic relationship, one in which he could grow into a more responsible partner.

I tried to spell this all out to Chris with the hope it might prod him to work with me to reset the frame. But it turned out he/we just could not do it. Chris was addicted to the affective response cycle associated with our unique original, supportive relationship.

When I first raised the prospect of terminating so that he could begin analysis locally, Chris was unequivocally opposed as well as angry about what he took to be my desire to get rid of him. After we had dealt with his transference-based anger and guilt about having given me so much grief, Chris's realistic arguments against terminating needed to be addressed. He and I had come a long way together. He had made gigantic psychological and interpersonal gains. We had co-created a solid therapeutic alliance within which we continued to make progress. He might not be able to establish as solid a bond with someone new and the new analyst would not know him initially as well as I did. Time and money would be lost.

Were the potential benefits of starting anew with another analyst worth the costs and risks?

I thought they were, though I had to fight against other, more self-interested desires that prodded me to agree with Chris's arguments against terminating. I very much wanted to keep going on together to see where we might get to. After good hours, I found myself denigrating the potential new analyst: he would never understand Chris as well as I did or would, I thought. But when I was honest with myself I knew that the work would have been better had it not been online.

After several months of intermittently interrogating the pros and cons of seeing a local analyst, Chris agreed to try working with a referral on a trial basis, on the condition that he could continue to see me while he was seeing the other analyst. He did not want to let go of our trapeze until he knew he could grab other hands that were strong enough to hold him, he confessed. I reacted to this poignant request from a place deep in Chris's psyche, by agreeing, before I had even thought it through, because a refusal would have been experienced by Chris as such a cruel rebuff. And I could not do that to him.

Later, as I struggled with what other analysts might think of such an unconventional dual analysis, I realized that it was ethically justified as a type of informed consent. Seeing both of us would make it possible for Chris to understand concretely what shifting analysts would mean to him affectively and practically before he made a final decision one way or the other. It would create the conditions for a more fully informed consent or dissent.

So, for three months, Chris saw both of us a couple of days a week each. Initially, as was to be expected. Chris was uncomfortable with the new analyst, which he handled by mocking his idiosyncrasies.

Sometimes he withheld important information and associations from the new analyst, which required my interpretative interventions to help push through the resistances and defensive barriers that kept him from developing trust in my replacement.

I was beginning to wonder whether the transition was going to work when Chris surprised me by admitting sheepishly that that there was something valuable about meeting in person that was missing in our online sessions. He felt more present. The other analyst was less "a figment of my imagination." Underneath Chris's grumbling about the other analyst's inflexibility I could see the benefit of his confronting lifelong problems with externally imposed rules and other limitations.

Our final parting was emotionally hard on both of us. Chris wept. I teared up. But our affects were muted by Skype. More intense affects would have been stirred up if we had been able to terminate in my actual analytic office, which, for me, reinforced why we were terminating, because he could have a more intense experience consistently by meeting in the same room as his local analyst.

Though we had both resisted, transitioning off the Internet was the right thing to do in this instance, because it maximized the patient's best interests in getting him the follow-up treatment he needed. Overlapping sessions with two analysts was certainly unconventional, and morally dubious in the minds of some, but it provided Chris with affectively dense experiences that enhanced the genuineness of the informed consent process involved in terminating treatment at a distance in favor of beginning analysis with a new therapist close to his home and work.

The chief ethical responsibilities in the cases of Brittany and Chris were much the same. The treatment decisions in both cases revolved around the ethical principles of non-maleficence ("above all, do no harm"), beneficence, truthfulness, and respect for autonomy. Brittany's online treatment ended up actually harming her (under the guise of a treatment justified by beneficence) by doggedly continuing a failing technique despite evidence that the patient's mental health was deteriorating and without considering the benefits of other options. Brittany's autonomy was disrespected during the two years her hometown therapist failed to inform her of alternative treatment options.

In marked contrast to Brittany, Chris benefited enormously from online treatment during the several years it took to lick his heroin addiction and to develop stronger self-maintenance, and self-affirming and self-reflective capacities. But, in time, when deepening the work was required, the benefit/cost ratio shifted in favor of in-person treatment. When this shift seemed evident to his analyst, Chris's autonomous decision-making was respected by a thorough exploration of the pros and cons of the available treatment options as well as a trial period with the new analyst that enabled Chris to feel comfortable choosing between continuing online or starting in-person with a new analyst. Brittany eventually reached a similar place in that her informed consent was respected after outside intervention, but this was accomplished without the assistance of her original therapist.

References

Buie, D. H. (2013). Core issues in the treatment of personality-disordered patients. *Journal of the American Psychoanalytic Association, 61*: 11–23.

Wallwork, E. (2012). Ethics in psychoanalysis. In: G. Gabbard, B. Litowitz & P. Williams (Eds.), *Textbook of Psychoanalysis* (2nd edition) (pp. 349–366). Washington, DC: American Psychiatric Publishing.

Wallwork, E. (2013). Ethical aspects of teletherapy. In: J. S. Scharff (Ed.), *Psychoanalysis Online: Mental Health, Teletherapy, and Training* (pp. 85–94) London: Karnac.

Wallwork, E. (2015). Thinking ethically about beginning online work. In: J. S. Scharff (Ed.), *Psychoanalysis Online 2: Impact of Technology on Development, Training, and Therapy* (pp. 83–92). London: Karnac.

INDEX

Ackerman, S., 172
affective resonance, 189
affective–intellectual upheavals, 22
Alizade, A. M., 37
Amati Mehler, J., 70, 171
Ambort, G., 2, 36
American Psychoanalytic
Association, 2, 85
analytic dialogue, 21–32
establishing, conditions for, 26–28
historical evolution, 23–26
initial reception of ideas, 22–23
real and virtual phenomenon, clinical material as, 28–30
teleanalytic dialogue, real and the virtual in, 21–22
ubiquity of voice in, 30–32
analytic dyad, 25, 69, 72, 75–76, 79, 81
anxiety
latent, 4
related to fantasy, 100
signs of, 13
Anzieu, D., 12, 15
"Arachne" (*Webs* song), 155
Argenmex, 57
Argentieri, S., 70, 171
Aryan, A., 6, 8, 17, 22, 25
atmosphere, lack of, 8, 72
attachment, 87, 89
early, 90, 166
insecure, 8, 184
theory, 170, 182
audio-visual functions, 70
auditory environment, 15, 188–189
auditory sphere, 189
auditory system, 187, 189
Avizia research report, 4

Bachelard, G., 89
Balick, A., 153, 163, 170
Baranger, M., 44, 88–90, 182, 189

Baranger, W., 44, 88–90
Barrow, J. D., 67, 75
Bayles, M., 175–176
Berenstein, I., 25
Bion, W. R., 29, 44, 69, 100, 158, 183
Birkerts, S., 86
bits, 67, 169
Björklind, C., 36
Black Lives Matter, 157
Bleger, J., 12, 35, 37, 43–44, 47
body/mind, 72 *see also:* mind and body
Bollas, C., 36–37
Bolognini, S., 3, 70
Bonfiglio, D., 41
Boston University, 86
Bouchard, S., 171
Bowlby, J., 181–182 *see also:* attachment: theory
Brainsky, S., 70
Brazelton, T., 175
Bridge, M., 37
Brockmeier, J., 92
Bui, T., 172
Buie, D. H., 217
Burdet, M., 2, 36

Cabanne, J., 28
CAPA *see* China America Psychoanalytic Alliance
Caparotta, L., 17, 36, 170, 184
Carlino, R., 17, 21–23, 25, 171
case studies
  Alana, 190–195, 198–205
  Brent, 105–127
  Brittany, 208–211
  Carlos, 56–57
  Cecilia, 79–80
  Chris, 211–220
  Danny, 135–138, 151
  Doreen and Oscar, 138–151
  Francesca, 76–79
  Giovanna, 74–75
  J, 158–159, 161, 165–166
  Marcela, 59–60
  Maya and Sam, 131–135, 151
  Mrs. A, 97–101
  S, 159–161, 166
  V, 163–166
Ceserani, R., 81
China America Psychoanalytic Alliance (CAPA), 2, 5, 85
Chodorow, N., 70
Churcher, J., 36–37, 41, 48
Citizenfour, 42
Civitarese, G., 37
Clark, A., 91
cognitive referents, 189
cognitive science, 91
Cohen, J., 36
Coleman, B., 67
communication studies, 91–92
Compaine, Benjamin M., 169
computer screen, 86–88, 90, 92, 181
conscious(ness), 27, 54, 66, 112, 164, 189, 214
  pre-, 101
consulting room, 38, 67–68, 70–72, 74, 81, 97, 165, 171, 180–181 *see also* "cyber-room"
  or computer screen, 86–88
COPE study group, 85
Corbett, K., 16
Cordess, C., 36
countertransference, 1, 10–11, 78, 105, 151, 179, 181–182, 205, 215 *see also:* transference
couple psychotherapy, 131, 169–170, 183–184
couple psychotherapy settings, 171–172, 184
  cyber-session, 177
  living abroad, 173
  relocating, 176–180

theory of change re: online, 182–183
therapeutic compromise, 176
traveling for work, 180–181
Voice over Internet Protocol (VoIP), 172–173
VoIP-mediated psychotherapy for couples, 173–182
war-torn zone, 174
cultural acquisitions of civilization, 62
cultural spaces, 88
culture, 63
Culture and Human Development (Valsiner), 87
Cundy, L., 161, 170
"cyber-room", 71 *see also* consulting room
cybersex, 154
cyberspace, 17, 66, 68–69, 94

Das Unbehagen in der Kultur (Freud), 63
Davies, R., 37
dazzling omnipotence, 74
De Carrica, A. I., 61
De Carrica, S. M. O., 61
De Varela, Y., 157
desmentida, 157, 161–162
Devor, A., 158
Di Chiara, G., 68, 71
digital
information, 95
media, 157
natives, 155
technology, 169
distance-mediated analysis, 200–201
Doyle, C., 39
drafts of analytic thought, 68
dreams, 28–29
dreamed, 28–29
remembered, 28
reported, 28
Drum, K., 171
Dryer, J. A., 153
Dylan, Bob, 66

electronic communication, 169
elusive reality, 26
emotional link, 100
emotional–affective communications, 68
emotions of love, 109
empathy, 189
end-to-end security, 47
Erikson, E. H., 158, 161
Estrada, T., 11
European Psychoanalytic Federation, 43
"e-world," 67

Faimberg, H., 48
Fairbairn, W. R. D., 199
fantasy, 12, 60, 78–79
anxiety related to, 100
hidden, 99
sexual, 101
transference, 97
unconscious, 101–102
Ferro, A., 18
Fiorentini, G., 76
Fishkin, L. P., 41
Fishkin, R. E., 41
Fitzgerald, T., 172
Fornari-Spoto, G., 170
Forrester, J., 36
Freud, S., 22–23, 28, 42, 47, 53, 55, 62–63
cultural acquisitions of civilization, 62
Frisch, S., 43

Gabbard, G. O., 36, 67
Gaburri, E., 78

Galli, V., 27
Garvey, P., 36
geopolitical landscapes, 156
"ghost relationship", 70
Giménez Noble, F., 2, 36
Girls (television series), 165
Gobby, C., 46
Goldberg, B., 67
Gordon, B., 171
Greenwald, G., 40, 42, 172
Guardian, The, 40, 42, 45

Habib, Y., 70
Hadjistavropoulos, T., 172
Haunting Melody, The (Reik), 55
Hautmann, G., 68, 72
Hayman, A., 36
Her (film), 162
Hirsch Hardy, J., 2, 36
Hoggett, P., 42–43
horcruxes, 162
Hunter, P., 172

IIPT teleanalysis research group, 198
Immigration Justice, 157
infant's processes of identification, 60
information and communication technology (ICT), 21, 23, 67
information technology (IT), 65
International Institute for Psychoanalytic Training (IIPT), 198
International Psychoanalytical Association (IPA), 2–4, 70, 85
International Psychoanalytical Association Congress, 54
International Psychotherapy Institute, 198
Interstate Medical Licensure Compact, 7

Jacobs, D., 85
Johnson, M., 91
Joseph, B., 181

King, P., 101
Klein, M., 153, 161, 181
Koocher, G., 172
Kreissl, R., 45
Kruse, P., 155

Labarthe, C., 37
Lakoff, G., 91
Lannemann, J., 92
latent anxiety, 4
latent content, 14, 16, 29, 31
Laura, P., 172
Layton, A., 36
Leader, C., 157
Lemma, A., 17, 36, 48, 74, 170, 184
Lev, A. I., 158
level of communication, 72
Lévy, P., 29
LGBTQ adolescents, 154, 156
LGBTQ community, xviii, 155
LGBTQ patients, 154
Lijtmae, R. M., 153
Lin, T., 4, 6, 10, 36, 100
Linell, P., 92
listening, 4, 188–189, 198, 205
  inner room of, 68, 71
Littleton, H., 171
long-distance psychoanalysis, 53–54, 57, 61
  analyst distance, 59–61
  development, 54–58
  transference in, 60
Lustig de Ferrer, S., 61

MacAskill, E., 40, 42, 172
Maheu, M., 171
Manguel, L., 25
Manhal-Baugus, 171
Martin, A., 65

Marzi, A., 68
Matte Blanco, I., 72
MegaChat, 47
Mellia, M., 41
Meltzer, D., 38
Meo, M., 41
Merriam-Webster, 16, 187
Mexico, 24, 58–59
mind, 68
  and body, 100–102 *see also:* body / mind
  disembodied and decontextualized model of, 88, 91
  extended model, 92–93
Mirkin, M., 73
Mizrahi, C., 54
mobile telephone technology, 170
mother tongue, 61, 78
multiverse, 67, 75
"mystic writing-pad," 62

Nafisi, A., 2
Naso, R. C., 153, 158, 161
negative transference, 6, 11, 110, 200, 204–205
  emergence of, 12
  projected into technology, 13–14
Nelson, E. T., 172
NPR radio program, 86

oedipal triangle, 16
Oedipus complex, 57
Ogden, T., 27
Ogden, T. H., 81
online
  analysis, 65, 75
  communication, 65
  couple therapy, 182
online analysis, light and shadow, 65–81
  elements, 65
  external connectivity, 80–81
  internal connectivity, 80–81
  negative opinions, 69–70
  positive opinions, 69–70
  Skype *vs.* telephone, 75–76
  special effects, 77
  technological crashes, 73–74
  virtual reality, 66–68
opinions
  negative, 69–70
  positive, 69–70

Panel Report, 72
Parsons, M., 37
Paz, R., 27
Petrucci, H., 28
phantom world, 44, 67
Philosophy Now, 93
phone analysis, 1–3, 12–13, 25–26, 36, 58, 72–73, 75, 105, 120, 190, 192–195, 199–205, 208–209
Pilecki, A., 153, 158
pillars of psychoanalytic theory, 57
pixels, 4, 6, 67
Poetics of Space, The (Bachelard), 89
Poitras, L., 40, 42
Polanyi, M., 38
polyhedral set of Chinese boxes, 68
Prensky, M., 155
present-body analysis, 54–56, 63
Pretty Good Privacy (PGP), 45
Prism, 40
privacy, 35
  breach of, 38–39
  conception of, 36
  confusion of, 36
  implications for, 37
  issues of, 48
  of conversation, 38
  preserving, 36
  telecommunication, 36, 45
private theories, 54

proper rapport, 188
psychical trauma, defence against, 35, 42
psychoanalysis, 65, 95
Psychoanalysis Online, 130
psychoanalytic
  couple psychotherapy training, 171
  field, 88
  method, 54
  practice, 59
  psychotherapy, 95
  sessions, 72
psychoanalytic setting, 35–49
  common sense in, 38–39
  endpoint security, 46–47
  good-enough telecommunications, 45–46
  ignoring risks in, 41–43
  insufficiency of common sense, 39–41
  José Bleger's view of, implications of, 43–44
  shared tacit knowledge, in 38–39
  societies/norms and, 45
  vulnerability of telecommunications, 39–41
psychoanalytic treatment, 85
  cognitive science and communication studies, 91–93
  human adaptability and expanding contexts, 93
psychodynamic therapists, 207
psychotherapy interactions, 94

quantum key distribution (QKD), 46

reality, elusive, 26
Reeves, N., 175
Reik, T., 55
remote therapy, 70–73
Riolo, F., 78
Rossi, D., 41
Rowling, J. K., 162
Rushe, D., 172
Russell, G., 17

Sabbadini, A., 48, 181–184
Sahovaler Litvinoff, D., 2, 36
Sandler, J., 54
Saporta, J. A., 92
Scharff, D. E., 157, 161
Scharff, J. S., 1–2, 8, 10, 15, 17, 36, 41, 72, 157, 161
Schlain, T., 165
Second Life (role-playing game), 155
Secure Sockets Layer (SSL), 45
Segal, H., 42
Sehon, C., 9, 105
self-destructive patterns, 199
semiotic demand settings (SDSs), 87
sexual
  dreams, 98
  fantasy, 101
  transference, 97
sexuality, 57
Shanyang, Z., 65
Shields, A. J., 46
Shotter, J., 92
Shuttle and Concentrated analysis, 70
Skype, 1–3, 25, 59, 70, 74, 79, 86, 131, 170, 172
  analysis, 73
  communication with, 4–5
  computer to computer connections, 5, 41
  packet-switching in, 41
  pros and cons, 4–5
  special feature of, 41
  therapy, 173
  vs. telephone, 75–76
Snowden, E., 35, 39, 42, 47

Snyder, E., 5
social media, 4, 155, 157, 163–166, 170
sociopath, 160
special effects, 77
Spencer, J. R., 39
spontaneous (unconscious) dynamism, 189
Stadter, M., 130
Steiner, J., 42, 102
Stevens, G. M., 39
Stimmel, B., 36
Sundelson, D., 36
Symantec, 41

Tallis, R., 93–94
technique of psychoanalysis, 59
technology, 129–151
  couple treatment, 139
  crawling age, 144
  cut-offs, 131–132
  fragmented conversation, 132–134
  high-quality broadband, 130
technological innovations, 171
technology and psychoanalysis, 61–62
teleanalysis, 1–18, 57, 189
  analysis of reactions, 14
  benefits of, 6–7
  contraindications, 8
  ethical considerations, 5–7
  frame and setting of treatment, 9–11
  indications, 8
  legal considerations, 5–7
  licensure, 7–8
  modes of resistance, 8–9
  objection to, 11
  of intimacy and distance, 2
  physical proximity, 11–12
  Skype, 1–6
  technical problems in, 6
  transference–countertransference, alliance and, 15–17
  unconscious communication through voice, 14–15
  virtual communication in, 15–17
  VoIP in, 1–2
teleanalytic
  sessions, 105
  work, 97, 100
telecommunication
  analytic dialogue via, 26
  good-enough, for psychoanalysis, 45–46
  implications for psychoanalyses conducted by, 47–49
  interception of, 38–39
  privacy of, 36, 45
  psychoanalysis via, 25–26, 30–31, 37
  security of, 35–36
  vulnerability of, 39–41
telephone analysis *see* phone analysis
teletherapy, xviii, 7, 69, 130
Temperley, J., 37
Tempora, 40
theoretical interest, 61
theorizing space and place, 88–91
therapeutic compromise, 176
Tofanelli, P., 41
Tomás, J., 61
traditional analysis, 57, 73
training programs, 66
transference, 1–2, 9, 12–14, 26, 28–30, 51, 58, 60, 66, 90, 98, 102, 107, 151, 163, 165, 181–182, 200, 204, 210
  alliance and, 15–17
  contextual, 14
  counter- *see* countertransference
  -countertransference, 12, 15–16, 70, 73, 88, 171, 182, 201, 210, 215, 217

fantasy, 97, 101
love, 57
maternal void, 134
negative *see* negative transference
neurosis, 60
perceptions, 10
primitive, 12
sexual, 98–99
split, 201
"Transference: The total situation" (Joseph), 181
transitional aspects of internet use, 154–157
transitional object, 156–157
transitional phenomena, 157
transitional space, 153, 155, 157–159, 161, 165–166, 196
Tronick, E., 175
Tuckett, D., 42
"turbo"-intersubjective dimension, 70
"turbo"-relational dimension, 70
Turkle, S., 158, 160

unconscious, 11–12, 14, 27, 54, 57, 62, 66, 71, 112, 127, 148, 189
communication, 2, 14–15, 17, 25, 73
dynamics, xviii, 105, 189, 217
fantasy, 101–102, 214
mental processes, 57
phantasy, 38
"uninvited guest", 75
US coastguard, 117
US Marine Corps, 117
utilitarianism, 66

Valsiner, J., 87
Varela, Y., 117
Venn diagram, 179
video conferencing, 75, 85, 170
video software programs, 85
video technology services provider, 5
video teleconference (VTC), 105–106, 118
virtual communication, 15–17
virtual reality, 66–68
virtual teleanalytic space, 100
virtualization capability, 19
voice, 187
Voice over Internet Protocol (VoIP), 1–2, 47, 67, 170
discussion, 181–182
mediated psychotherapy, 170
mediated software, 177
-mediated therapy for couples, 173–181
software, 182
theory of change, 182–184
VSee, 5, 25, 47, 86, 176

Wallwork, E., 215
Wanlass, J., 2–3
web camera, 1–2, 4, 9–10, 13–14, 31, 56, 73–74, 87, 97, 106, 176, 182
Weber, C. B., 61
Webs (musical play), 155
Weintrobe, S., 42–43
Werbin, A., 2–3, 36
Wertsch, J. V., 92
WhatsApp, 24
Winnicott, D. W., 67, 127, 153, 156–157, 183, 161
Winocur, J. O., 61
Wright, D., 45

Ylander, F., 43
Yuan, Z. L., 46

Zimmermann, P. R., 45
Zoom, 5, 25, 86
Zwischenreich, 78